Investment Titans

Investment Titans

Investment Insights from the Minds That Move Wall Street

Jonathan Burton

McGraw-Hill
New York   San Francisco   Washington, D.C.   Auckland   Bogotá
Caracas   Lisbon   London   Madrid   Mexico City   Milan
Montreal   New Delhi   San Juan   Singapore
Sydney   Tokyo   Toronto

Library of Congress Cataloging-in-Publication Data

Burton, Jonathan.
   Investment titans : investment insights from the minds that move Wall Street /
Jonathan Burton.
     p. cm.
   Includes index.
   ISBN 0-07-135496-4
   1. Investments—United States. 2. Investment analysis. 3. Securities—United
States. I. Title.
HG4910.B863 2000
332.6—dc21

                         00-062447

McGraw-Hill

A Division of The **McGraw·Hill** Companies

1 2 3 4 5 6 7 8 9 0   DOC/DOC   0 9 8 7 6 5 4 3 2 1 0

ISBN 0-07-135496-4

This book was set in Fairfield by Tina Thompson.
Printed and bound by R. R. Donnelley & Sons Company

This publication is designed to provide accurate and authoritative information in
regard to the subject matter covered. It is sold with the understanding that neither
the author nor the publisher is engaged in rendering legal, accounting, futures/secu-
rities trading, or other professional service. If legal advice or other expert assistance
is required, the services of a competent professional person should be sought.

> —*From a Declaration of Principles jointly adopted by a Committee*
> *of the American Bar Association and a Committee of Publishers*

McGraw-Hill books are available at special quantity discounts to use as premiums
and sales promotions, or for use in corporate training programs. For more information, please write to the Director of Special Sales, Professional Publishing, McGraw-
Hill, Two Penn Plaza, New York, NY 10121-2298. Or contact your local bookstore.

This book is printed on recycled, acid-free paper containing a
minimum of 50% recycled, de-inked fiber.

For Lisa, Nicholas, Daniel and Ava:

The Most Rewarding Investment of All

Contents

Preface

A finance professor and his student were walking on campus one afternoon, deep in discussion about money and investing, when the student spied a $20 bill on the ground. Eagerly, he reached down to pick it up. "Don't bother," the professor said blandly. "If it were really there, someone would have taken it already."

Opportunity presents itself in unusual places. This book is a story of opportunities gained and lost. Its foundation was set in late 1996, when Barry Vinocur, editor in chief of what was then *Dow Jones Asset Management*, came to me with a unique idea for a series of question-and-answer interviews. What if I contacted pioneers of finance and investment and talked with them in-depth about their groundbreaking work, their insights about investing and their current view of the financial markets?

These great thinkers, many of them Nobel Prize winners and would-be winners, created the theories and concepts that Wall Street later turned into investment products and strategies. It would seem that these authorities would have much to say about how to be a better investor.

As a business and personal finance journalist, I was familiar with the research and published papers of luminaries like Harry Markowitz, Paul Samuelson and William Sharpe. But I had never actually spoken with them about the innovative ideas that had brought them fame.

"Leaders in Finance" debuted in January 1997, featuring a spirited conversation with Nobel Prize–winning economist Gary Becker about stock-market volatility and people's ability to cope with adversity. Over time, the series developed into regular discussions of investment risk and reward, the lessons of history, and the unique advantage that comes from being an informed investor. Many notable economists and investment professionals have contributed their sagacious insights, including Markowitz,

Samuelson, Sharpe, Peter Lynch, the late Merton Miller, Eugene Fama, Jack Treynor, Gary Brinson and Peter Bernstein.

Asset Management is a bimonthly magazine for institutional investors and investment advisers—a relatively sophisticated readership. My challenge for the series—and for this book—has been to make complex subjects accessible to people who might not have an MBA. Investing is not rocket science, despite Wall Street's best efforts to make it so—except for the fact that launching a rocket also requires a good deal of common sense and informed judgment.

It is my hope that readers of *Investment Titans* will learn more about investing than they already knew, regardless of their expertise. Buying and selling stocks is hard work—your hard work. This book offers a concrete and helpful understanding of investment strategies, as seen through the eyes of some of the most unique thinkers in the investment business.

Investment Titans also is a story of risk and how we handle it. Investors tend to focus on investment returns and ignore the inherent risk. To the investment manager who boasts proudly, "We beat the market," the question should be: "Did you take above-market risk?" Unwelcome as it may be, there is always a trade-off between risk and reward. Investors need to make a realistic and honest assessment of their risk tolerance, for portfolio risk is one of the few factors within their control. Portfolio return, unfortunately, is not.

Through exclusive interviews, the nine distinguished subjects of *Investment Titans* generously have offered their most lucid ideas and insights to help people invest more wisely. Each chapter covers a different aspect of investing, including:

- Stock-market risk and reward
- Time horizon and the long-term power of stocks
- Indexing
- Value versus growth investing
- Investor psychology
- International investing strategies
- Determining your risk tolerance, hiring a financial adviser and using the Internet to manage your portfolio

Underlying each of these themes is a central question: "Can you beat the market?" If not, why? If so, how? Finance experts are split on this issue. Many of the investment titans in this book contend that the answer to "Can you beat the market?" is a resounding "No." It's nearly impossible to predict stock prices, they claim; throwing darts at the stock pages or taking a "random walk" across a list of ticker symbols would generate about the same results. Markets are too efficient; mistakes are instantly spotted.

For these "efficient-market" disciples, the investment landscape is cut and dry. Since most professional investors fail to hurdle their benchmark, individuals have even scarcer hope of finding undiscovered gems that will make them rich. Any famed investor who has consistently outperformed, like Warren Buffett or Peter Lynch, is a statistical quirk—a sideshow to Wall Street's Big Top. So stop trying. Instead, invest in passively managed mutual funds that track a market index. Asset allocation—how much you confer on stocks and bonds—not stock selection, is most important to meeting financial goals.

The random walkers present a strong case. But other respected thinkers in this book argue that stock price movements are in fact predictable, markets can be exploited through diligent research, and gold can be mined by those who dig hard and deep. Yet if it is possible to go "One Up on Wall Street," as Peter Lynch outlined in his 1989 best-seller of the same title, it's also true that many well-informed people are chasing similar opportunities. *Investment Titans* aims to tear down the Wall and steer you safely across the Street. Here are highlights of what to expect from each chapter:

• Harry Markowitz is an unlikely father of modern finance. As a young graduate student at the University of Chicago in the early 1950s, Markowitz was waiting to meet with his dissertation adviser when he struck up a conversation with a stranger sitting next to him. The man, it turned out, was a stockbroker, and he encouraged Markowitz to study the stock market—perhaps the best advice a broker has ever given.

Markowitz soon was researching existing ideas about investment strategy, and in 1952 published a road map for investors to gauge the risk of their *entire* portfolio. To reduce exposure to unwanted risk, he argued, diversify holdings across many types of investments. Better to hold a basket of unrelated investments, Markowitz suggested, so that when one group is tumbling, another is appreciating. Diversification offers a smoother and happier ride over time. Sure, this sounds elementary now—Investing 101—but that's because of Markowitz, who shared the 1990 Nobel Prize for economic sciences. Before him, no one had explained why diversification mattered; there was no such animal as a "financial adviser." Memories of the Depression were fresh, and few Americans owned stocks. Indeed, a popular view of investing was simply to put all of your eggs in one basket and watch that basket carefully. Markowitz showed how shaky that basket can be.

• Paul Samuelson, another Nobel Prize winner and professor emeritus of economics at the Massachusetts Institute of Technology, takes issue with the notion that if you hold stocks long enough—10, 20, 50 years—you will not, cannot, lose money. He is familiar with statistics that show that the U.S. stock market has not suffered a loss in any given 15-year period since 1926. And he can see how statistics like this can convince investors that if they stay in equities long enough, they will endure less market risk and be assured of netting at least the long-term historical average annual return from stocks.

A nice idea, but untrue, Samuelson counters. Time does not heal all stock-market wounds. While he concedes that over the long term stocks likely will fare better than other assets, to invest on that assumption is dangerous. Risk does not go to zero over long periods, Samuelson contends. To think otherwise paints a false sense of security and complacency. And when stock prices crumble, your sweetheart investments could look scary. That could lead to poor short-term judgments and even outright panic. Indeed, Samuelson advises: "You shouldn't spend much time on your investments. That will just tempt you to pull up the plants and see how the roots are doing, and that's very bad for the roots."

• Jeremy Siegel, a professor of finance at the Wharton School, is the author of the best-selling *Stocks for the Long Run*. What exactly is the "long run"? Siegel explains that the long run is a lifetime, where the risk of being out of the game actually is greater than the risk of playing.

Siegel shares some bold views about stock-market risk. While Samuelson charges that stocks are riskier than bonds, regardless of time horizon, Siegel disagrees. His startling premise is that a stock portfolio held for more than 20 years is less risky than a portfolio of bonds. How can that be, when bonds are supposedly much more stable? Because over time economic inflation eats away at fixed-income returns, while stocks have beaten inflation handily.

• John C. Bogle, the founder of the Vanguard Group of mutual funds, is the closest thing that individual investors have to a folk hero. For half a century, this iconoclastic fiduciary has worked diligently to make investing simpler for people. Not that making money in the stock market is easy, because investing is no sure thing. Bogle just makes buying and selling funds easier to understand.

One of the easiest investment rules for people to follow, and Bogle's all-consuming passion, is minimizing expenses. As with portfolio risk, investment costs, such as the fees paid to mutual funds, are another crucial factor within an investor's control. "This business is all about simplicity and low cost," Bogle says. "I'm not into all these market strategies and theories and cost-benefit analyses—all the bureaucracy that goes with business. In investing, strip all the baloney out of it, and give people what you promise."

• Josef Lakonishok, a finance professor at the University of Illinois and a respected institutional money manager, is a staunch supporter of value investing. To a value investor, what goes down must come up. Value investors search for situations where they strongly believe that others have the picture wrong. Unlike investors who gladly fork over premium prices for shares of popular "growth" stocks, shareholders of value stocks refuse to pay homage and dollars to Wall Street's darlings. Instead they are devoted to Wall Street's dogs. In this chapter, Lakonishok shares his top investment secret, an inside tip that may surprise many stockholders. You'll also learn to recognize attractive value stocks and to analyze their current and future prospects.

• Are markets ruled by cold, calculated reason or heated, helter-skelter actions? Efficiency or emotion—which is it? Richard Thaler of the University of Chicago believes that investor psychology and human behavior dominate stock price movements. That means the market can be bested by those who stay cool when others overreact. Thaler ministers over a budding discipline called "behavioral finance," which contends that efficient-market models are seriously flawed. Investors are not always rational. Psychology matters. Emotions matter. And before the efficient-market types came along, legendary investors like John Maynard Keynes and Benjamin Graham routinely factored human nature into their investment strategies. In this chapter, you'll learn about the mind games that people play with money and the impulsive investing mistakes they tend to make—from trading too much to not trading enough.

• To Gary Brinson, the chairman of influential Chicago-based investment manager UBS Asset Management, stocks should be chosen according to business sectors, not borders. Where a company is based doesn't much matter, as long as it's a leader. Globalization will make borders and trade barriers obsolete, he claims, and stocks will trade around the clock on every major exchange.

Still, many savvy investors are convinced that their portfolios get enough international exposure from holding U.S.-based multinational corporations with worldwide reach. Indeed, giants like Coca-Cola generate most of their revenues outside of the United States. Investment sage Warren Buffett has taken this very approach with Berkshire Hathaway's stakes in Coca-Cola and Gillette, for example, a strategy that Brinson challenges with two sharp words: "Warren's myopic," he snaps.

Investors will increasingly accept a broad, borderless view of the world, Brinson counters, and will become more comfortable with the stocks of companies that are not so close to home. And he offers fundamentally sound investment advice on how to navigate this developing trend and profit from it.

• As a chronicler of the history of investing and its guiding theories, best-selling author and investment counselor Peter Bernstein is a one-man Greek chorus for the events, people and principles that have shaped finance and investment over the past half-century.

Bernstein has been described as a master of the "art of holding hands." He is a voice of reason for those many investors who have not yet experienced a full-fledged bear market. "The stock market doesn't know you're there, and it's not going to be considerate," he warns. "You don't *deserve* to get anything, really. The market is not an accommodation machine. It owes you nothing."

In Chapter 8, Bernstein talks at length about the characteristics of a good investor. Be realistic, and accept uncertainty, he advises. He also has plenty to say about the giddy love affair with stocks that has swept so many people off their feet during the past few years.

• William Sharpe has rolled out an assembly line of useful investment tools, including the Capital Asset Pricing Model, or CAPM, and the Sharpe Ratio. Want to know how much risk a mutual fund manager is taking with your money in an effort to beat the market? The CAPM tells you. It says that just being in the stock market is a risk you can't eliminate, so the way to get superior, market-beating investment returns is to take on bigger risks—for which you could incur big losses. Don't want to compete? The CAPM gave rise to passive investing through index funds.

Sharpe later developed the Sharpe Ratio, which is now a standard measure of whether fund managers are good at their jobs.

The higher the ratio, the better the fund's risk-adjusted return. Today Sharpe, a computer buff, is democratizing finance through the Internet with an investment-planning vehicle called Financial Engines—revolutionizing individual investing as he shook professional money management in the early 1960s.

It has been a true privilege and a tremendous professional opportunity for me to speak with each of these pioneers. I have tried in this book to interpret their views in ways that many people can appreciate. Owing to space considerations, three important interviews with prominent investment titans regrettably were not included. These men are: Burton Malkiel, author of the influential *A Random Walk Down Wall Street*; Roger Ibbotson, the innovative founder of securities data firm Ibbotson Associates; and Martin Leibowitz, vice chairman and chief investment officer of the teachers' pension fund TIAA-CREF.

Malkiel's salient views and Ibbotson's work and data are referenced in several chapters. Leibowitz is a towering force in fixed-income investing, the man who literally wrote the book about how to understand and value bonds. But after a gracious, informative talk with him, I decided to keep the spotlight of this book exclusively on stocks. The responsibility for any other omissions and errors, and may there be few, is mine alone.

Yet in the end, one piece of eloquent investment advice from Leibowitz stands out: "Good ideas can slip between the cup and the lip," he said. "In this business, one can have a great cup, a wonderful brew, and it doesn't get turned into reliable long-term returns. And just because something works out well and turns out to be a wonderful investment doesn't mean one should automatically take a victory lap. The overall process is the key to long-term results. So don't crow when you have a success. Think hard about where that success really came from."

Be thoughtful and appreciate your success—such judicious counsel applies to so much more than investing.

Jonathan Burton

Acknowledgments

Writing may be a solitary pursuit, but gathering the important and illuminating information necessary to create a compelling work is always a collaborative effort. This book is no exception.

Heartfelt thanks are due first to Barry Vinocur, former editor in chief of *Dow Jones Asset Management*, who had the vision to create the "Leaders in Finance" series and the confidence to let me use my best judgment to shape and edit often-complex interviews into colloquial and approachable magazine pieces.

Over three years and many lengthy discussions with Barry about strategy and direction, "Leaders in Finance" developed into a must-read for the institutional investors and financial advisers who receive *Asset Management*. To the many readers who took the time to write an appreciative note about the series, I'm pleased and grateful that you consistently found the interviews as informative to read as I have found them to write.

To the pioneers of finance and investing who opened their minds to me so that I could write this book, you have my deepest gratitude. I hope this finished work accurately reflects the wisdom of your words and insights.

To the other incomparable thinkers who have been profiled in "Leaders in Finance," thank you for helping bring an idea to fruition. Many of you are university professors, and this series— now in its fourth year—has been my graduate school. You have taught me much about what it means to be a better investor. I have tried to incorporate these lessons in my reporting about personal finance and investment trends and tactics. If only space and time would have permitted me to feature each of you in this book.

Special thanks is due to Charles Ellis of Greenwich Associates, one of the brightest assets of the investment management business. In a casual conversation a couple of years ago, he suggested that "Leaders in Finance" could be turned into a noteworthy book, and put me in touch with an editor at McGraw-Hill named Jeffrey Krames.

I have worked with many editors during my journalism career, but few with Jeffrey's tenacity and inspiration. He saw this book's potential from the start, and has stood by it every step of the way. Jeffrey has been the singular driving force behind the scenes of its production, challenging and encouraging me to create an even better work than I originally envisioned. Thank you, Jeffrey.

Some portions of this book appeared in similar form in pieces that I wrote for *Dow Jones Asset Management, Bloomberg Personal Finance, Individual Investor* and *Online Investor*. Thanks to Barry Vinocur, Steve Gittelson, editor of *Bloomberg Personal Finance*, Paul Libassi, editor of *Individual Investor,* and Jan Parr, editor of *Online Investor*, for allowing the essence of these articles to reach a wider audience. Thanks also to my good friends Brian Maddox, Alexis Sinclair and Ken Krimstein—each creative writers and confidants—who gave me intelligent advice about managing a book project, and to Daniel Kornstein, who provided astute professional counsel. At research firm Ibbotson Associates, Jamie Martin and Alexa Auerbach graciously provided invaluable investment data, as did Annette Larson at mutual fund- and stock-rating service Morningstar.

My time is given primarily to reporting assignments and to my family. Lisa and the kids have been understanding and supportive throughout this period, making room in a busy schedule so that I could work. For that, and much more, I am most appreciative. And so, to my three wonderful children, who would never cease to ask innocently, "What chapter are you on, Daddy?" I can now say, "The last one, honey."

Investment Titans

CHAPTER 1

The Efficient Frontier: Harry Markowitz

"You've got to look at the portfolio as a whole, not just position by position. And if you're trying to reduce the volatility or uncertainty of your portfolio as a whole, then you need more than one security obviously, but you also need securities which don't go up and down together."

Risk and return are inseparable twins—joined at the gut. Additional risk promises greater gain, but stiffer losses. Stay close to the middle of the path, and your ride will be smoother. Unfortunately, people can get into trouble and make poor decisions when they either don't take enough risk to be satisfied when markets are rising, or take too much and become frightened at the first whiff of danger. Accordingly, investors nowadays are encouraged to assess their tolerance for risk as realistically as possible, and to build a diversified portfolio they can live with. In this straightforward way, you strike a balance between risk—how much you're willing to give up—and return—how much you get as compensation for the market's uncertainty.

These guidelines weren't always so clear. Until the early 1950s, investors didn't have much of a physical framework to deal with this fundamental trade-off between risk and return. Not that investors were entirely in the Dark Ages. Diversification was a common way to control investment risk. John Maynard Keynes, the legendary economist and a highly successful investor in his own right, cited diversification as one of the three most important principles of successful investment. "The ideal investment portfolio," he wrote, "is divided between the purchase of really secure future income (where future appreciation or depreciation will depend on the rate of interest) and equities that one believes to be capable of a *large* improvement to offset the fairly numerous cases that with the best skill in the world, will go wrong."[1]

Although Keynes was speaking sensibly to a typical investor, he didn't outline how to insulate a portfolio from damaging shocks with an adequate proportion of "really secure" bonds and "large improvement" stocks. Not that he should have. While most investors understood that diversification was a logical way to off-set risk, their actual asset allocation—how they diversified—was haphazard at best. A mutual fund might hold 50 or 100 different stocks, but fund managers had no formal tool to tell if their picks would perform independently or as virtual clones of one another. Ideally, you want a diversified portfolio of stocks that "think" for themselves—when some are down, others are down less or even up, and each has its role in a greater effort.

This concept seems elementary today—Financial Planning 101—but only because of a young University of Chicago economics graduate student named Harry Markowitz. Before Markowitz put his pencil to paper, neither Keynes nor any of the other great minds of the investment profession had developed a concrete, verifiable way to determine if a portfolio was properly positioned to capture the most return for the least amount of risk. The "mix-and-match" approach to diversification that was typical of the time served only to produce a rudderless portfolio of securities—and not very secure, at that. Investors received scant clues about how single holdings, when taken together, affected their portfolio results—if they even bothered to consider the portfolio in its entirety. The legendary folk humorist Will Rogers obviously figured he was speaking for many when he dished up the following homespun investment wisdom: "Buy stocks that are going to go up. After they've done that, sell them. If they aren't going to go up, don't have bought them." Recalling those days, Markowitz is still struck by the limitations that investors brought to their portfolios:

> **People did diversify, but intuitively. There was in practice a notion that you shouldn't put everything into one industry. But financial theory didn't explain this practice. The future is uncertain. Nature keeps doing things it never did before.**

Suppose that you divided your money among several securities, and any particular security had a certain probability of being wiped out. Are they all going to be wiped out at the same time? Or are some going to do well when others do poorly? That makes a big difference as to how stable your portfolio is as a whole.

Markowitz showed investors how to create a more desirable, dynamic stock portfolio. His work added texture and depth to what had been a fairly one-dimensional view. From his conclusions, investors finally could see whether a group of chosen stocks cooperated together or not, and how they impacted a portfolio's *overall* risk and return.

For an insight that would revolutionize investing and earn Markowitz a Nobel Prize in 1990, this stroke of genius began with barely a ripple. In 1950, Markowitz, just 22, devised a tool for investors to understand how much risk they would have to bear to achieve a specified expected return, and to minimize that risk through thoughtful diversification. This blueprint—sketched in a single afternoon at the University of Chicago business school library and later refined—formed the basis of what would become known as "Modern Portfolio Theory," or simply, "Portfolio Theory." His essay outlining this groundbreaking concept was published in the influential *Journal of Finance* in 1952. "Portfolio Selection" filled 14 pages of mostly mathematical equations, but its message was deceptively simple: If you are uncomfortable with above-average investment risk, then diversification, not concentration, will give your stock portfolio a strong foundation and provide you with a level of managerial control that you otherwise would not enjoy.

Modern Portfolio Theory prods investors to create a portfolio of stocks that are not related to one another. In this way, each individual security brings a unique strength to the collaborative effort known as your investment portfolio. Owning shares of both homebuilders and grocers, for example, is a good bet when the economy is booming. But in a recession, when growth is scarce, construction companies suffer more than supermarkets. That's because in bad times people don't rush to build, but they do need to eat. And since no one can predict when prosperity will come or go, how the stocks in your portfolio react to changes in market conditions is more important than how many securities you own. In a winning portfolio, certain players will have stronger talents than others: some play defense, others play offense, while a smaller and versatile third group is able to cover many positions and situations. Suppose a baseball player is a star fielder but an average hitter. He still makes the lineup because his sharp defense gives your long-ball sluggers an edge. Portfolio Theory shows how your own particular managerial style and risk tolerance can help you field an effective team. Markowitz explains:

> **You've got to look at the portfolio as a whole, not just position by position. And if you're trying to reduce the volatility or uncertainty of your portfolio, then you need more than one security obviously, but you also need securities which don't go up and down together. You can do risk control much better if you have mathematics to provide a framework, rather than just have a rule of thumb not to put your eggs in one basket.**

As investors, we want independent holdings to cooperate together for a greater good—our financial good. Owning dozens of different stocks may seem like a safe harbor against stormy market conditions, but quantity doesn't guarantee quality. If you and 10 coworkers perform a single task well but excel at nothing else, your company isn't likely to thrive. Adding another 10 associates with the exact same skills would only make things worse. Similarly, buying shares of 50 or even 150 computer companies doesn't protect you when consumer sales sag and the technology sector implodes. With comparable stocks, there's no safety in numbers.

The Accidental Theorist

That Markowitz should be in the business school library at all was the result of a chance conversation with a stranger in the waiting room outside the office of Markowitz's dissertation adviser. It came out that Markowitz was stymied about finding a subject for his Ph.D. thesis. As it happened, the man was a stockbroker, and he encouraged Markowitz to study the workings of the stock market—perhaps the best tip a broker has ever given.

Markowitz soon found himself poring over the popular ideas about investing in stocks that were prevalent at the time. Memories of the 1929 stock-market crash and the subsequent Great Depression were still fresh, and relatively few American households owned equities. Stocks were considered highly risky—too volatile for anyone but professional hands who could analyze securities and keep trained eyes on Wall Street's unpredictable bouncing ball. And while some investors practiced diversification to offset market volatility, others preached the idea that holding a few carefully selected stocks was the best route to achieving the greatest returns for the least amount of risk. "The intelligent and safe way to handle capital is to concentrate," the respected Wall Street pundit Gerald M. Loeb expounded. "The greatest safety lies in putting all your eggs in one basket and watching the basket."[2]

If concentrating investments in a few stocks promises high expected return, then it follows that focusing on one top-performing stock would be an even better bet. Indeed, if all you cared about as an investor was raking in reward, then you should just put your entire savings into a single security and stand back with an upturned palm, ready to collect. Of course, most people don't invest this way. Instead, they spread their bets across many holdings.

Why would anyone diversify, Markowitz wondered, if it meant settling for lower returns? Something else must be compelling investors to make such a trade-off. Economists like Markowitz frame the world in terms of trade-offs—what the rest of us call "fate." Every choice is a road not taken, and you must accept the consequences of your decision. So it goes in the stock market, where not only is there no free lunch, there's also no all-you-can-eat special.

Diversification's appeal, Markowitz reasoned, must have to do with stock-market risk. From that intuition, he rooted Portfolio Theory in a crucial and insightful assumption: All investors are risk-averse. Investing all your money in one stock might bring a huge payoff, but what if you're wrong? What if, instead of making 10 times your investment from one of those glorious "ten-bagger" stocks that come to a lucky and patient few, you instead were left holding the bag? According to this reasoning, investors must be compensated for taking on the additional risk of owning stocks versus a more stable short-term choice like cash or U.S. government bonds. This sweetener is known as a *risk premium*—the difference between a risk-free return and the total return from a risky investment.

Decades later, researchers in the nascent study of behavioral finance—which focuses on how human psychology influences personal investment choices and stock prices—would corroborate what Markowitz had implied: People are risk-averse because they fear losing. This tangible emotion is known as "loss aversion": The pain of a loss outweighs the pleasure of a gain. The economist Paul Samuelson—who discusses his own theories on investing and investor behavior in the next chapter—once offered a colleague the following bet on the flip of a coin: Heads, you win $200; tails, you lose $100. The colleague turned down the bet, explaining that he would feel the $100 loss more acutely than the $200 gain. Indeed, one advantage of investing in a mutual fund is that you aren't forced to face your losers head-on; the portfolio manager shoulders that responsibility.

Now, loss aversion is an essential, hard-wired survival mechanism that is triggered when people face uncomfortable risks. It's that inner voice of reason that reminds us to "stop, look and listen," and clearly has been invaluable to the survival of the human race. But in the stock market, loss aversion can lead investors to take greater risks to avoid losses in their portfolio, and not take enough risk to generate gains. If you doubt this, think about your own stock portfolio. Do you tend to sell winners—locking in a profit—and hang on to losers, hoping to break even? You're not alone. Most people find it difficult to sell a stock when it's under water, even though it's more advantageous to take a tax loss on the sale and let your winners ride. Why? Because the appreciated stock is a victory; the shares that have tumbled represent defeat.

Elsewhere in this book, University of Chicago professor Richard Thaler, a leading voice in the popular research field of behavioral finance, gives advice on how to overcome inherent psychological biases and barriers that stand in the way of better investing. Half a century ago, Markowitz implicitly understood that diversifying your investments can eliminate a good deal of personal distress. With a diversified portfolio of stocks, bonds and cash, you'll sleep better knowing that if the market crashed tomorrow, your most stalwart stocks are likely to withstand the brunt of the blow even as the high-flying start-ups crumble. As Markowitz points out:

If you invest equally in a large number of securities that are correlated, then your risk doesn't approach zero. Then risk approaches the average, which is very substantial. You have to diversify, and diversity means looking for things that aren't too highly correlated. And in the process, investors are forced to think about a lot of important things, like why do markets or securities go up and down together?

Put Risk in Its Place

Once Markowitz understood why people diversify, he needed to show them how to build a portfolio in a way that balanced their risk tolerance against the investment returns they expected. This challenge was much more complex, for although people will sweat and shake when faced with unfamiliar risk, we don't always follow our best instincts. When it seems like everyone is making more money in the stock market than you are, it's tempting to take on more risk than you ordinarily would. After all, if you don't play, you don't score. And if everybody's doing it—well, why not? So you tell yourself it's all right to take a chance—you only live once. You bury the rational gut feeling—and jump into an investment abyss without really considering the terrain below.

Just as you imagined, the view from 10,000 feet is indeed spectacular—unless you haven't properly packed your parachute. Markowitz recognized that many investors stuff their portfolios with securities in the offhanded way they toss clothes into a laundry basket. With Portfolio Theory, Markowitz urged investors to look at their decisions in the big picture. His suggestion—radical at the time—was that investors should treat a portfolio as an integrated unit, not an array of loose parts. You do yourself a great disservice by simply throwing together a handful of hot stocks and mutual funds, adding a sprinkle of bonds and cash, and calling it a portfolio. Even if the returns from this fiery blend singed the corners of your monthly brokerage account statement, you still wouldn't have an idea of the risk levels you tolerated to get those results. Markowitz explains:

> **When I was doing my research, the way you judged a portfolio manager was to say: "Suppose I had two portfolio managers and 10 years ago I gave each of them $10,000. One made my $10,000 become $20,000; the other made my $10,000 become $40,000. Obviously, the one who made it become $40,000 was twice as good." What this ignored was whether one of them exposed me to greater ups and downs during the course of the 10 years.**

Investment return drives us; investment risk deters us. The prospect of losing every cent you pumped into a single investment is certainly frightening, but risk doesn't have to control you; the goal is to control risk. When approaching an investment decision, be realistic about what the market can give you in exchange for the risk you take.

Markowitz received a Nobel Prize in economic sciences in 1990 for quantifying this unavoidable tug-of-war. Strike a balance, he implored. "The notion that investors ought to be concerned with both risk and return, and the basic formulas for risk and return, came in one afternoon," he recalls. Sitting at his desk in the University of Chicago library that day in 1950, Markowitz drew a broad curve on a sheet of paper from the bottom left to the top right. Its sweeping trajectory resembled an airplane's elegant takeoff, ascending to the left at first, then banking right in a gradual climb toward a higher altitude.

On the far left side of the page, Markowitz noted a series of numbers in percentages from low to high and labeled this *expected return*. With investing, there is no sure thing, and each investor has a preconceived notion of what return he should get for his effort. Expected return is less emotional. It takes the historical returns from an investment, then figures an average future rate from a range of possible outcomes.

Across the bottom of the page, Markowitz jotted another succession of percentages and called this set of figures *standard deviation*—which is a way to measure a portfolio's volatility and range of performance. With a mutual fund, for example, standard deviation shows how much a portfolio might vary in the future from its average historical return. The higher the number, the greater the volatility—the short-term ups and downs of a security. When a portfolio has a large standard deviation, its expected return will be more variable and reactive than a portfolio that operates within a narrower, predictable band. An investment with such a wide range is capable of terrific feats—and sinking disappointments.

Standard deviation is an important risk measure that will be discussed in greater detail later in this chapter. One useful analogy to understand it better might be to think about people you've known in your life. At one end of the spectrum are the boulders—

the Rocks of Gibraltar; at the other extreme are the skipping stones, and most fall somewhere in between. Investment portfolios have similar "personalities." Some you can count on through the storms, others go with the wind, and most are a changeable blend.

Ideally, we try to construct investment portfolios that match our basic temperaments. As a guide, investors could trace the bold arc that Markowitz created, a horizon that became known as the *efficient frontier*—a set of points that contains portfolios with the highest returns for a given level of risk. To build a portfolio where risk and return expectations were aligned with his comfort level, an investor heeding Markowitz's advice needed only to gauge his risk tolerance off the bottom of the page and then find a corresponding return point along the efficient frontier. Conversely, he also could choose a hoped-for rate of return and see how much risk he'd have to shoulder in the effort to achieve it. In this way, investors could more intimately understand their own trade-off between risk and reward, and build an "efficient portfolio." Here's how Markowitz describes his invention:

> **Portfolio Theory recommends that people take a portfolio off the efficient frontier. You choose your point on the efficient frontier according to your willingness to bear risk. It's no free lunch. As you go up the trade-off curve, you get more return, but you also get more risk. If you don't want that much risk, you have to go down the curve, but you give up return.**

The highest point on the efficient frontier—in the upper right corner—is an undiversified portfolio that maximizes expected return. Investing only in small-capitalization U.S. stocks, for example, would offer high potential gains, but also saddles you with concentrated risk. As you move across the frontier, you begin to mix U.S. equities with unrelated assets—large-capitalization and mid-capitalization U.S. stocks, international stocks, bonds, cash, precious metals, natural resources—that follow an orbit different from that of small stocks and accordingly bring diversification and lower risk. Changing the asset blend doesn't knock your portfolio off the efficient frontier, but the diminished volatility brings down the noise and risk levels. The sound quality becomes richer, more resonant. Indeed, as Markowitz explains, finding a comfortable place along the efficient frontier is similar to adjusting the volume control on a stereo:

> As you turn the button one way, you're getting more risk and more return; the other way is less return, less risk. Depending on your risk tolerance, you may want to pick the portfolio with maximum return, which is the riskiest one on the curve, or you may want to come down the curve, as long as you are maximizing expected return for a given volatility.

By the time you get to the bottom end point of the efficient frontier, you're holding a portfolio consisting entirely of U.S. Treasury bills, considered the safest of all investments. It's the point of least resistance, to be sure, but it's also the point of low return. Moreover, being 100 percent in Treasuries, contrary to what you might assume, is not the least risky investment portfolio you could hold. That distinction belongs to an asset mix of 10 percent stocks and 90 percent bonds. Why? Because exposure to 100 percent of *anything*—even solid U.S. government debt—packs a full wallop. A smattering of equity with the fixed income produces a more satisfying result. Notes Markowitz:

> When they look at risk-return trade-off curves, people want to go to the very high return points, because they say "I understand what it means to be making this much per year in return on average." They don't consider the risk that involves. A trade-off curve should show expected return, but being at the "right place" also means there is a chance that if they're not lucky, they could lose.

The Specifics of Risk

Portfolio Theory focuses squarely on risk. Investors naturally gravitate toward return. And when stock prices are hitting new highs and people are convinced that owning equities is a license to print money, people begin to believe that being out of the stock market is riskier than being in. It's a twisted logic that measures risk not by what you might lose, but by what you might not win.

Risk, by any definition, is the chance of loss. Professional portfolio managers are well aware of this fact. The fear that poor investment performance could cost them their jobs, along with heightened competition from increasingly agile rivals, has sent many money masters running to make use of sophisticated risk-management tools they hope can carve an edge. At the same time these professionals are obsessed with risk, individual investors have appeared remarkably complacent about it. Not that no one cries, "The sky is falling"—there are always doomsayers; it's that many U.S. investors at the century's turn had reached the happy conclusion that the sky could not possibly fall. "The tricky thing about risk," noted James Grant, editor of the fortnightly newsletter *Grant's Interest Rate Observer* and an astute commentator on money and finance, "is that it is more threatening as it seems less obvious, and less threatening as it seems more obvious."[3] Markowitz takes a similar view of investors who linger too long at the punch bowl:

> **There's too much feeling of certainty. My feeling is that it's like nature is drawing from a deck of cards. Somewhere in that deck is a 1929, when the market crashed. I don't know the probability of that 1929. Maybe it's one in 100 years or one in 200. But there is a 1929 in this deck of cards we're being dealt.**

You can't predict the future, and you can't expect to dodge a market crash. But like a motorcyclist, you can enjoy the ride even while wearing a helmet. In fact, with added safety, most people would enjoy the ride more. The investment parallel is a diverse portfolio that matches risk with your tolerance for it, coupled with a methodical investment approach. Later in this chapter, you'll learn more about understanding risk tolerance. First, you need to concern yourself with the two distinct types of risk that you face: *systematic risk* and *specific risk*.

Systematic risk, commonly known as "market risk," is the risk of being invested in the market itself. Market risk cannot be diversified away. It is the price of the bet. Every risky security carries an element of danger that its price will drop. Put simply, every stock is sensitive to market movements—swoons that can cost you money. This fear of failure keeps many investors underweighted in equities despite the stock market's long-term wealth-building effect, while some people are so risk-averse that they myopically avoid stocks altogether.

Specific risk, also called "unsystematic risk," is the risk of investing in a particular company or industry sector. Specific risk is a layer of uncertainty on top of market risk—but unlike market risk, it can be mitigated through diversification. Because specific risk is diversifiable, investors shouldn't expect to be compensated for taking it. Market risk, because it always exists, is the only risk that is rewarded. Accordingly, investors have strong incentive to avoid the specific risk of owning just a couple of stocks and instead make their portfolios more reflective of a broader market.

Suppose you believe strongly that people are going to be driving gasoline-powered automobiles for decades to come. For your own car's immediate needs, you regularly stop at the local Exxon station, and you're happy with its prices and service. So you figure that as long as you're sharing your paycheck with Exxon employees, maybe you should own some of the company's stock. Now, ExxonMobil is a global oil giant that competes with other multinational oil producers such as BP and Chevron. If you invest in ExxonMobil alone, there's always a chance that the company's fortunes may stumble and it will lose out to better-managed rivals.

You can buffer the specific risk of owning ExxonMobil by also holding shares in several other major oil producers. But even having stakes in other oil companies diversifies only part of the specific risk; there's still the chance that calamity will strike the entire industry. Maybe overproduction and slower global economic growth will constrict crude prices and take down the sector. You just don't know. To diversify specific risk even further, mix in assets that have little to do with oil and energy. Add companies in technology, financial services, telecommunications, health care, real estate, transportation and consumer goods, and your portfolio's risk profile starts to resemble that of the market as a whole.

You Beta, You Bet

Once you're familiar with these two distinct risks of stock ownership, you then should measure the volatility of an individual security or portfolio in relation to other common stocks. Again, volatility is the tendency for a security to rise or fall sharply in price over a brief time.

There are several key yardsticks of investment risk to understand: *beta, standard deviation, Sharpe Ratio, R-squared* and *alpha*.

Beta, so named because it uses the Greek letter as its symbol, offers a handy mirror of how risky a stock or fund has been compared to the overall market that an investor hopes to outperform. But beta is at best a rearview mirror. Beta cannot predict future patterns of a stock or mutual fund; it merely reflects past behavior and suggests what might be.

You need to know that a beta of 1.0 is assigned to a major market index. For stocks and stock mutual funds that invest in larger companies, the market benchmark is the Standard & Poor's 500-stock index; investors in smaller stocks often use the Wilshire 4500 or the Russell 2000 stock indices, which include companies not found in the S&P 500. Bond investors benchmark against the Lehman Brothers Aggregate Index. The S&P 500 is often called "the market." In fact, these 500 stocks are only a representative sample. The total U.S. market actually consists of more than 7,200 big, medium and small companies. A mutual fund that tracks the S&P 500, such as the mammoth Vanguard Index 500, also will have a beta of 1.0. This means its risk is roughly equal to its benchmark. In general, portfolios with betas above 1.0 are riskier than the market; those below 1.0 are less risky.

Accordingly, if the market beta is 1.0, an investment with a beta of 1.1 can be expected to perform 10 percent better than its benchmark in up markets and 10 percent worse in down markets. Conversely, a beta of 0.90 offers below-market risk—meaning the portfolio will trail in up markets by 10 percent and act 10 percent better in down markets. For example, at the end of April 2000, White Oak Growth Stock Fund, which invests in large-growth companies, posted a beta of 1.28. Immediately you know this is a higher-risk investment with a wide range of performance that could swing at least 28 percent above or below its S&P 500 benchmark. For the three years that ended in March 2000, White Oak Growth returned 47.7 percent annually—20.3 percentage points, or about 43 percent, better than the S&P 500.

In contrast, investments with betas of less than 1.0 fare better in bearish markets but typically will lag behind the powerful bullish trends. Dodge & Cox Stock Fund, for instance, has a beta of 0.89; its value-stock portfolio tends to rise and fall at a slower rate than the market. Dodge & Cox finished the three years through March 2000, a bear market for value stocks, with a 16.8 percent annualized return—10.6 percentage points below the growth-stock-oriented S&P 500.

Dodge & Cox and low-beta funds like it typically would be most appropriate for more conservative and patient investors, while White Oak Growth and its racier counterparts would appeal to more aggressive shareholders. A simple analogy to think about personal investment style is to compare it to the type of car you choose to drive. In fact, people would be advised to give as much careful thought to buying stocks as they do to buying a car. The good news about investing is that, unlike the car, you aren't

constrained by budget. Your investment dollars will buy a prag-
matic Honda or a dramatic BMW. Just think of your portfolio as
a large garage, and there's room for both. The Honda is the reliable core of the portfolio, and the BMW is for fun and expeditions.
Maybe you work a straight, 40-hour week and spend evenings and
weekends with family; maybe you work 60 hours a week and
cherish free time alone. People make these choices, combina-
tions and trade-offs every day; there's no reason why a lifetime of
investing should be any different. Investing is serious—and fun.
But you're the only one who can determine when hard work ends
and fun begins.

These rules hold as well for common stocks. Internet service
provider America Online, for example, with a beta in March 2000
of roughly 2.5, is nearly two and a half times as volatile as the
S&P 500 index to which it belongs. If the market rises or falls 10
percent, AOL tends to swing 25 percent to either side. In contrast, energy giant ExxonMobil carries a beta of just 0.54. Exxon-
Mobil is a more stable investment than both AOL and the S&P
500, typically gaining or losing only 5.4 percent when the index
advances or declines 10 percent.

Because the performance prospects for AOL seem chancier
than for ExxonMobil, the stock would attract aggressive investors
who expect a higher return to compensate for the perceived extra
risk. That is, investors insist on being paid a premium for going
out on a limb with AOL, knowing that the market value of
such a fast-growing company could be slashed if it failed to
meet Wall Street's expectations. Maybe the Internet will become
just another utility, and AOL will have to lower its monthly access
fee in response to mounting competition. Again, you just don't
know.

For effective diversification against volatility and risk, take
additional risk. Not greater risks, necessarily, just more of them.
An airplane with a broad wingspan will have a smoother flight
than a craft with a narrow wingspan. Spread your wings. As
Markowitz aptly described, it pays to hold several asset classes

with little or no correlation. Each can be volatile and risky in their own right—no need to stuff cash in a low-yielding bank certificate of deposit—but they likely will display volatility at different intervals. Over time, this strategy actually makes a portfolio less uncertain and potentially higher-performing.

Adding lower-beta stocks to a portfolio lessens its volatility. If you invested $10,000 each in AOL and ExxonMobil, for example, the two will offset each other neatly. AOL's business does not overlap with ExxonMobil's. Indeed, the beta of a portfolio that held those two stocks alone in March 2000 is 1.5—shaving off more than one-third of the risk of holding AOL by itself. Add an equal dollar amount of telecommunications bellwether AT&T and the beta falls further, to 1.26. Couple this with like investments in health care giant Merck & Co., banking powerhouse Citigroup, and consumer products leader Johnson & Johnson, and you have a highly diversified, large-capitalization stock portfolio with a reasonable beta of 1.16. Over a five-year period through March 2000, this portfolio, in fact, posted an average annual return of 46.6 percent, according to Morningstar—nearly double the 26.8 percent annual result from its S&P 500 benchmark in exchange for roughly 16 percent more risk.

Stock screening tools can help individual investors strike a balance between the risk and reward of their portfolio, and find securities that fit their risk tolerance. The Internet is a great resource; many financial Web sites offer screening options free of charge. Good choices include Wall Street City (www.wallstreetcity .com), Quicken (www.quicken.com) and MSN Money Central (www.moneycentral.msn.com).

Deviating Standards

Remember how Markowitz used standard deviation to help create the risk-return trade-off known as the efficient frontier? Think of investing as pitching a quarter into a glass of water from a few feet away. Sometimes the coin will land in the glass; other times it will fall wide of the mark. Standard deviation determines the range of possible outcomes for a given investment, expressed as a number, which is then measured against its return. Assets with above-average standard deviations will have higher highs and lower lows.

The S&P 500 over the three years through March 2000 returned 27.4 percent annually with a standard deviation of 21.9. An investment with a similar standard deviation should be expected to achieve at least the benchmark return of 27.4 percent. If you fare better, you're ahead compared to the risk you've taken. A portfolio that is 1.5 times more volatile than the market would have a standard deviation of 32.8. To compensate, investors should expect a commensurate return.

The Janus Mercury fund, for example, carries a three-year standard deviation of 39.9. As such, the fund is nearly twice as volatile as the S&P 500, and so it should provide substantial above-market returns. Mercury's three-year average annual gain over the three years ending in March 2000 was 60.9 percent—more than double the return of the S&P 500. This fund has covered its risk well.

But high standard deviations can also indicate serious under-performance. PBHG Growth is an aggressive fund with a standard deviation of 55.9—about three times that of the S&P 500. Such a high level of risk exposure promises big gains in a given year—like in 1993 when this fund returned 46.7 percent, beating the S&P 500 by 36.7 percentage points. But in the late 1990s PBHG Growth fell on hard times, posting an average annual return of just 2.4 percent in the three years through 1998. Then, true to form, it came roaring back, gaining 92.5 percent in 1999.

Look Sharpe

The Sharpe Ratio, named for William Sharpe, the Nobel Laureate who created it, is a pure measure of risk-adjusted return, expressed as a figure. Technically, the Sharpe Ratio is the return achieved for each unit of risk. For instance, you can safely assume that an investment in Coca-Cola is less risky than an investment in Internet portal Yahoo!. Coca-Cola therefore would have a lower standard deviation. Now, if Coca-Cola returns 12 percent a year and Yahoo! returns 13 percent, Coke will have a higher Sharpe Ratio because it has achieved that return with less risk.

You can use the Sharpe Ratio to compare two funds directly, and determine how much risk a fund had to bear in order to earn an excess return. Look for investments with the highest Sharpe Ratio relative to their peers. But figuring out the Sharpe Ratio is complicated. A quick way to make a ballpark calculation is simply to divide the total return of an asset by its standard deviation. The S&P 500, with its standard deviation of 21.9 and three-year average return through March 2000 of 27.4 percent, has a Sharpe Ratio of roughly 1.25 (27.4 divided by 21.9). Janus Mercury's 60.9 percent three-year average gain and 39.9 standard deviation gives it a Sharpe Ratio of about 1.53. The Janus fund had a three-year performance similar to that of Fidelity New Millenium Fund, which returned 58.9 percent over the same period. But the Fidelity fund had a standard deviation of 56.3, contributing to a subpar Sharpe Ratio of 1.05. Investors in Janus Mercury got their return with far less risk. That's what makes a fund look sharp.

Are You Square?

An often-overlooked measure of portfolio risk is called *R-squared*, which compares an investment's correlation to its benchmark. The importance of R-squared becomes clear in a search for above-average mutual funds that dare to be different.

Shareholders of actively managed equity funds are paying a professional for stock-picking skills. Ideally, you want an active fund manager to add value over a comparable, passively managed index fund. Index funds mirror the return of a benchmark, less expenses. To surpass a benchmark by any commendable distance, an active manager must take calculated, thoughtful risks. Perhaps this means concentrating assets in a particularly attractive stock or sector. Maybe it means buying when everyone else is selling, or vice versa. No matter what, fund managers must be willing to make executive decisions with clear conviction, and to stand behind those choices until they decide on a more appropriate course of action. The quest for profitable nooks and overlooked crannies is how they earn their keep. Otherwise, you might as well buy an index fund and accept what the market gives.

The trouble is that for some managers, a strong stance poses what to them is an even greater danger: being wrong. Nowadays there is increasing pressure on managers not to stray far from their benchmark. A manager's compensation and bonus package are linked to performance, and the penalty for underperformance is harsher than the reward for outperformance. This toe-the-line message leads all but the bravest and most iconoclastic managers to take a path of least resistance. They don't want to get paid for taking risk—they just want to get paid.

When you assume an investment risk—no matter how educated—there's always the danger that the stock will turn out to be a disaster that blows a hole in your portfolio. Some fund managers don't want to go anywhere near that risk. They run in the middle of the pack, blending with the herd and avoiding extremes. The return of these portfolios stays close to the market, though always with a slight lag.

If this sounds like one of your funds, be careful: The portfolio manager could be "index hugging," otherwise known as "closet indexing." Index huggers charge for the cost of tailored active management, but they give you an off-the-rack portfolio that looks and acts like an index fund. What's wrong with that? Nothing, if you don't mind paying more for the same results. The average large-cap U.S. stock fund charges 1.4 percent a year for management, or $140 on each $10,000 investment. The bill for a like-minded S&P 500 index fund is just 0.6 percent, or $60. The Vanguard 500 Index fund collects just 0.18 percent, or $18 for a $10,000 account.

Closet index funds will never venture far from the market average. Yet because of their higher expenses, returns for index-hugging portfolios will be lower than for real index funds. If you want an investment to follow an index, buy an index fund. Don't pay a closet indexer for management services that you're not getting.

How do you unmask a closet index fund? First, you want to track a portfolio's return according to its beta. Then compare a fund's performance against its benchmark. That's where R-squared comes into play. In portfolio-speak, R-squared measures the relationship between a fund and its best-fit index. It's expressed as a number from zero to 100. As the R-squared increases, the fund begins to resemble its benchmark more closely. Index funds have an R-squared of 100, pegging them as market clones.

Insightful research and knowledge on R-squared and other risk measures is readily available on the Web from fund-data companies such as Morningstar (www.morningstar.com). A Morningstar study, in fact, shows that the average stock fund more closely correlates with the S&P 500 than it ever has—particularly for large-cap funds. In 1994, only one in 12 large-cap portfolios had an R-squared of 90 or higher; by the fall of 1999, two of every five did.

Bottom line: If an actively managed fund has an R-squared between 95 and 99, and a beta hovering near 1.0, leave it in the closet where it belongs.

Alpha One

Another measure of performance relative to beta uses the first letter of the Greek alphabet, *alpha*. A positive alpha means an investment did better than its beta suggested it would. A negative alpha shows that a fund manager didn't earn enough to compensate for the risk taken.

Ideally, you want an investment to deliver above-average returns for below-average risk. Weitz Value Fund, for example, carries a beta of 0.65, which suggests that this mid-cap value portfolio has low risk and should therefore underperform its benchmark in bull markets. The S&P 500 averaged 27.4 percent gains in each of the three years through March 2000. With a beta of 0.65, Weitz Value could be expected to gain 17.8 percent annually over the same period (0.65 times 27.4 percent). Instead, the fund returned 27.2 percent on average during those three years— in line with its benchmark, but with one-third less risk—earning a positive alpha. In other words, the fund's manager added significant value to the portfolio without assuming inordinate risk.

Understanding Your Risk Tolerance

Suppose that in early 1995, you saw the future and concentrated your stockholdings into equal dollar amounts of technology bellwethers Microsoft, Intel, Dell Computer, Cisco Systems and America Online. In exchange, you got a high-octane portfolio capable of blowing the doors off any measurable index—but one that could crash and burn when technology stocks fall out of favor.

By all rights, this would be a high-risk portfolio. Investing $10,000 in each of these five high fliers would have delivered a blistering 108 percent annualized return in the five-year period through March 2000, according to Morningstar—83 percentage points better than the S&P 500 benchmark average. But the standard deviation of this gilded group was an extremely volatile 88.7, versus a more temperate 21.9 for the index. The portfolio's beta of nearly 1.7 meant it took on 70 percent more risk than the market average.

Maybe that's a trade-off you can live with. If not, then it's unlikely that you would have been able to hang on to such a portfolio through five years of leaps and dives. So come to terms with the facts of investment life—before you buy. For although it is one of the few investment factors within their control, many investors don't realistically assess their risk tolerance.

We'll look at ways to anticipate investment outcomes when

we meet William Sharpe in a later chapter of this book. Sharpe studied under the tutelage of Markowitz and was instrumental in gaining recognition for Portfolio Theory and putting his own stamp on it. For now, the two main questions you need to worry about as an investor are: What must I do to meet my investment needs, and how do I manage the risk involved?

The answers hinge on how much risk you're prepared to take and the trade-offs you are willing to make. Successful investing is not picking the next Microsoft—although that sure would be great. For most people, investing is simply about establishing an asset allocation that achieves certain goals within a set time frame. Motivations are different if you're 35 years old, or 45, or 55. Will you accept more risk or not? Do you want to save more or less? What if all doesn't go as planned? Are you able to work longer in order to meet your expectations, or diminish your expectations and accept a lower standard of living?

Financial planners typically try to box clients into a risk profile. You're asked a prepared series of seemingly random questions that deal with attitudes toward spending, saving and dealing with money. From these results, planners typecast you as a high-, moderate- or low-risk investor. Then they assume a historical annual rate of return for stocks, bonds and cash, your life expectancy, how much income you will make and what you'll need to live on in retirement. With this knowledge, they choose a point on the efficient frontier where you belong, and attempt to tailor a portfolio that fits your "personality."

Frankly, this information is so general that it's virtually meaningless—another example of paying a high price for off-the-shelf advice. The notion that you're a daredevil, a wallflower or somewhere in between may determine the kind of fun you have at parties or the vacations you take, but it has little bearing on your investment needs and results. What you usually get from such rote analysis is a generic portfolio that doesn't answer the key question: Will I make it? Markowitz contends that investors deserve better:

> The process is too automatic. Advisers say, "We've taken all these facts about you—and this is the right portfolio for you." That bothers me, because then the individual doesn't realize that there is risk involved. Even if it is the right portfolio, there is a chance that 20 years from now, he won't have anywhere near what he is counting on having. He should understand that maybe, if he saved at a higher rate or took a different portfolio, this chance could be made smaller.

When investors consider the best way to construct a portfolio, they aren't looking for a date with Mr. Right; they want a long-term relationship with Mr. Market. People want to know the range of outcomes they might face from a toss of the dice today. How much can I gain? How much can I lose? And can I live with these possibilities?

Which Type of Investor Are You?

Investors are generically viewed as being either conservative, moderate or aggressive. But what does that mean?

- Conservative investors tend to keep their risks small, committing most of a portfolio to cash and high-quality bonds. They may include income-producing, relatively secure stocks like utilities and telephone companies that pay regular shareholder dividends.
- Moderate-risk investors will follow the lead of conservative investors, but mix in more volatile growth stocks and mutual funds.
- Aggressive investors tolerate speculative investments that offer highly unpredictable outcomes but a potential for turbocharged returns.

Most people possess a bit of each of these qualities. We take risks and are cautious. We break molds and are malleable. We play to win and know how to lose. Don't accept common categorization from so-called investment experts. They can't possibly know you better than you do. Being honest with yourself is the first step toward becoming a sophisticated investor. The key is to take sensible risks, to be prepared. It doesn't matter if you drive a Honda or a BMW—you still have to keep the engine tuned.

A good place to start is with your cash holdings. Emboldened by the bull market for U.S. stocks and below-average inflation in the 1990s, people with long time horizons have tended to shun cash and stay fully invested in the market. Buying stocks for the long term—U.S. stocks, really—is a can't-miss strategy, the thinking goes, especially if you won't need the money for another 25 years. Just sit back and ride out the bumps. For diversification— if you even get that far—there's always foreign stocks, real estate investment trusts, natural resources and energy stocks, and perhaps intermediate-term bonds.

Cash, it's true, is no way to make money. Inflation cruelly whittles away the value of supposedly fail-safe bank certificates of deposit. But cash is not trash. A prudent asset-allocation strategy has always included some cash liquidity to cushion an investment portfolio. Cash won't get hit like stocks and bonds when interest rates rise. It also fares better during bouts of high inflation because it rolls over at correspondingly greater yields. And cash is nice to have when stock prices fall and there are bargains to scoop up. It's easy to forget years like 1994, when cash outdid the broader U.S. stock market. That year, the S&P 500 rose 1.3 percent, while U.S. Treasury bills—a cash equivalent—returned 3.9 percent.

How much cash in a portfolio is reasonable? That depends on your age and risk tolerance. Generally, the more time you have to let your investments grow, the more you can earmark for stocks. If the market collapses and doesn't recover for several years, people with steady jobs and long futures can better absorb such a blow. Cash would be a more immediate concern for older and nonworking people with greater income needs. Money that you'll use in a relatively short time, such as to buy a house or send a child to college, should also be kept liquid.

Yet even the youngest, most aggressive long-term investor ought to have some cash available. Many investment professionals recommend a cash allocation of between 5 percent and 10 percent of investment assets—or at least one year's worth of living expenses. A blend of 60 percent stocks, 30 percent intermediate- and long-term bonds, and 10 percent cash or U.S. Treasury bills is considered a standard allocation model, give or take a few percentage points.

Secure with a 10 percent cash base, for instance, you can begin to build a portfolio that can generate real wealth. Many people fill the bulk of a portfolio—say, 80 percent—with low- to moderate-risk U.S. and international blue-chip stocks, a large-cap index fund, top-performing actively managed funds and high-quality bonds. The remaining 10 percent can be given to several high-risk, speculative plays, including smaller growth companies, Internet and biotechnology hopefuls, and emerging markets. Just be prudent, Markowitz cautions:

> **An individual investor should not put too much money into individual securities. He should at least put the majority of his equity money into a well-diversified actively managed fund or an index fund. If he thinks he understands certain things better than the market on average, or his adviser does, then take a *little* bit of money and play games with it.**

Optimal Portfolios

Studies show that asset allocation, even more than which stocks and bonds you own, is the most important determinant of investment return. To illustrate this point, Ibbotson Associates, a Chicago investment research firm, estimated the net value of three separate $100,000 portfolios over a 10-year period ending in June 2000. Over that time, the average yearly pretax return for the S&P 500 was 13.8 percent, 11 percent for long-term corporate bonds and 7.3 percent for cash.

The results? A mix of 10 percent S&P 500 stocks, 30 percent long-term corporate bonds and 60 percent cash would have been worth $201,557 at the end of the period. A blend of 30 percent stocks, 60 percent bonds and 10 percent cash was valued at $283,892. And as could be expected, a portfolio with 60 percent stocks, 30 percent bonds and 10 percent cash fared the best of the three, with an ending value of $364,477.

Which industries hold the most promise? Which stocks and bonds do you buy? Spread the risk. Think about diversifying among 10 industries, paying special attention to areas or companies about which you have a keen understanding. The S&P 500 sectors and industries include: *Materials*, such as chemicals and steel; *Industrials*, like engineering and aerospace; *consumer discretionary*—department stores, restaurants, automobiles; *consumer staples*, such as food, beverages, cosmetics and household products; *energy*—oil and gas drilling and exploration; *financials*, including insurers and banks; *telecommunications services*, like wireless and broadband providers; *Information technology*—computer software and hardware, semiconductors, Internet and telecommunications equipment; *health care*—pharmaceuticals, biotechnology, medical products, hospitals, and *utilities*, like electric and gas companies.

As an example, some investment experts suggest that the best performers for the next few decades will be companies in financial services, health care, technology and leisure. Why are they so confident? They're just following the life cycle in the United States, which for the next 30 years or so will continue to be dominated by the 76 million members of the so-called baby boom generation. Spending and savings habits evolve with age, and baby boomers take these patterns to exponential extremes.

If you agree that these four broad areas are the engines of future growth, it would be smart to own a selection of promising growth and value stocks in each category. You'd want large stocks with established market leadership, coupled with shares of well-managed small companies that have a chance to become bigger. Since an aging population also is a pressing issue for developed Europe and Japan, you would do well to consider non-U.S. stocks that can benefit from this trend. An international fund that invests worldwide can provide adequate diversification. Or if you're especially bullish on one part of the globe—say, Latin America or Europe—you can narrow the field with a specialized regional fund. Plus international holdings can lower total portfolio risk, since stocks overseas tend to move independently from U.S. stocks.

Of course, the experts could be wrong. As a rule, mitigate specific sector risk by putting no more than 10 percent of the portfolio into any one industry. In 1999, the S&P 500 rose 21 percent, but many sectors fared poorly. Mutual funds that specialized in financial services lost 1.4 percent; those that bought real estate–related stocks lost 3.7 percent, according to Morningstar.

But with a 10 percent cap on investment in a given sector, even a 50 percent loss would mean an overall portfolio decline of just 5 percent. Additionally, to offset specific company risk, keep investment in any single stock to a maximum of 5 percent of the portfolio. That way, even if a stock drops 50 percent in value, the hit to the portfolio would be only 2.5 percent.

Markowitz's own portfolio is a balanced 50-50 blend of stock mutual funds and individual bonds. His main exposure to domestic and international stocks comes from the highly diversified College Retirement Equities Fund, which is exclusively for employees of educational and research institutions. He also owns a few individual stocks, including an investment made decades ago in International Business Machines. The fixed-income portion he handles himself.

Diversification demands a big canvas. Owning just two or three growth stocks and a growth-oriented mutual fund is not enough. What happens when growth stocks falter? You could easily experience what's known as a shortfall to the market—not keeping up, essentially. The only way to avoid a shortfall is with a well-diversified portfolio that can maneuver through all market conditions.

How Much Diversification Is Enough?

Portfolio risk decreases as the number of assets increases. But how much diversification is enough? At what point does diversification become a drag on performance? Here's what Markowitz has to say:

> If you're trying to reduce the volatility or uncertainty of your portfolio as a whole, then you need more than one security obviously, but you also need securities which don't go up and down together. It turns out that you don't need hundreds and hundreds of securities. Much of the effective diversification comes with 20 or 30 well-selected securities.

When it comes to both individual stocks and mutual funds, less may be more. A heavyweight critic of broad portfolio diversification is Warren Buffett, who focuses his sights on a solid-looking business, loads up on its shares and holds long-term. "Diversification, as practiced generally, makes very little sense for anyone who knows what they're doing," the Oracle of Omaha has decreed. And a growing number of fund managers have concluded that if they can't be Buffett, they can at least invest like him. So they have dispensed with broad-based diversity and instead sink 50 percent or more of their shareholders' assets into their top 10 promising stocks, rounding out the remainder with smaller "farm team" positions.

Focused-fund managers view concentration as powerful leverage to help them hurdle their benchmark index, distinguishing them from peers and the predictability of index funds. Concentrated funds are at opposite poles from indexed offerings, which hold a bit of virtually every name found in their universe. The idea is that a skilled stock-picker has a better chance of beating the market with his best ideas than with a diluted collection of names.

In fact, a body of research suggests that the benefits of diversification taper off as the number of stocks in a portfolio rises. A famous 1970 study by Lawrence Fisher and James Lorie showed that risk declines noticeably as stocks are added to a portfolio. But once the portfolio holds more than 20 stocks, further additions have a minimal effect on risk.[4]

The "sweet spot" of a portfolio, the point where specific risk is most effectively diversified away, falls between 12 and 20 distinct holdings. Adding more stocks, as Fisher and Lorie indicated, has little or no impact on volatility, as measured by standard deviation. Yet the average diversified U.S. stock fund has 138 different stocks, Morningstar reports. Are investment managers too cautious? Many are. From Charles Ellis of Greenwich Associates, whose wise counsel is widely respected in the financial services industry, comes this advice: "As investors, we will make better decisions if we concentrate our skills and energies on making fewer and better investments, deliberately searching for the Great Decisions."[5]

Mutual fund investors have similar concerns. Buying a fund is a proven way to own a group of diversified securities. But don't go overboard. Choosing one or two actively managed funds or an index fund from each of several broad categories offers plenty of diversification. Many investors are looking for exposure to stocks of big, medium and small companies—both growth and value— in U.S. and foreign markets, along with an offsetting allocation to fixed income, natural resources and real estate. Resist the temptation to "guarantee" diversification by owning a smorgasbord of like-minded funds. That flawed strategy only gives you an expensive index clone—and guaranteed sub-benchmark performance.

Concentrated funds may be an antidote to overdiversification, but they come with their own consequences. The "con" in concentration is that the fund manager might take too much risk, loading up on shares of a company that seems promising but instead runs headlong into trouble. For a broadly diversified fund, this specific risk isn't a major problem; it can be for a focused fund. High volatility is another factor. These funds tend to have above-average standard deviation from their category averages. Another warning: Managers of concentrated funds tend to be rather iconoclastic in their decisions. Investors can spend many years in the wilderness with them—to the point where patience and loyalty are sorely tested.

When considering a concentrated fund, be sure the manager has a long record of sharp stock-picking. He should also be willing to take the chance of holding on to the fund's big winners and watching them win again—and again. Good choices include: Oakmark Select, Marsico Focus, Torray, Papp America-Abroad and Weitz Partners Value.

Risk is shifting sand. Staying on top of it is the challenge. Through Portfolio Theory, Markowitz put a foundation under risk. He showed investors there are many choices, depending on their personality and perspective, to steer them from uncertainty. Of course, diversification has its limits. In the end, there's no getting away from risk—but a big-picture view can keep it at bay. With investing, remember to see both the forest and the trees; don't go out on a branch—branch out.

CHAPTER 2

Time and Money: Paul Samuelson

"You should take money seriously. In fact, you shouldn't enjoy investing. That's a trap. It makes you too active. You churn your own portfolio. You listen to stories, and most of the stories are not worth listening to."

For much of the 1990s, investors enjoyed extraordinary, double-digit stock-market gains year after year. Not surprisingly, a popular belief developed among even more sophisticated shareholders that if you hold stocks long enough—10, 20, 50 years— you will not, cannot, lose money in the market. What a nice idea. There's just one problem, says Paul A. Samuelson, the celebrated Nobel Prize–winning economist: It's not true.

The chance that the stock market will sack you with a sharp, crippling setback does not diminish with each passing year, Samuelson contends—no matter how luxurious a time horizon you have. Market risk never disappears. Investment experts religiously preach portfolio diversification to soften the impact of an unforeseen blow—typically advising a tailored blend of common stocks, plus bonds and cash. Rightly so, but broad diversification is only a partial defense. Holding more stocks doesn't eliminate all risk, just as insurance companies don't operate risk-free by writing more and more homeowner policies. There's just no avoiding systematic risk—the unpredictable consequences of being in the market itself. As Samuelson reminds us, those dice are rolled each day:

> The meter is always running with respect to risk. The argument people use—that the long-term investor doesn't have to worry about risk the way the short-term one does—is not correct. It is not true that risk erodes toward zero as the investment horizon lengthens. Every year that comes up is the first year of what's left.

Market risk is not the same as market volatility—those violent gyrations that can send stock prices soaring or plunging. The volatility of a portfolio does tend to smooth out over long periods. A patient, buy-and-hold stock investor who stays in the market and faithfully reinvests dividends will see clearly how time burnishes rough edges. If you chart a mutual fund's month-to-month returns over 20 years, it will resemble sylvan rolling hills. A monthly tally of its performance over the past two years will be a snapshot of jagged peaks and deep valleys. The pastoral big picture blurs the prickly details.

Wouldn't it be great if you could artfully dodge the market's hardest punches? In fact, Samuelson points out, leapfrogging in and out of the market actually adds to your overall investment risk. As a short-term strategy, market timing is inherently volatile. You're likely to miss the big, wealth-building rallies. And you still have to contend with market risk. The history of the world's greatest market-timers is a slim volume indeed. More often than not, timers are busily patting themselves on the back when stocks stage a stunning rebound.

So you want to be in the market on its best days, but no one can predict when that will be. As the comedian Woody Allen once said, most of success in life is just showing up. Large-company stocks—U.S. companies, that is—have richly rewarded those who stayed the course through the swings, hits and misses of the twentieth century. The Standard & Poor's 500-stock index has not suffered a loss in any 15-year period going back to 1926, according to Ibbotson Associates, a Chicago-based investment research firm. This basket of the 500 largest-capitalization stocks, with dividends reinvested, delivered average annual gains of 11.3 percent between January 1926 and December 1999—handily beating inflation, the nemesis of all investors that over time can destroy the value of a dollar.

What does an 11.3 percent return, compounded each year, mean in real money? Plenty. Ibbotson's calculations show that a $1,000 stake in the S&P 500 in January 1926 would have grown to $2,845,628 by the end of 1999, not counting the cost of taxes. Even one decade of staying in stocks through the market's fits and starts can make a huge difference in return. Investing $10,000 in the S&P at the end of December 1989 would have begun ominously. Stock prices had crashed in October 1987, but the benchmark Dow Jones Industrial Average clawed its way back over the following year. By the middle of 1990, the Dow had risen well above its precrash levels. But as the U.S. economy slumped into recession, the market tumbled sharply, losing roughly 20 percent between July and October 1990. After that, the tide turned, and for much of the next eight years the stock market never looked back. By December 1999 the portfolio would have been worth $53,243, before taxes. Time is money.

The extraordinary power and popularity of U.S. stocks as an exceptional, inflation-fighting asset class is a short history at best, Samuelson asserts, one that holds up only with the benefit of hindsight. The future offers no similar guarantees, he adds, and to invest on any other assumption is dangerous. Czarist Russia bonds might have seemed a fair play in 1912, but you'd have lost the entire investment five years later in the Russian Revolution. In the 1950s, conservative investors believed that U.S. bonds were the safest and best-performing investment. Stocks were too speculative to be left to individuals. In 1951, only 4 percent of U.S. households directly owned equities. Thirty years later, just 16 percent did.[1] Not long ago, even pension funds, university endowments and other institutions were restricted on how much of their investment portfolios could be allocated to common stocks.

Yet for more than 50 years now, that risky, inscrutable U.S. stock market has been extremely kind to investors. In the 54 years between 1946 and 1998, inflation-adjusted returns on the large-company stocks in the S&P 500 were positive 38 times, according to Ibbotson. That translates to a 70 percent win rate. Most people would take those odds to the track. You would have gloated during cakewalks like the S&P's 53.4 percent inflation-adjusted gain in 1954. But you also would have endured agonizing periods like 1974, when that same bellwether index dropped 34.5 percent. But those were the exceptions. For most of the past half-century, investors have experienced large-cap U.S. stock returns in any given year of between negative 10 percent and positive 30 percent.

Will the next 50 years—or even the next five—be as generous? Who knows? Believing otherwise leads to a false sense of security and complacency. The Scottish economist Adam Smith, one of the greatest observers of people and money, noted this essential point more than 200 years ago in *The Wealth of Nations*: "The chance of gain is by every man more or less over-valued, and the chance of loss is by most men under-valued."[2]

The Securities Blanket

Peace of mind, however, is exactly what we hope the stock market will give us—the kindly market will take care of our children, our retirement, our heirs. Stocks have become a trusted friend, a rock and redeemer that we can count on for the rest of our lives. If only that were so. As author and astute investment veteran Peter Bernstein will explain in a later chapter of this book, the market owes you nothing. The trend may be your friend, but a stock isn't. You can become infatuated with a stock, embrace it—even understand its personality better than you know your own family's. But it's a one-way relationship. A stock doesn't care that you own it. And though a hot stock might make you enough money to afford an expensive dinner, it will never pick up the check.

Of course, the long run is full of hope, as well it should be. But hope alone is not an investment strategy. Everyone wants to be worth more in 10 years than they are today. But judgment is clouded when we confuse chance with certainty. The stock market is a whirlwind bazaar of fabulous choices, and many investors understandably become kids in a candy store around it. Buy and

hold—and buy some more. Except the proprietor—Mr. Market—
often gives service with a snarl. On Wall Street, the customer is
not always right, even if you've been a regular for years.

Time does not heal all of the market's wounds. Bear markets—
prolonged price declines of at least 20 percent—are miserable
and unforgiving water tortures. The S&P 500 lost 41.2 percent
between January 1973 and December 1974. The only choice
when trapped in such a quagmire is to hunker down until the
storms pass—the S&P roared back with a 61 percent gain over
1975 and 1976.

But most investors in the depths of a market depression find
that after weeks and months and years of waiting and hoping for
salvation, courage becomes increasingly rare. Famed British
economist John Maynard Keynes, ever quick with a rapier wit,
captured this sentiment best in his jab at the fact that a lengthy
investment horizon may not always live up to its star billing: "In
the long run," he announced, "we are all dead."

While Lord Keynes was opining how short-term events can
mottle one's long-term perspective, Samuelson was a young Harvard University graduate student, just beginning to develop his
own views about how money is saved, spent and traded. This was
the 1930s, and the United States had implemented President
Franklin Roosevelt's New Deal recovery program to help end the
Great Depression. This blend of grassroots populism and fiscal
pragmatism left a strong impression on Samuelson, who was born
in 1915 in Gary, Indiana, and still retains the steely bearing of his
midwestern upbringing.

Samuelson has described himself as the "last generalist" in economics. In fact, he is one of its most ardent generals, though his
battle gear is a scholarly sport coat and signature bow tie. His *Economics: An Introductory Analysis*, first published in 1948 and now in
its 16th edition, is considered the definitive college-level overview of
what is frequently called the "dismal science." For his many contributions and theories that advanced the study of money and its uses,
Samuelson won the Nobel Prize in Economics in 1970.

Now professor emeritus of economics at the Massachusetts Institute of Technology, Samuelson has devoted considerable energy toward educating investors about the benefits and costs of a broad-based stock portfolio. He aims to clarify and demystify complex questions of finance and investing—an absorbing effort he modestly has called his "Sunday painting."[3] Central to that focus is an understanding of how stock prices behave over time and the impact of a long-run time horizon on investment risk. He observes:

> **People believe that history shows conclusively that in dozens of 15-year periods, there's never been a time when you didn't do better in equities. That makes it almost a sure thing. And if you're investing for 500 years, it would be a sure, sure thing. If you just don't pull up the tulips by their roots but just hold, the long pull is your friend and your risk erodes with the time of your investment horizon. It's a leading dogma of the spreading taste for equities.**

Bring a group of bullish investors together and they'll talk about gains, not losses. That's human nature. Virility—and its bragging rights—has become an obsession, particularly among aging, competitive baby boomers. "I invest; therefore I am." Many people vainly believe that if you just hold on long enough, a stock portfolio somehow will attain a kind of legendary investment immortality. If only Grandpa hadn't sold International Business Machines in 1968. How much more dearly he'd be remembered! That's easy to say now, but it conveniently ignores Big Blue's many lonely years in Wall Street's wilderness. Then Grandpa would have been remembered, all right—as a bumbler who didn't sell IBM when he'd had the chance. Samuelson muses:

> **The trouble with this current dogma is that if it's true as stated, then being 60 percent in equities is better than 50 percent. Being 70 percent is better than 60 percent. Being 100 percent in**

equities isn't best of all, because 110 percent is really better. But the moment you're over 100 percent, you not only can be wiped out of your principal, you actually go into debt. Yet so many people believe the dogma about equities that they'll still say in their old age, "I'm a patient buy-and-hold investor, and I'm going to enjoy the higher means." Once you've been successful in equities and until you cease to be successful, you begin to believe there isn't any risk in them.

Wall Street Goes Main Street

Achieving some personal investment nirvana is a utopian ideal. But for much of the 1990s, many investors felt they had already been to the mountaintop. The S&P 500 returned 26.8 percent each year on average between 1995 and 1999—more than twice its normal reward, according to Ibbotson. An equity culture flowered, although at times it seemed more of an equity cult. By early 1999, 48 percent of American households directly owned stock, largely through mutual funds, versus just 19 percent in 1983.[4] Each 1,000-point ascent of the Dow Jones Industrial Average brought larger headlines and heightened investor interest in stocks. Individuals hungered for shares, and the rising demand was self-fulfilling as the stock prices quoted on Wall Street spiraled upward.

On Main Street, expectations surged about the magic the market could weave. In one remarkable survey of 750 individual investors taken in August 1997, respondents nationwide expected average annual gains of 34 percent on stock mutual funds over the subsequent decade—*triple* the historical norm.[5] That year, the S&P 500 returned 33.4 percent, not counting inflation. In 1998, it tacked on another 28.6 percent. By early July 1999, the price-earnings ratio of the S&P 500 index had reached a record 27.3 times its expected full-year operating earnings—a P/E ratio of about twice the historical parallel.

To be sure, the U.S. stock market advance in the 1990s had

some solid underpinnings. Corporate earnings were strong, the economy was growing and Treasury bond yields had not climbed enough to lure investors away from stocks. Those three factors led columnists James K. Glassman and Kevin A. Hassett to assert in a controversial *Wall Street Journal* article in March 1999 that the Dow, which had then just crossed 10,000 for the first time, would be more appropriately valued at 36,000. Later that year, Glassman and Hassett coauthored *Dow 36,000: The New Strategy for Profiting from the Coming Rise in the Stock Market*, which attempted to establish that stocks are no riskier than U.S. Treasury bonds—considered the safest of all investments. Among their chief contentions: Stocks have outperformed bonds over nearly all 20-year horizons. Therefore, in the long run stocks are only as risky as—even less risky than—bonds. As stock investors appreciate that they are free at last from excessive risk, they will no longer demand a premium return to hold stocks. The Dow should climb to a point at which stock returns equal bond returns. "The risks of stock investing—never so great as imagined—really have declined," the two scholars asserted in their *Journal* piece. "Investors today are rationally exuberant. They are bidding up the prices of stocks because stocks are a great deal."[6]

At the very least, investors in the latter part of the 1990s were buying a great deal of stock. Their love affair with equities, like any budding romance, was lighthearted and giddy. And while a good portion of their money was in tax-deferred retirement accounts like 401(k) plans, which force long-term holding, these newcomers hadn't yet felt the disruption that a short-term shock can deliver to the best-laid plans. While it's been true that over longer periods of time stocks have outperformed bonds, stock-market volatility has hardly disappeared. In any given year, stocks are not always the top-performing asset. For such a heightened level of uncertainty, investors rightly should be paid more to hold stocks, as has long been the case, and stocks should continue to bring a higher annual rate of return on average than bonds.

When inflation is low, however, the risk premium on equities can be expected to shrink, because there is less perceived risk in the economy. Inflation is the Grim Reaper; it strikes at the heart of bonds and cash. As the value of money erodes, and a dollar can buy increasingly fewer things, investors expect stock returns to outpace inflation as compensation. But when inflation is in check and the Federal Reserve isn't pressured to raise interest rates, stockholders will accept a lower risk-premium over bonds.

Glassman and Hassett's bold prediction appeared during a period of abnormally low U.S. inflation, to be sure. But their argument that over time stocks are no riskier than bonds, however well-presented, suggests that we can be secure about the long run simply because the short run has been so good. Forget all you've been told; past performance *is* a guarantee of future returns.

Were this the case, there would be no reason for anyone to diversify against risk by holding bonds or cash—just back up the truck and shovel in the stocks. This idealistic notion recalls the now-infamous speech that respected Yale University economist and market forecaster Irving Fisher gave to the Purchasing Agents Association in New York on October 14, 1929. "Stock prices have reached a permanently high plateau," he stated firmly. Two weeks later, the market crashed. History did not repeat itself immediately after Glassman and Hassett's article was published in the *Journal*, but overoptimism doesn't follow any set timetable. Samuelson sounded a cautionary note:

More and more people are being converted to this doctrine that it's prudent to hold equities if you are a long-term, patient holder. As that doctrine spreads, that's going to raise the price-to-earnings ratio of the market. If it became universal, it would actually create no anchor. What P/E ratio is wrong? When people believe you can't lose money in equities, that may become true in the short run. But it will self-destruct if the P/E gets high enough.

Gearing for the Long Run

The long run is a self-winding mechanism. We have no control over what will happen later today, let alone years from now. The problem with the long run is that investors are caught up in the short run. We don't want the romance to end. When it invariably does, the relationship gets rocky, and we try to find a smoother rock. The long run is demanding. It asks for self-interest, not selfishness; trust, not trysts. If we allowed such openness and understanding, we would settle in for a lifetime of ups and downs with money. We would spread investment dollars across small, mid-size and large U.S. stocks, with a tilt toward the biggest and most liquid companies. A sprinkling of international stocks would provide added diversity, with bonds and cash serving as income-producing anchors. Then we'd hold out hope that a bear market for U.S. stocks won't cut our retirement to ribbons. But since wishes unfortunately are nothing more than ideals, we simply would go about our business and wouldn't check the investment portfolio twice a day to see how we're doing in the personal wealth department. Warns Samuelson:

> **You shouldn't spend much time on your investments. That will just tempt you to pull up the plants and see how the roots are doing, and that's very bad for the roots. It's also very bad for your sleep. The future is longer than the present, and you should be concentrating on long-run performance.**

Instead, if stocks swoon for even a few trading sessions, a jarring reality—"I can lose, and lose big"—hits close to home. Instinctively, we run for cover. The grandchildren will have to find their own way. So you sell at precisely the wrong moment. Sir John Templeton, founder of the fund group that bears his name and a keenly astute investor, has long extolled the wisdom of buying stocks at the point of what he calls "maximum pessimism." Having the guts to act on that instinct is a rare quality, which makes it all the more valuable.

No question, losing is painful. Just thinking about the prospect can be paralyzing. Here you invest heart, soul and wallet into a portfolio, and you're snubbed. Investment, after all, means commitment. And the fact is that when we commit, we open ourselves to hurt. Don't expect something in return for your attentions. The importance of keeping investment expectations within reason cannot be overstated: The market doesn't care if you're six months from retirement or about to buy a house. IBM doesn't know that you own it, and doesn't feel indebted to your grandfather. The market isn't concerned one bit about you or your family. For this "partnership" to succeed, Samuelson charges, you must be the one who cares:

You should take money seriously. In fact, you shouldn't enjoy investing. That's a trap. It makes you too active. You churn your own portfolio. You listen to stories, and most of the stories are not worth listening to.

You don't get something for nothing. In fact, sometimes you don't even get something for something. Investing is all about trade-offs. The ever-practical Samuelson has remarked: "Even children learn in growing up that 'both' is not an admissible answer to a choice of 'which one?'" Or as Gerry Goodman—who writes under the pseudonym "Adam Smith"—said in *The Money Game*, "If you don't know who you are, the stock market is an expensive place to find out." Know what you are giving up. Then it will be easier to outline what you really want, and to accept the reality of what the market offers. Samuelson is critical of those who regard investing as a quick way to turn dreams into dollars:

Most people take investing as kind of a game. Now, everybody may have a little gambling spirit. And, if you do, take a few hundred dollars and go to Las Vegas and blow it. But don't gamble with your most important savings, which is your life-cycle savings. We're all born dependent; we get trained and educated, and we have a period of working life. Increasingly these days,

that's followed by an ever-longer period of retirement. We need to live on what we saved and invested earlier. The savvy investor understands, from the beginning, the virtues and costs of diversification. You have to understand what you're giving away.

For investors to accept the trade-offs of an investment lifetime, it's important to understand one major risk over which they do have control: risk tolerance. How willing are you to invest outside of the safest choices? Can you stomach loss—even a temporary one—if those decisions go against you? How do you react to unexpected bad financial news? What is the biggest drop in the value of your total investment portfolio that you could tolerate? Ten percent? Fifty percent? Knowing these answers will keep you on track at times when it seems there are no answers, a point that Samuelson hammers home:

> **Your risk tolerance is a feature of you, like your nose. I tell people to think about how badly you would feel if, at the time you retired or during your retirement, the market went against you. How much would you resent coming down in the world? Pit against that how much you would like going up in the world. And always keep in mind not the worst-case scenario, but likely, possible scenarios of adversity.**

Conventional wisdom suggests that stock investors should ratchet down exposure to equities and increase fixed-income holdings as they age. With time as an ally, it makes sense to many experts for a 35-year-old to be more risk-tolerant than her retired parents. Samuelson disagrees. There's no magic formula, he explains. Investment risk-tolerance is not a function of age, he adds, but of circumstance and personality:

> **Suppose you're the sort of person who really hates coming down. There's a certain minimum retirement nest egg that you would hate to go below. You can then say, "I'm really risk averse**

to that degree." So you set aside an amount of money in safe, compound interest to guarantee you that minimum, and you play with the rest in equities.

At issue is not time itself, but how you use it. A worker living paycheck to paycheck to support a family probably will be more risk-averse than someone with extra money to save. But years later, as his children leave home and cost pressures ease, this now-retired worker may, in fact, take greater investment risks.

Typically, Samuelson avers, younger investors can be more tolerant of market risk because if stocks go south and their standard of living follows suit, they have old-fashioned sweat equity to see them through. They're able to work harder and longer through the dry spells. Adds Samuelson:

> **Risk is affected by what you do now. When are you going to use that money? When are you going to retire? When you're young, because there's so much compound interest to build up, you can afford to be more risk-tolerant. This means you will have a higher equity position.**
>
> **But it is not automatic that when you turn emeritus you should say, "I don't have so many years to go and so I can squeeze way down on my equity fraction." First, you may not understand the number of years you actually have. If you retire at 65, you still have 20-odd years, and to be without equity holdings may be a misunderstanding of your own risk-tolerance.**

Timing Is Not Everything

Samuelson also has concerned himself with a key conflict that frequently affects investors: market tolerance versus market timing. Do you stay in a diversified portfolio of stocks and bonds continuously over time—a classic buy-and-hold investor—or dart in and out of the market in an attempt to beat it?

Timers try to predict changes in a market. Are prices going up or down? Which begs the question—are stock prices predictable? Is it possible to figure how a stock will fare in the future given its past performance? To a technical chartist, recent price history is a security's bloodline. To Samuelson, history is bunk. "If one could be sure that a price will rise, it would have already risen," he has said. "What can be perceived about the future," he added, "must already be 'discounted' in current price quotations." Keep a cool head, Samuelson advises:

> **What will happen tomorrow cannot be known. When your broker says, "Hurry, hurry, you have just time to buy," you know that's almost certainly wrong. The price is already in the market, unless he has inside information. If a broker calls and says, "General Motors is going to pay a dividend tomorrow. Buy the stock," don't believe him. Everybody knows General Motors is going to pay that dividend. That's already priced into the market. There are people who look at the screen all day long, and if they see a temporary aberration, are motivated to act on it. And in acting on it, they wipe it out.**

"The market is never wrong," goes a well-worn Wall Street adage. Mr. Market makes few mistakes to begin with, and can easily become Mr. Fix-It when called. That's the meaning behind the joke about the finance professor and the student who spied a $20 bill on the ground and eagerly reached for it. "Don't bother," the professor chided. "If it were really there, someone would have taken it already."

This belief that prices react quickly to reflect new information forms the core of Efficient Market Theory. Efficient-market types contend that if you watch a stock trade for a few hours and carefully plot a graph of each tick, the results would be no more conclusive than a Rorschach inkblot. You would see a pattern of advances and retreats, but the movements would be aimless, a "random walk" that seems like the stock-market version of the game Twister. Random walkers believe that stock selection is just a high-priced fishing expedition. They are convinced that even the best investment managers are unlikely to outperform a benchmark index year after year—and most shouldn't even bother.

Bubble, Bubble, Boil and Trouble

Samuelson belongs to the camp that says that markets are—as he describes—"near-perfectly efficient." Pricing discrepancies and anomalies, when they surface at all, are short-lived, he adds. Still, he concedes with a grin that if by luck or charm you do stumble upon such a rare opportunity, grab it. Often these misalignments occur when ordinary rallies metastasize into speculative manias. The craze for Internet stocks that exploded in 1998 and charged into 1999 is a good example. During this time, increasingly higher market valuations were awarded to fledgling young companies with even shorter histories as publicly traded stocks. Actually, a fair amount of the activity in these Internet plays came not from fundamental investors, but from so-called online "day traders" who try to turn a quick profit jumping in and out of a stock numerous times throughout a market day. But the white-hot sector also rewarded longer-term players. An investment in online retailer Amazon.com at the end of August 1998 would have returned 346 percent a year later. In the same period, Internet portal Yahoo! dazzled shareholders with a 328 percent return.

Enthusiasm for Net stocks continued through 1999 and into 2000 as a steady stream of buyers pounded the door. At the end of September 1999, Amazon, a young firm with no profits, enjoyed a market capitalization four times that of established consumer leader Avon Products, with strong earnings and a string of unbroken quarterly dividend payments going back to 1919. Yahoo! was valued more highly than Merrill Lynch & Co., Wall Street's largest brokerage.[7]

The Internet is becoming a powerful force in daily life, much as the television and the personal computer have before it. But bubbles can rise only so high before they pop—as ultimately happened to Internet stocks in April 2000. Yet as prices for these untested companies soared in 1999, and a chorus grew that this time it really was different, Samuelson looked on with the experience of someone who has seen this type of speculation come and go.

Still, he is ever mindful of the conventional Wall Street wisdom that says, "Don't fight the tape." Market bubbles and irrational investor behavior is part of human nature. In 1634, Holland went mad over tulip bulbs. One anxious speculator offered 12 acres of land in exchange for a single, rare tulip root.[8] The Japanese real estate market rose so high in the late 1980s that the value of the land under Tokyo's Imperial Palace was said to be worth more than the entire state of California. But like all manias, these also came to an abrupt and sad end. As historian Charles Mackay reported in his 1841 classic *Extraordinary Popular Delusions and the Madness of Crowds*, the Dutch tulip mania collapsed under its own foolish weight, and by early 1637 tulip bulbs sold for one-tenth of their peak value.

In each postmortem following a market crash, pundits try to reconstruct the pieces in an effort to make sense of it all. Supposedly the impetus is to help us learn from mistakes. "Dwell on the past and you will lose an eye," goes an old Russian proverb. "Ignore the past and you will lose both of them." But ignore we do, blissfully. "This time, it's different" has been a rallying cry for many baby-boomer shareholders, who are old enough to know better. In truth, no one can foresee when or how a bubble will burst—only that eventually it will. In the meantime, we walk in tighter and tighter circles, hoping to find an empty chair when the music stops. Samuelson, for his part, frames the issue with characteristically wry perspective, quipping: "When everyone is insane, 'tis folly to be wise."

The Quest for the Holy Grail

Speculation, like a fairy tale, is not rooted in reality. Neither is it investing. Speculation is found money—that $20 bill on the campus lawn. Do people win lotteries? All the time. Will you? It's doubtful. Such are the laws of probability. Flagging the next Yahoo! would be quite a feat, but how do you know when you've found it? Most people would sell too soon. A typical individual investor doesn't have many clues about how long the long term should be, and Samuelson brashly wagers that even a highly trained professional investment manager also is unlikely to have a golden timepiece:

> **I'm constantly asked, "Where can I get disinterested, expert financial advice?" And I have no answer. There's essentially no such thing. People who offer financial advice come in two brands: those who charge you, and those who don't but earn their money as commission on what they sell you. The most reputable money manager will sell you anything that's sellable. The churning of portfolios, which is done consciously and unconsciously, and some of the tactics followed by people who think that they're ethical and respectable, are really unconscionable.**

Samuelson's assessment highlights one of several deadly investing sins that consistently plague mutual fund managers who actively buy and sell their portfolios. Investors expect that these professionals will decide on an investment strategy and stick to it. And since these highly paid stock-pickers are smart and savvy, they surely won't follow the herd. Like their shareholders, portfolio managers supposedly are focused on the long term, so of course they won't chase performance.

Yet chasing after a soaring stock is exactly what some managers do in an attempt to make themselves and their track records look better. They dress up a portfolio to produce eye-catching returns, but shareholders get stuck with the charges. Performance-chasing managers are really shirtsleeve traders in button-down disguise. Their computer screens flash winners in bright, money-spinning green. Their stocks are on a tear. Red lights—stocks in a tumble—are for the other guys. They buy. They sell. They fool themselves and their shareholders into thinking that all this noise actually adds value.

In truth, these trigger-happy managers can do considerable harm to their shareholders. Their inconsistent behavior is unpredictable, so investors can't count on the fund to fulfill its role in a portfolio. Frequent trading adds to transaction costs and generates painful short-term capital gains taxes. Short-term gains are levied on shares held for one year or less, and taxed as ordinary income—as if you'd earned the money on the job. Ironically, many of these same peripatetic managers admonish shareholders to invest in their fund for the long run. In contrast, fund managers who hold a stock for longer than 12 months before selling will generate long-term capital gains, which are taxed at a more favorable 20 percent rate.

Be wary of funds with high portfolio turnover. A turnover rate of 100 percent means the fund, on average, holds an investment for 12 months. At 200 percent, portfolio holdings are being replaced every six months; at 300 percent, the entire portfolio is bought and sold in just 16 weeks. Morningstar, the Chicago-based mutual fund–rating service, identifies 48 domestic stock funds with turnover ratios above 300 percent. You might ask, rightly, how anyone can come up with so many replacement ideas so fast. And if the ideas were so good to begin with, why isn't the manager hanging on to them?

Patience is a virtue—especially among fund managers. You'll need to allow some leeway for turnover, depending on a fund's investment style. For instance, the average turnover rate in late 1999 for funds that own small-capitalization value stocks was 59 percent, against 128 percent for small-cap growth funds, according to Morningstar. That's understandable, since value investors typically own stocks whose fortunes are turning around slowly and methodically. Growth stocks, in contrast, usually tell a positive story that investors eagerly reward with rapidly appreciating prices. Faced with milking another 10 percent from a popular stock or locking in a profit, growth-fund managers may heed a smart bit of market advice and get out when they can, not when they have to. But if they sell, they should have a better replacement ready to go. This strategy also applies to individual investors. Before you sell a stock and incur short-term capital gains, ask yourself why you're unloading the shares. You should be confident that any substitute will give you similar capital appreciation, as well as offset the capital gains tax that you're paying.

In general, look for funds with turnover ratios below 100 percent. Investors with taxable portfolios especially should regard above-average turnover in a fund as a potential liability. People with tax-deferred accounts don't have to worry about taxes just yet, but the rest of us do. And if your fund's turnover should suddenly soar, it's likely that something serious has happened with its operation or management. Find out, and then decide whether or not to remain a shareholder. Managers who manage best, manage least, an adage with which Samuelson clearly would agree:

There's too much active management. There's too much trading and too much self-deception. Few people or organizations have any presumptive edge over a low-cost, no-load set of index funds, particularly on a risk-corrected basis. For the ordinary person who isn't looking for thrills, it's not hard to give prudent advice, but it's very dull advice. With indexing, you can sleep well knowing that you've done all that a sensible human being can do for the good cause. Your equity tolerance should be down to your sleeping point.

Millions of investors have heeded this counsel and have committed their financial futures to funds that attempt to mirror a specific stock index. If the fund does its job, their reward will be the index's return, less expenses, which generally are negligible. Most index-fund shareholders nowadays have cast their lot with the S&P 500. These investors are in "the market"—though really it's only a proxy. The 500 large companies in the S&P index, however diverse, are not the total market, any more than two wings make an airplane. The same is true of the 30 large companies in the Dow Jones Industrial Average. While the S&P 500 accounts for most of the market—about 75 percent of its value—thousands of small- and mid-sized companies are not included. For maximum representation, you'd want a fund that mimicks the Wilshire 5000 Equity Index of virtually all U.S. stocks.

As Jack Bogle, founder of the Vanguard Group, explains later in this book, the essential idea behind indexing is to own the total stock market through an inexpensive mutual fund. Costs are one of the few variables within an individual investor's control. With mutual funds, you get what you *don't* pay for. High expenses eat away return year after year—money that comes straight out of your pocket. Adding insult to injury, on average in the 1990s, only about one-third of U.S. diversified stock-fund managers were able to beat their S&P 500 benchmark in any given year. Moreover, these lucky few are rarely ever the same each time.

People say: "You're settling for mediocrity." Isn't it interesting that the best brains on Wall Street can't achieve mediocrity? They say: "Look at the 10 percent that beat the index." What they don't realize is that generally those are not the same 10 percent. The hotel rooms of capitalism are always full, said the economist Joseph Schumpeter, but they're full with different people.

If only high expense-ratios automatically meant better mutual fund performance. But as Nobel Prize–winning economist William Sharpe details in Chapter 9, there's precious little evidence that higher expenses net you a better return. The thorny issue brings to mind the old story of the country bumpkin on a first-time visit to Manhattan. He accompanied his city friend to the harbor near Wall Street and was struck by row upon row of gleaming boats. "Here are the bankers' yachts," the urban dweller announced grandly. "And here are the stockbrokers' yachts." His naive visitor eyed the streamlined vessels with significant awe. "But where," he asked, "are the customers' yachts?"

All Horse Players Die Broke

For meaningful, wealth-accumulating stock-market gains, you must invest for the long term. That means stepping into the market today and staying for a lifetime. Samuelson argues this case with his Time Diversification Theory, which supports a long-term disposition and dispels the active timer. To compare, he separated the investment horizon into two distinct paths: diversification *within* time and diversification *across* time.

"Within time" means always keeping a properly allocated portfolio, spread across many securities and suited to your risk tolerance and investment horizon. "Across time" investors rely on heavily concentrated sector bets, flipping from one industry to another, or from cash to stocks and back. Explains Samuelson, "Monday, Wednesday and Friday I'm in equities. Tuesdays and Thursdays I'm in bonds. That's not the same as being always 60 percent in equities and 40 percent in bonds."

Samuelson likes to tell the story of a colleague at MIT some years ago who was smitten with a provision in the university's retirement investment plan that allowed free telephone switching between stocks and fixed-income assets. This professor bounced into all-equities from zero-equities and back 16 times in one year. "He can't do any harm to himself," an incredulous Samuelson surmised when he heard this piece of gossip. "Nobody's so stupid as to guess wrong all the time." So while his patient colleagues were content to hold half in stocks and half in fixed income for the year, this across-time professor seemingly achieved a similar result with his market acrobatics. Or so Samuelson thought. But the jitterbug is not ballet. On further reflection, he realized that the professor's timing not only was inefficient, it also was much riskier. "He accomplished no market-timing," Samuelson concludes. "He was just taking on extra variability, because you don't get the same reduction of risk."

> **The moral is this: If you must be a timer, be a very modest timer. If a trader goes back and forth on sector funds—health funds, banking funds, financial services funds—he might say, "I've had a well-balanced portfolio over the year." That's wrong. He's never been diversified. He hasn't made the mistake of taking a chance on one thing. But he's not getting the advantages of diversification within time.**

A folktale is told of two men who were entrenched in a heated argument they could not resolve. They decided to take their disagreement to the village wise man. The first man told his story, and the sage said, "You're right." The second man then related his version, and the arbiter said, "You're right." Whereupon both men left feeling satisfied. A young scholar who had been watching this exchange looked askance. "How can they both be right?" he asked. The wise man thought a moment, then said, "You're right!"

The point of this story is that there is no "right" answer; there is only yours. Investment perspective and risk tolerance are unique for everyone. How will the future treat your money? Will inflation rear its ugly head and thrash stocks and bonds? Will your investments generate enough income to see you through retirement? Are you prepared to work longer if you must? The outcome will be only as good as the ongoing choices you make. Naturally, we all want to be confident about the future. But overconfidence, behavioral studies show, leads people to believe they have control over fate, and to confuse chance with skill. As Adam Smith pointed out more than two centuries ago, people underestimate the possibility that they will lose.

In truth, no one knows when any bull market will end or begin. In that sense, the risk of being out of the market is actually greater than the risk of being invested. That 11.3 percent annual gain from large U.S. stocks between 1926 and 1999 is frequently touted to portray the stock market's long-term superiority. But what's not often said is that if you missed the best-performing month in each of those years by shifting completely into cash, your annualized portfolio return over that time would have been a meager 2.7 percent. This minuscule return would not even have kept pace with a 3.1 percent average annual inflation rate. Clearly, it's important to heed Samuelson's warning against the pitfalls of market-timing—diversification across time—at least with the core of your portfolio. If you want to speculate in stocks with a small amount of money, fine, but have no illusions about your ability to be in the right place at the right time. For more often than not, investors who persist in the fantasy of precision timing end up bearing the cross of time.

The Equity Premium: Jeremy Siegel

"When I say 'long run,' I'm thinking not of a particular stock or mutual fund, or even staying with a particular broker or money manager. I am talking about holding financial assets so you can enjoy growth and income throughout your life. One of the biggest mistakes investors make is underestimating the holding period of their assets. It's really 'stocks for a lifetime.'"

THE STOCK MARKET constantly tests your faith. Good news, bad news; soaring gains, swooning losses—how can something so volatile, so nerve-racking, be so welcome in our lives? Jeremy Siegel wants us to focus more on the positive attributes of stocks. A financial markets historian and author of the best-selling *Stocks for the Long Run*, Siegel encourages investors to look past the market's short-term hazards and blows. He isn't unrealistic; he just wants people to stay with stocks. When U.S. stock-market activity is viewed over a couple of decades and longer, he contends, equities actually are safer and more stable than any other investment, even bonds or cash.

Stocks safer than bonds or cash? It's true that stocks have outperformed other investments over time, but how are they less risky? Because of inflation, Siegel says. Higher wages, prices and manufacturing costs chip away at the value of a buck. Adjusting for inflation, a dollar saved is not a dollar earned.

Bonds and cash simply don't retain their purchasing power once inflation takes its toll. Inflationary spikes also take a swipe at stock valuations—anxious investors tend to shun most equities in favor of short-term holdings like cash, which can be reinvested at increasingly higher yields. "Hard" assets such as real estate and precious metals are also in demand, as they provide a cushion against rising prices for goods and services.

But stocks are unique in their ability to recover strongly from bouts of high inflation. Companies usually can raise prices to keep pace, plus they have real assets and working capital that can generate earnings to carry them over the rough spots. Seen over many years, in fact, stocks have proven to be a solid hedge against inflation.

In that light, having little or no exposure to stocks runs the serious risk that your investment portfolio won't keep up with inflation. Years from now, a dollar won't buy as much as it does today. The value of your investments must grow enough to offset inflation. If not, you'll either have to keep working, make do with less—or both.

Siegel, a professor of finance at the Wharton School of the University of Pennsylvania, became a bright beacon for investors with the publication of *Stocks for the Long Run*. This investing tome, first published in 1994 and now in its second edition, features historical research and charts to proclaim the long-term superiority of a diversified stock portfolio over fixed-income and other assets. Bonds and cash are pleasant-enough chaperones, according to Siegel, but stocks are the life of the party. Given the burst of stock buying in the late 1990s, it seems that more than a few people have agreed.

But if all good things come to those who wait, how many years must we wait for the stock market to deliver good things? "In the long run we are all dead," famed economist John Maynard Keynes once quipped. How many years exactly is the "long run"—10, 20, 50? Buyers of Japanese stocks at their peak in 1989 were still hoping to recoup their losses more than a decade later. In the United States, the Dow Jones Industrial Average suffered through a parched spell between 1966 and 1982, punctuated by a grisly bear market in 1973 and 1974.

What if the end of your long run coincides with the end of a bull market? In Chapter 2, noted economist Paul Samuelson criticized the increasingly popular notion that stocks are a can't-lose proposition if you just hang on long enough. "The meter is always running with respect to risk," Samuelson says. "It is not true that risk erodes toward zero as the investment horizon lengthens. Every year that comes up is the first year of what's left."

Most investors view a holding period in terms of how long they own a certain stock or mutual fund. For Siegel, the "long run" is not a set length of time—although much of his research is based on at least 20 years of history. And it doesn't mean that people should invest all of their money in the shares of a few carefully chosen companies, or even a stock-index fund that tracks the total market. The long run is a commitment to investing, a state of mind. Actively buy and sell securities over the years if you want, but can you go the distance? Are you willing to hold on to stocks over your working career, through sometimes intolerable conditions, so that you can live off the portfolio's income and principal in retirement? Siegel explains:

> When I say "long run," I'm thinking not of a particular stock or mutual fund, or even staying with a particular broker or money manager. I am talking about holding financial assets so you can enjoy growth and income throughout your life. One of the biggest mistakes investors make is underestimating the holding period of their assets. It's really "stocks for a lifetime."

Timely Horizons

Own stocks not just for the long run, but for a lifetime. Yet Siegel contends that investors today expect too much from stocks. In fact, he claims, the market's run in the near future won't be as good as its recent past.

We're frequently told that the compounded average return for large-capitalization U.S. stocks between 1926 and 1999 is slightly more than 11 percent a year. Not often quoted is the real return from stocks *after* inflation: roughly 8.3 percent, according to Ibbotson Associates, the Chicago-based investment data firm. Over that time, the Consumer Price Index for all urban consumers (CPI-U)—a standard barometer of inflation—rose roughly 3.1 percent each year, which cut into total return. But put this in perspective: Over the same period, Ibbotson reports, inflation-adjusted returns on long-term U.S. government bonds averaged 2 percent annually, and just 0.7 percent a year for cash.

Siegel's own research places the long-term, after-inflation rate of return for equities at about 7 percent a year, going back to 1802. Clearly, stock-market returns far exceeded that figure during the high-octane, low-inflation 1990s. In the decade through June 2000, the post-inflation real rate of return from stocks was a well above-average 14.6 percent, Ibbotson calculates.

Don't expect those outsized returns to continue, Siegel cautions. While pleased to see an increased public awareness about the long-term power of stocks, Siegel says he's concerned that some investors might believe that equities promise more than they realistically can deliver—especially those who have not seen a ferocious bear market. For them, "In the long run we are all dead" has become "In the long run we are all rich." Adds Siegel:

> **Some people are talking about Dow 15,000 or 20,000 in a matter of a few years. I'm concerned about that. The market will offer substantial returns to investors in the future, but I do not believe it's going to match the returns we've had since this grand bull market began in 1982.**

Why should stock returns be lower? Because, Siegel explains, investor demand for stocks is higher. The so-called equity premium exists in part because risk-averse investors frequently overreact to short-term events and discount stock prices too heavily. Investors demand compensation for the uncertainty they accept, and prices will fluctuate until a buyer is satisfied enough to take a chance.

Higher risk usually is commensurate with potentially higher returns. When few people want to own stocks, the equity premium is greater. But as people have realized how well the U.S. stock market has treated investors over recent decades, they have become buyers themselves. When that happens, prices are bid up, as they were throughout the 1990s, and potential return on investment comes down.

The equity premium is a basic supply-and-demand story. If

people perceive less risk in shares of Internet titan Yahoo!, for instance, they will pay the going rate for a stock that seemingly can do no wrong. If prospects for Internet-based companies crumble, along with investor demand for Internet stocks, then the price of Yahoo! shares will ratchet down to a point at which investors perceive that the stock's potential reward outweighs its risk.

Since these vagaries of the market are largely unpredictable, it really doesn't pay to jump in and out of stocks. Spend time in the market; don't market time. Investors who believe they can time the market are frequently discouraged. While stocks might have some predictable patterns, the market does not exactly advertise which weeks and months will be its best and worst. But if you really must rely on past performance as a guide to jumping in and out of the market, here is some statistical insight: The two best months for stocks since 1926 have been July, with a 1.8 percent average return, and December, at 1.7 percent, Ibbotson reports. The worst month? September, with a negative 0.9 percent return. The top-performing three-month period has been November, December and January, with a 4.7 percent average collective return, followed closely by a 4.3 percent total gain in June, July and August. Which indicates that being fully invested during just those six months and out of the market at the other times would have captured about 80 percent of the market's 11.3 percent average annual gains before taxes.

It might be tempting to mark your calendar. The big trouble with such crude timing mechanisms, of course, is that no one really knows when stock prices will climb. Siegel describes what could go wrong:

> **What often happens with timing is that an investor is out of the market when stocks are advancing. That can lead to discouragement, because then you don't go back in. Instead, you wait for prices to dip back down. As a result, a lot of timers find themselves out of the market when the market is rising, and this leads to far lower returns.**

For someone who eschews market timing and trumpets the long run for stocks, Siegel closely watches daily market activity. He even interrupts a conversation to peer intently at the screen of a laptop computer in his office that is displaying up-to-the-minute stock prices and market news. "I am fascinated with the short-run drama of the market," he confides. "The emotions that play into the movement of the market; how stocks react to news; how markets interconnect. Following the markets on a short-term basis is something I enjoy."

Siegel is not a trader himself, although he does acknowledge a market-timing tool that he contends has more reliability than others: a 200-day moving average strategy—which is the average of the last 200 days of prices for an index. This established technical market indicator provides returns that are nearly identical to a traditional buy-and-hold strategy, Siegel claims, but with considerably less short-term risk. Here's how it works: Add the last 200 days of closing prices for any index and average them. When the daily price of the index stays above its moving average, you keep holding. If it breaks below the average, it's a bearish signal.

In *Stocks for the Long Run*, Siegel reported that he tested this buy-sell tactic using this specific criterion: If the Dow Jones Industrial Average closed at least 1 percent above its 200-day moving average, stocks were bought. If the Dow closed at least 1 percent below its 200-day moving average, shares were disposed. Siegel found that over the past century this strategy has kept investors in bull markets and out of bear markets, and in fact was most effective in avoiding the October 1929 market crash. Wrote Siegel: "On a risk adjusted basis the return on the 200-day moving average is quite impressive."[1]

But there are several important points to remember here. First, any timing strategy is far from perfect. Monitoring the 200-day moving average would have narrowly skirted the October 1987 market crash, Siegel found, but would not have signaled a reentry point until June 1988, when the Dow had recouped all but 5 percent of its October losses.[2] Timing also involves high transaction costs that will reduce returns, and for taxable accounts, the tax hit will further diminish results. Finally, and perhaps most important, how concerned should anyone be about short-run risk when your goal is to own stocks of quality companies over the long haul? Says Siegel:

> **There are many timing strategies that don't work—that result in not-as-good returns without much reduction in risk, and you have transaction costs on top of that. So one has to be very careful about pursuing these short-run technical strategies.**

Indeed, a conservative buy-and-hold investing strategy actually requires considerably more courage than market timing does. Buy and hold is not easy. To stay in the market when conditions are bleak is difficult, to say the least, and is in fact why many investors exit the market when the going gets tough. This aversion to short-term loss drives people into the perceived safe haven of cash and bonds, but they're often out of the market when inevitable rallies occur. Over many years, Siegel notes, short-term thinking can leave investors with substantially less than they would have gained by staying the course in stocks.

Short-term losses are painful, to be sure. But market slumps are precisely the wrong time to panic. Sage investor Warren Buffett has advised that if you expect to be a buyer of stocks in the future, "you should be elated when prices fall and depressed when they rise."[3] Siegel agrees that investors would do well to view down markets as opportunities to add to portfolio holdings. He says:

> **If you need the money within the next year or two, a decline in the market hurts. Then you probably should stick with bonds for that big expenditure—your children's education, for instance, or to buy a business—where you need cash and know when you're going to need it.**
>
> **But if you are looking way into the future, a declining market helps. You can reinvest at lower prices. If your horizon is 15 or 20 years in the future, then you can still be in equities and be pretty assured that you're going to do better than bonds,**

because over a 20-year period, stocks do better than bonds over 90 percent of the time. So maybe what we have to do is realize that what we perceive to be pain is actually opportunity.

Inflated Views

The risk inherent in stocks never disappears—no matter how long you are invested. What does diminish over time is the risk of holding stocks versus that of bonds. Notes Siegel:

> The relative risk of stocks is below that of bonds. Over long periods, stocks were much more stable than would have been expected from their year-to-year volatility. That did not hold for fixed-income investments. There's very little place for bonds, primarily because of inflation risk. Stocks, being claims on real assets, respond much better to inflation in the long run. For portfolios of 20-year horizons, stocks are actually less risky than bonds in terms of purchasing power—return after inflation. And for 30-year horizons, the risk can be as much as one-third lower than for bonds.

Consider how inflation can erode the value of a bond. Suppose you invest $50,000 in a 10-year U.S. Treasury bond. Benjamin Franklin may have frowned upon borrowers and lenders, but even Old Ben would not likely have spurned the venerable U.S. Treasury. You can't get any safer, more secure debt than a piece of paper backed by the U.S. government. Now say the U.S. Treasury promises to pay you $50,000 in 10 years, plus 6 percent annual interest, or $3,000 a year. While there's no guarantee, you still can be reasonably sure that you'll receive regular interest payments plus the original $50,000 a decade from now.

While the 6 percent dividend should offset much of inflation's scourge, the truth is that $50,000 in 10 years won't buy all it does today. That said, inflation was unusually low during the 1990s—

about 2.8 percent annually on average—and the menacing double-digit inflation that plagued the United States in the 1970s is unlikely to resurface anytime soon. But inflation does seem to be creeping back toward its historical average of 3.1 percent. Adds Siegel:

We don't think about inflation risk today, with inflation being so low. People forget about it and say that their dollars are safe. But that has not been true through history. When you go out 10, 20, 30 years, you have to be very concerned about what those dollars are going to be worth. You don't need very much inflation to cut severely into the yields of fixed-income assets.

Over time, equities are very good hedges against inflation. You don't have to worry about the erosion of purchasing power. If you're long-term oriented in terms of accumulating assets and savings, the equity imperative is much stronger.

Tipping Risk

Investors were skeptical when the U.S. government introduced inflation-indexed bonds in January 1997. Around that time, deflation seemed to pose the greatest threat to U.S. economic health. Goods from abroad had become cheaper and better, consumers had more choices than ever, and the flood of new competition made it difficult for U.S. companies to pass along higher prices to consumers.

Siegel was among the few early and enthusiastic proponents of these unique bonds, which the government calls Treasury Inflation-Indexed Securities but everyone else has dubbed TIPS, for Treasury Inflation-Protected Securities. Like conventional Treasury bonds, TIPS pay a fixed rate of interest every six months. The bonds also offer preset maturity dates ranging between 2002 and 2029. But unlike standard-issue Treasuries, TIPS are designed to shield investors from the ill winds of inflation by keeping pace with fluctuations in the Consumer Price Index. Siegel explains a main reason to hold these securities:

TIPS is a very important asset, because what has hurt the bondholder's portfolio in the long run is inflation. The risk from inflation to the bondholder goes up over time, because the bondholder is only promised dollars—but you don't have any idea what that money can buy.

Investors are promised two unique guarantees from TIPS. First, the Treasury increases the principal you get back at maturity to reflect changes in the CPI. Rising inflation normally would diminish your purchasing power, but TIPS will return your principal—plus the amount lost to inflation. Semiannual payments also increase, since they are made on the readjusted principal value. You won't get that perk from a regular Treasury.

Second, the Treasury will return the face value of the inflation-indexed bond at maturity if consumer prices decline instead. During such a deflationary period, the regular income stream from TIPS would slow, but if you invested, say, $1,000, at least you'll get $1,000 back.

While TIPS may expose you to greater income risk than traditional government bonds, inflation-protected securities do eliminate a key element of the interest-rate risk that can negatively impact any fixed-income investment. Generally, when interest rates rise, bond prices fall. As rates decline, bond prices rise. If, for instance, you own a 10-year bond that pays 6 percent interest, and the 10-year yield falls to 5.5 percent, income-hungry buyers will pay a premium for your 6 percent debt. If the yield climbs to 6.5 percent, your 6 percent paper is not so appealing and will trade at a discount to face value.

Interest-rate risk itself is divided between two components: the actual interest-rate portion and the inflation-rate portion. Over time, inflation has been far more volatile than interest rates. Since inflation-indexed bonds adjust for swings in inflation rates, they effectively neutralize the inflation-risk component of the security, leaving you exposed only to relatively more stable interest-rate changes.

When you buy TIPS, the inflation protection begins immediately. Say the 10-year U.S. Treasury bond is yielding 6.5 percent. Now suppose you pay $10,000 for a 10-year TIPS with a 4.25 percent annual coupon. Inflation is running at 2.5 percent annually. If yields and inflation are both constant, then six months from now the TIPS will pay $215.16, which is half of its coupon interest (2.125 percent) on principal that has grown by half of the yearly inflation rate (1.25 percent), to $10,125.

Your payment in another six months will be 2.125 percent of the full-year's inflation-adjusted principal ($10,250), or $217.81. Adding interest from the two coupons, $432.97, plus the $250 gain in principal, equals a yearly income of $682.97, or a total annualized risk-free return of 6.83 percent. The inflation-indexed bond would have been a better deal than the $650 annual payout from the 10-year Treasury.[4]

The 2.25 percentage-point difference in yield between the 10-year Treasury and the 10-year TIPS is the break-even inflation rate. In this example, inflation was running at 2.5 percent, 0.25 percent higher than the implied inflation rate on the traditional 10-year Treasury. If inflation continued at this rate or higher over the next decade, income from the TIPS would move up in lockstep, but income from a standard bond would decrease in real terms. But if inflation declined to 2 percent, then the annual income from the TIPS would sink to $631.40, for a 6.3 percent total return.

While Siegel certainly would not avoid stocks, he does speak admiringly of the benefits of inflation-indexed securities as diversification against market uncertainties. He notes:

The long-run return from inflation-indexed bonds may not be as good as stocks, but you do get inflation protection. The final payoff depends on the path of inflation over the next 30 years. If inflation averages less than 2 percent per year, there's no particular reason to buy them. But if inflation is more than 2 percent, not just this year, but over the next 30 years, you'll be better off in the inflation-indexed bonds than in U.S. Treasuries. And my feeling is when we talk about 30 years, inflation is going to aver-

> age over 2 percent. Inflation will come back—maybe not the vir-
> ulent type of inflation like the 1970s, but inflation of 4 or 5 per-
> cent over a period of several years is a likely event sometime
> over the next 30 years.

The major downside to TIPS is taxes. You have to pay ordinary income taxes on the inflation adjustments, even though you actually won't be able to pocket the cash until the bond matures or is sold. Therefore, TIPS are best suited for tax-deferred accounts.

You can postpone the tax issue with inflation-indexed Series I savings bonds, known as "I-bonds." These securities are exempt from state and local taxes, while federal income tax can be deferred until they're cashed. Plus, the bonds are tax-exempt when used to pay for college tuition by taxpayers on a limited income.

TIPS can be purchased for a fee from banks and brokerages, or without a commission in $1,000 increments through the government's Treasury Direct Program (www.treasurydirect.gov). Information about I-bonds is available online from the Bureau of the Public Debt (www.savingsbonds.gov).

Several mutual fund companies also offer inflation-indexed bond funds, which would be a good avenue for investors who want a diverse portfolio of these products. Pimco Real Return Bond and American Century Inflation-Adjusted Treasury are two established offerings. Low-cost fund giant Vanguard Group in June 2000 launched a contender, Vanguard Inflation-Protected Securities Fund, which charges an annual management fee of just 0.25 percent. An especially alluring aspect of these funds is that they can pay out the inflation adjustment each year, so although you're still taxed, you see the money right away.

The New Nifty Fifty

When it comes to stock prices, when does the air get too thin to breathe? A central part of Siegel's research involves stock valuations, in particular the often-stratospheric growth stocks with price-earnings ratios that sometimes hit triple digits.

The leadership of the market has shifted dramatically since the mid-1960s. During those go-go years, big firms like General Motors, AT&T and Standard Oil of New Jersey were profitable but didn't grow very fast. A generation later, the Standard & Poor's 500-stock index is led by dynamic enterprises like Cisco Systems, Intel, Microsoft, Wal-Mart, Merck and Pfizer, to name a few. As we will see throughout this book, earnings aren't everything to investors, they're the only thing. Above-average corporate earnings growth can support correspondingly higher stock valuations, Siegel contends:

These firms are growing much faster than the overall economy, and this deserves a higher price-earnings ratio. Along with their current growth rate, there are unprecedented circumstances with respect to global expansion and global markets that justify the multiples they're selling at.

Siegel frames his case for growth stocks through the lens of the so-called Nifty Fifty. These 50 highfliers defy the conventional strategy of buying growth at a reasonable price. Instead, eager institutions and individuals alike will pay for growth at any price, driving valuations to new and uncharted heights.

During the original Nifty Fifty era of the late 1960s and early 1970s, shares of photographic market leader Polaroid, for example, were valued at 95 times earnings, with earnings per share growing at 40 percent annually. Computer titan IBM, then the world's largest company, traded at 50 times earnings on the strength of consistently impressive annual earnings growth of 20 percent. As a group, the Nifty Fifty sold at an average P/E of 41.9 in 1972, more than twice the valuation of the S&P 500.[5] Investors rationalized the extreme valuations by regarding these rarefied companies as "one-decision" stocks that you could buy and hold forever without fear.

As it happened, forever came early for these darlings. The most vicious bear market since the 1929 crash hit Wall Street in 1973 and lingered into 1974, and the gold-winged Nifty Fifty tumbled hard. Investors in Polaroid suffered through a negative return for nearly three decades, Siegel reports, and IBM's total return to investors was less than half of what the S&P 500 delivered.

Wall Street in the first quarter of 2000 chillingly reminded Siegel of a new Nifty Fifty era. Of the 33 stocks that had a market capitalization over $85 billion, nine sported P/E ratios of more than 100, including six in the top 20, Siegel noted. The consensus among Wall Street analysts at the time was that these companies would grow earnings at better than double the expected rate of the S&P 500 over the next five years, but Siegel remained unconvinced. Few companies can achieve such superior performance, and fewer still are large-cap stocks. And even if these companies could continue to post such extraordinary growth rates, Siegel concluded, they would still be priced at twice the projected level for the S&P.[6]

Writing in *The Wall Street Journal* that March, Siegel warned: "Our bifurcated market has been driven to an extreme not justified by any history. The excitement generated by the technology and communications revolution is fully justified, and there is no question that the firms leading the way are superior enterprises. But this doesn't automatically translate into increased shareholder values. There is a limit to the value of any asset, however promising. Despite our buoyant view of the future, this is no time for investors to discard the lessons of the past."[7]

That lesson, he explains, is straightforward:

There is no history that supports a P/E of over 100 for a big-cap stock. I can see the average being 60, 70 times earnings for a couple dozen of the best technology stocks, though you're not buying on the cheap. Above that, they're vulnerable.

Just how vulnerable became evident only weeks after Siegel's essay was published. The technology stock–laden Nasdaq 100 index, which had soared to 5048 in mid-March, was trading at 3321 a month later, a 34 percent hit. Dearly priced Internet stocks fared worse, with some losing 60 percent and 70 percent of their value. By mid-July, the Nasdaq was still 20 percent off its peak, and the Internet sector was limping along. Says Siegel:

What happened to the Nasdaq in the spring of 2000 showed how vulnerable some of those high P/E stocks can be. They're priced to perfection, and anything that's not picture perfect is taken out ruthlessly. One must be aware of that.

Boomer Years

Owning stocks for a lifetime seems sound enough advice. But what sort of lifestyle can most of us anticipate in the years to come, and how might specific quality-of-life choices affect the type of investments we make?

Between now and 2010, the gigantic baby boom generation will move through their 40s and 50s—76 million people, nearly one of every three Americans, all at similar points in their lives. These children of the post–World War II era, born between 1946 and 1964, have driven consumer spending and corporate earnings since birth. Their middle age will be no different.

Cradle-to-grave spending among generations is generally predictable: toys, games and fast food for kids; fashion, music and apartments for twenty-somethings; starter homes, household goods and gadgets in your 30s; trade-up homes and investments in your highly productive 40s and 50s; and leisure time and health care for the retirement years. The baby boom generation is on the same life path that others have taken before and will again—but since they're so numerous, boomers don't walk through life so much as stampede. As has been true for half a century, what baby boomer wants, baby boomer gets.

The U.S. Census Bureau estimates that 22.2 percent of the

population currently is between 45 and 64 years old. Another 12.6 percent are aged 65 and over. By 2010, the 45-to-64-year-old crowd swells to 26.5 percent of all Americans, while the over-65 bracket expands to 13.2 percent of the population. Put simply, by 2010, four of every 10 people you see in this country will be at least 45 years old.

At the same time, the boomers' children—the "baby boom echo" also known as Generation Y—are entering their teens and 20s. Baby boomers, owing to sheer numbers, often overshadow the echo boom, which began about 1976 and peaked in 1990. And certainly, elder boomers, not their children, hold more money and power. But Gen Y, though smaller than the baby boomers with roughly 60 million members, is hardly insignificant. Currently, about 35 percent of the U.S. population is under 25 years old, the Census Bureau reports. While that percentage won't change much by 2010, it nonetheless represents a sizable market.

Most boomers are now in their 40s and 50s, railing against middle age. These are their peak years of productivity, earnings and investing. Many expect to work well beyond their 65th birthday. "Do not go gentle into that good night," wrote the poet Dylan Thomas. Not to worry—boomers won't.

Think of baby boomers as "sonic boomers," an economic and political thunderclap. These mostly affluent Americans are big spenders, especially on services and other conveniences. Their consumption has helped boost corporate earnings, which in turn has contributed nicely to rising U.S. stock prices. And once boomers start collecting inheritances from their affluent parents—in what promises to be an epic transfer of wealth—expect much of that money to land in stocks.

To uncover potential market winners, you first should understand how the baby boom generation plans to live. If you're thinking lazy retirement with park benches and weekday golf, try again. Boomers are going to want to be where the action is. Domestic industries that could benefit from an active aging population include technology and the Internet, financial services, health care and biotechnology, and leisure and entertainment. Older boomers have more money than time, so they will buy quality timesaving services and devices. Young echo boomers, with more time than money, will want inexpensive housing, transportation, fashion, food and fun.

Investment advice clearly is something that baby boomers, facing retirement and estate planning issues, will continue to demand. The percentage of people who consider themselves an investor rose from 36 percent in 1998 to 50 percent in 1999, according to a Yankelovich poll. They'll need guidance about accumulating and protecting their wealth—a positive for banks, brokerages, mutual funds and insurance companies.[8]

Technology also should remain a major investment theme. Boomers like technology's bells and whistles, but they particularly covet its convenience and flexibility. Their openness toward change—a trait that boomers have all but branded—will dovetail nicely as the echo boomers mature into their 20s. This young and restless generation is entering its most rebellious years, and its best and brightest will drive technology in nontraditional ways— much as then twenty-something boomers Steve Jobs and Steve Wozniak achieved in 1984 with a radical innovation in computing called the Macintosh.

Newly minted college graduates tend to be at the height of their innovation cycle, so expect echo boomers to create numerous quality-of-life improvements. Advancements in technology and biotech will keep people looking and feeling younger. Baby boomers have an urgent desire to postpone physical aging. When the Fountain of Youth proved elusive, boomers created one through genetic and biological engineering. The first decade of the twenty-first century could see even greater interest in preventative and restorative medicine and treatments, giving people real chances to live longer and better.

In such an entrepreneurial environment, the stocks of small technology and biotechnology companies would have excellent prospects. Pharmaceutical companies, along with suppliers, distributors and retailers, also would be likely to enjoy a continued sales surge.

But economic conditions change, and the punch bowl crashes to the floor. One thing is sure: No one's getting any younger. The peak of the baby boom, born in 1961, will turn 50 years old in 2011. At the same time, the leading edge of the boomers, born in the late 1940s, will be approaching retirement. Then this powerful consumer bloc could begin to trim its spending, and echo boomers wouldn't be numerous enough to pick up the slack. Many companies would feel downward pricing pressure, crimping earnings and sending stock prices lower. If this grim reversal of fortune actually occurred, you would want to rotate investments into high-quality bonds and innovative small-cap companies that can find shelter in niche markets.

Siegel is paying close attention to this potential hiccup in the long-run scenario. He says:

> **We are going to be coming to a point of distribution of stocks by the baby boomers as they enter into retirement. The rich will be leaving money to their children or to charitable organizations. But the vast majority of people will run down their savings during retirement and have only a residual to give their children. The average person who saves a few hundred thousand dollars and stops working at age 65 is going to need that money— especially as they live longer.**
>
> **So a lot of these assets are going to be sold; it's not going to be just donated to the next generation. We have to be concerned with who is going to buy those stocks—and at what price. If there were not any buyers, we could have a bust toward 2030.**

But the outlook doesn't have to be so bleak, Siegel claims. He points out that, unlike the developed world, developing countries don't have an "age wave" of elderly citizens. In fact, for the next several decades, most of the population of countries like China,

India, Indonesia and Latin America will be in their productive 40s and 50s. They could be buyers of U.S. stocks. And if U.S. productivity growth continues to increase, then echo boomers could become rich enough to afford to buy the baby boomers' assets. As Siegel observes:

> When the baby boomers will be selling their net assets, the rest of the developing world will be buyers of those assets. The developing world will be in a strong accumulation stage at the same time the developed world is in a decumulation stage. That is a very important force in the capital markets.

Going the Distance

Let's briefly review some of the key points that Siegel suggests can help people to become better investors:

- Maintain a diversified portfolio.
- Avoid short-term market timing.
- Don't underestimate your true holding period.
- Developed, mature relationships are tested time and again. Even in the darkest moments, stocks are to have and to hold.

Adds Siegel:

> Statistics that show the superiority of stocks don't show the superiority of *every* stock. They show the superiority of a diversified portfolio of stocks. As a result, if you want to capitalize on what we have found is true of the stock market, you have to construct a portfolio that tends to replicate the market. I've always been a great fan of index funds. Their record speaks for itself. I would say that probably the best investment advice—I don't recall who gave it to me—was when I realized the intrinsic logic of the index fund.

As you might expect, Siegel's personal investment portfolio is largely a reflection of what he preaches. His holdings include index funds, with a smattering of inflation-indexed bonds. But he also includes small bets on several actively managed funds and individual stocks. Siegel won't name names, but says he's been impressed with a few fund managers who appear uniquely qualified:

> **Their investment tilt or opinion convinces me to move into their funds. I do a little bit of large- and small-cap funds and growth and value funds. I also try to shade one way or the other, depending on where I think the market is going. I don't recommend this to the average person, because even I am not convinced that I'm gaining a lot of extra return with it. But I think a major way to explain why people outperform or underperform has to do with which style they cling to. There's the total market and how it moves, and then just beneath the surface, there's the investment style—the class of stocks.**

Siegel persists with these actively managed investments even though he's of the opinion that markets are mostly efficient. True, he admits, markets are not perfectly priced, but he adds that it's still extremely difficult to find those rare moneymaking market anomalies before everyone else catches the scent:

> **Everyone is trying to find stocks that promise to become big winners, and these get overpriced. For most shareholders, they will disappoint. Value stocks, on the other hand, don't attract as many of those investors. Stock pickers will do better with small-capitalization stocks, because many of these companies don't have analysts following them. But you'll spend a lot of time searching. I would commit only a small fraction of my portfolio toward these pursuits, and don't think that if you have a few successes you're a genius. Just because someone who doesn't know much about blackjack wins five hands in a row, it doesn't mean you can beat the dealer.**

CHAPTER 4

The Average Outperforms: John C. Bogle

"Why can't managers beat the market? Where's the value added? In terms of industry-wide statistics, it's just not there. One reason is because of cost. The cost is a handicap on the horse. If the jockey carries a lot of extra pounds, it's very tough for the horse to win the race."

I F MUTUAL FUND shareholders have a folk hero, it's John C. Bogle, the founder and former chairman of fund industry titan Vanguard Group. Bogle is an outspoken, iconoclastic, in-your-face champion for low-cost, buy-and-hold investing—a populist in a business suit who has spent five decades criticizing, cajoling and challenging his fund industry colleagues to give small investors what he calls "a fair shake."

He certainly looks the part—tall and lanky with a sonorous voice, a Princeton-educated everyman hammering out liberty and justice for all. It's a role that, quite literally, Jack Bogle was born to play. His father came from a well-to-do family that had prospered in business, but he had no great aptitude for it.

Instead, the younger Bogle took after his maternal great-grandfather, Philander B. Armstrong, a maverick who conceived of mutual insurance in the property field and in 1875 formed a company called the Phoenix Mutual Fire Insurance Co. He would spend his career railing against excessive industry fees and expenses.

Try to guess the speaker of the following passage from a fiery speech—Bogle or his great-grandfather: "Gentlemen, you must recognize (1) that companies having the smallest expense will have the ultimate advantage; (2) that companies having this advantage are the most desirous of correcting present abuses and (3) that companies which cannot long survive the present condition of affairs are determined to nullify every effort for reform. To save our business from ruin we must at once undertake a vigorous reform. To do this, the first step must be to reduce expenses."[1]

The words belong, in fact, to Armstrong, who delivered them in 1885 to a meeting of fellow insurance industry leaders. But the sentiments could easily have been his great-grandson's. Says Bogle, with characteristic bluntness:

> **This business is all about simplicity and low cost. I'm not into all these market strategies and theories and cost-benefit analyses—all the bureaucracy that goes with business. In investing, strip all the baloney out of it, and give people what you promise.**

Especially low cost. Bogle rarely misses an opportunity to pound home the direct and clear relationship between low management fees and superior investment returns. In 1975, a century after his great-grandfather started his insurance company, Bogle opened the doors of Vanguard as a mutual fund company in the truest sense of the ideal. Shareholders of Vanguard funds "own" the management company that administers the funds. Unlike other fund companies, Vanguard operates at cost, with each fund paying its share of the corporation's expenses for management, portfolio trading, salaries, marketing, advertising and other charges.

It's not a big tab. Vanguard's broad menu of several dozen indexed and actively managed stock and bond portfolios is nothing fancy—and dirt cheap. The firm has a well-deserved reputation for nickel-and-dime management fees on its passively managed index funds, but even its actively managed portfolios are generally priced at half to one-third of what the competition charges. The annual expense ratio of a Vanguard fund at the end of 1999 averaged a paltry 0.28 of 1 percent on assets under management—or just $140 on a $50,000 investment. In contrast, the cost for the average mutual fund was 1.37 percent—$685 to handle that same $50,000 commitment.[2]

Like many funds, Vanguard's offerings are "no load," avoiding the additional fees common to funds sold through brokers and some financial planners. But Vanguard's self promotion is modest by fund-industry standards, so its portfolios aren't saddled with

"12b-1" marketing fees—"killer B's," they're called—that are increasingly common even among no-load funds. You're also not likely to see splashy television commercials and full-page newspaper ads touting Vanguard—another plus for shareholders. Nor will you find Vanguard products in the giant no-transaction-fee fund "supermarkets" that some brokerages feature; Vanguard won't fork over the fees they demand for shelf space. Bogle explains:

> **Distribution has to be paid for. If you want bigger distribution—more sales—you have to pay more. More money for brokers, more money for advertising, more fees to the mutual fund supermarkets. There's a huge additional cost for distribution. The fund's shareholders are bearing it. And if the adviser can afford to give fund assets away to the supermarket, why didn't he preserve them for the fund shareholders?**

Vanguard does pass cost savings to its fund shareholders—and to their advantage. If you keep personal expenses to a minimum, you have more money to save and invest. The same is true of the fund business. Money that isn't funneled to cover management, sales, distribution and marketing stays in your account and works for you. Over time, this can make a big difference in your total wealth. And as you will discover later in this chapter, when buying funds it pays to be cheap—shareholders of low-cost funds tend to enjoy better returns than do high-cost-fund investors.

The House That Jack Built

The world according to Bogle is a soapbox of homespun common sense—a "Field of Dreams" notion that if you give investors quality service at a reasonable price, they will remain loyal, long-term customers. For anyone who has run a business, that's not so revelatory—except in fund management, it can be, Bogle contends. "We used to be a business that sells what it makes," he has noted. "But we've become a business that makes whatever sells."[3]

Bogle is the author of two popular investment books, *Bogle on Mutual Funds: New Perspectives for the Intelligent Investor*, published in 1994, and *Common Sense on Mutual Funds: New Imperatives for the Intelligent Investor*, published in 1999. The titles speak volumes about Bogle's deep-seated sensibilities toward investing, borrowing as they do from *The Intelligent Investor*, Benjamin Graham's classic 1949 treatise that provided individual shareholders with straightforward, simple investment insights.

Also in 1949, Bogle, a Princeton University undergraduate on an academic scholarship, was in need of a topic for his senior thesis in economics. True to form, he was determined to tackle a subject on which no Princeton thesis had ever been written. But he wasn't sure where to turn. In December 1949, he happened to read an article in *Fortune* magazine titled "Big Money in Boston." The story described the mutual fund business as a "rapidly expanding and somewhat contentious industry that could be of great potential significance to U.S. business."[4]

Bogle says he had never heard of mutual funds before, let alone invested in them. Perhaps he identified with the "contentious" label. Whatever the motivation, he decided right then to make this nascent industry the subject of his thesis. This "remarkable accident," as Bogle refers to it, sparked a remarkable career that has dramatically influenced how people approach investing and markets. "If I hadn't opened that magazine, I wouldn't be in this business today," he muses. "I don't know where I'd be raising hell. Maybe I'd be a bank clerk somewhere."

A bank chairman, more likely. Bogle's intuitive grasp of money-related issues and circumstances is difficult to overlook. His senior thesis was published in April 1951 and titled "The Economic Role of the Investment Company." Read today, the factually based essay is long on idealism. It commends the fund industry's efforts to represent shareholders fairly and honestly, and notes unique advantages that funds give to individual investors—such as diversification and liquidity. But certain passages foreshadow how this nonconformist author would one day shake the status quo of active money management with an innovative upstart called an index fund.

In his thesis, Bogle introduces two themes that would become synonymous with his professional life: performance and costs. He exhorts the fund industry not to boast that it outdoes the market: "Funds can make no claim to superiority over the market averages," he writes. Then he suggests that fund companies might be overvaluing their services: "There is some indication that the cost of management is too high," Bogle ventures. He concludes with the admonition that the fund industry's continued success hinges on giving shareholders a financial break: "Future growth can be maximized by concentration on a reduction of sales loads and management fees," he asserts. Half a century later, Bogle clearly is proud of a work that in many ways is still in progress, noting:

The thesis said that mutual funds should be run in the most honest, efficient and economical way possible. You could argue that that's the callow idealism of a twenty-one-year-old senior in college. You could also argue that it's the grand design for Vanguard.

Live Rich, Invest Cheaply

Many financial experts contend that a fund's bottom-line return is more important than its fees, but remember that fees directly impact the bottom line. Though an annual expense ratio of 1.5 percent may seem insignificant atop a 25 percent annual return, fees alone would decimate a return of 2.5 percent. And in the glow of the tremendous bull market of the late 1990s, it's easy to forget that as recently as 1994, the Standard & Poor's 500-stock index returned a grand total of 1.3 percent for the entire year.

With mutual funds, less is often more. Over longer time horizons, even half a percentage point difference in fund expenses can make a significant impact on your accumulated wealth. Consider a $150,000 investment divided equally between three diversified U.S. stock funds and held for 20 years. One portfolio levies an annual expense ratio of 1.5 percent, a second charges 1 percent, while the third takes just ½ of 1 percent.

As it happens, all three funds post a total return of 11.3 percent each year over the holding period, before factoring inflation—in line with the blue-chip S&P 500's historical average between January 1926 and December 1999, according to Ibbotson Associates, a Chicago-based financial research firm. Ibbotson calculates that the $50,000 in the highest-cost fund would be worth $327,319 after the two-decade holding period. The investment in the next-most-expensive fund would grow to $358,440—a performance gap of roughly $20,000. But the results for these two funds would pale against the $50,000 invested in the cheapest fund, which after 20 years would have a value of $392,359. Put another way, choosing the most expensive fund instead of the cheapest offering in this example would cost you $65,000; even the middle ground would subtract nearly $34,000 from your best result. Says Bogle:

All investors fall short of the return of the market by the amount of their costs. You see that fact come home to roost in years like 1987 and 1994, when the index actually went up but the average fund went down. Sure, there have been some terrific managers: Peter Lynch, Michael Price. John Neff, who ran Windsor Fund for 30 years, beat the index over that time, although not for the last 10 years. What does that tell you about the next 10 years? It's not clear. The relationship of past performance to future performance is very marginal.

A mutual fund's expense ratio is the most important factor within an investor's control. The fact is that shareholders in actively managed funds have little say over the course of their investments. A professional manager picks the stocks or bonds, and can trade them without regard for the costs and tax implications of frequent buying and selling.

Comparing the five-star Strong Large Cap Growth Fund and the Vanguard 500 Index is illuminating. For the five years through July 2000, Strong had a pretax average annualized return of 25.8 percent—besting the S&P 500 by 3.2 percentage points each year. The Index 500's pretax return over that time was 22.6 percent. For a tax-exempt investor, Strong wins. But after-tax, the picture changes. Strong returned 20.9 percent annually over that five-year span; 500 Index's post-tax return—the dollars that taxable investors keep—was 21.7 percent.[5] Bogle remarks:

You're paying capital gains taxes as they occur instead of deferring them over the long run. If you can defer gains over 10 years, the compound return you earn within that 10-year period without the money going out to the tax collector is very considerable.

And most fund managers do seem to enjoy frequent buying and selling. Unearthing winners and paring losers, after all, is what they're paid to do. The turnover ratio for U.S. stock funds averaged 89 percent at the end of 1999, meaning that stock jockeys in effect were replacing each stock in their portfolio once every 13 months. Some leading fund families are even quicker on the draw; average fund turnover runs 108 percent at industry titan Fidelity Group, for example, or a complete portfolio makeover every 11 months. Besides the additional expense, high turnover can stiff shareholders in taxable accounts with a painful tax bill unless a manager takes care to balance capital gains against losses.

In contrast, the annualized portfolio turnover rate among Vanguard's buy-and-hold–oriented actively managed equity funds at year-end 1999 averaged 45 percent, or a new crop every 27 months.[6] Compared to most fund companies, Vanguard seemingly employs a bunch of couch potatoes. That's fine with Bogle. Where is it ordained, he wonders, that the "active" part of fund management should also include trading? He chides:

> **Can't portfolio managers sit still for a minute? Just take a time-out. The industry used to say it was for the long-term investor. It now should say, "for the short-term speculator." That's what mutual funds are about today. A holding period of a year and a month on average is short-term speculation, not long-term investing. It's ridiculous. It verges on insanity.**

Why pay more? If you think your fund company charges too much for mediocre management, vote with your wallet and find a better-priced alternative. Choose among excellent-performing funds with the lowest possible expenses. Fund investors have more frugal choices now than ever. Vanguard boasts a complete lineup of thrifty offerings, but other large fund companies are notably cost-conscious, including TIAA-CREF, Janus, T. Rowe Price, Dodge & Cox and American Funds Distributors.

Vanguard, however, is the undisputed cheapskate champion. The flagship large-capitalization Vanguard 500 Index Fund, which mirrors the S&P 500 benchmark, carries an expense ratio of just 0.18 percent—a miserly $90 a year on a $50,000 investment. Even its actively managed U.S. Growth Fund charges just 0.41 percent to invest your money in large-cap growth stocks—$205 annually for each $50,000. The average U.S. diversified stock fund at the end of 1999 was weighted down with an expense ratio of 1.43 percent, or $715 a year on that same $50,000[7]—hundreds of extra dollars for fund management that could line shareholders' pockets instead.

Getting What You Pay For

Some investors might wonder what Bogle's fuss over costs is all about. Surely, they conclude, above-average performance will compensate for high expenses. If only fund investors got what they paid for. But quite often they don't. In fact, five-year, load-adjusted results for 15 Morningstar equity and fixed-income investment categories—including large-, mid- and small-cap, value and growth, U.S. and international—show that with rare exception, cheap funds fare better than their costlier rivals. Specifically, stock and bond funds with expense ratios at or below their category's average are more likely to outperform the group's five-year average return.[8]

At the same time, active managers continue their ongoing yearly struggle to beat the S&P 500 benchmark. Most fail. In 1994, when the S&P 500 returned a threadbare 1.3 percent, three of every four actively managed U.S. diversified equity funds fell short. Over the five years through 1999, only one in six active managers in this group were able to deliver results above the S&P 500's 28.5 percent yearly average. Active strategies would have fared more poorly if not for a strong showing in 1999, when one of every two managers scaled the S&P 500.[9] Bogle, not surprisingly, is unimpressed:

Why can't managers beat the market? Where's the value added? In terms of industrywide statistics, it's just not there. One reason is because of cost. The cost is a handicap on the horse. If the jockey carries a lot of extra pounds, it's very tough for the horse to win the race.

Where is the value added? That's a good question for any smart businessperson to ask. Bogle found his answer with low-cost index funds that strive to match the returns of a target benchmark, less fees. Index funds don't try to beat the market or buy and sell the latest hot stocks. They just own a representative sampling of all the stocks in an index and go along for the ride. If index funds ever do outperform their bogey, which happens occasionally, it's only by a few hundredths of a percentage point. Their main attraction is the ability to capture nearly all of a benchmark's return efficiently and inexpensively—which, as Bogle implies, is more than can be said for many actively managed funds:

> What is everybody paying all this money for—nearly 150 basis
> points [1.5 percent] for the average fund—when we can run
> index funds for 20 basis points? Fund sponsors shun indexing
> because while it's very profitable for the mutual fund share-
> holder, it's not profitable for the fund adviser.

Vanguard cast its lot with indexing in August 1976 when Bogle
launched the Vanguard First Index Investment Trust, later
renamed the 500 Index Fund. A fund that matched a market
average was an untested and uncertain breed—Vanguard's offering was the first retail product of its kind. But Bogle needed a
bold statement. He had opened the doors of his new fund company barely a year earlier, forced to go it alone after a falling-out
with new partners ended his 20-year career with venerable fund-
manager Wellington Management. The old-line firm had given
Bogle a job upon graduation from Princeton, partly on the
strength of his senior thesis. By his mid-30s he was running the
entire organization. Now he was on his own.

Bogle named his new firm The Vanguard Group of Investment
Companies after the HMS *Vanguard,* a famous eighteenth-cen-
tury flagship of the British navy. He had not yet begun to fight.
Bogle's early move at Vanguard was an attempt to gain managerial
control over Wellington Management's popular fund portfolios,
which included the stalwart Windsor Fund. The plan failed,
although Vanguard did secure a role to handle the Wellington
fund family's back-office functions.

Vanguard needed to do more than just push paper in order to
thrive. But investment management was not part of its mandate.
Enter the index fund—tailor-made for the young administrative
company. An index fund needs no active investment management—it requires only diligent maintenance to minimize any
deviation from the benchmark index.

Bogle was familiar and comfortable with the concept of a fund
that tried to replicate a market average. Indeed, if anyone in the
fund business ever would make this leap, it was Bogle. Unlike his

colleagues running actively managed fund shops, Bogle had little to lose. The prospect was made even more attractive because the notion of indexing a portfolio was new and controversial, yet another opportunity for Bogle's contentious side to shine.

Then, as now, the virtues and limitations of indexing were hotly debated. In his classic 1975 essay "The Loser's Game," Charles Ellis, managing partner of investment-industry consultant Greenwich Associates, hit money managers broadside with the blunt assessment that it was increasingly difficult for them to outperform a market index. Wrote Ellis: "The investment management business is built upon a simple and basic belief: Professional money managers can beat the market. That premise appears to be false."

Ellis explained that with so many bright and talented people running portfolios, investing had become a game of tough-minded institutions competing not with rank amateurs, as in the past, but with one another. How often do traders from Fidelity, Capital Research or Goldman Sachs make mistakes? Not often. Winning such an even match requires you to make fewer mistakes than your opponent. You score a higher return than the average, not because you were so much better, but because others played worse—a "loser's game." So don't try too hard, Ellis admonished money managers. "It appears," he noted, "that the *costs* of active management are going up and that the *rewards* from active management are going down."

In a misguided attempt to justify their fees, Ellis added, managers frequently trade too much and shoulder excessive risk—erratic behavior that only increases their chances of miscalculating and suffering a painful year. As Ellis presciently observed: "This would suggest to investment managers, 'don't do anything because when you try to do something, it is on average a mistake.' And if you can't beat the market, you certainly should consider joining it. An index fund is one way. The data from the performance measurement firms show that an index fund would have outperformed most money managers."[10]

Ellis at the time was just one of several influential proponents for indexing. The year before, Nobel laureate Paul Samuelson had challenged institutional managers to "set up an in-house portfolio that tracks the S&P 500 Index—if only for the purpose of setting up a naive model against which their in-house gunslingers can measure their prowess."[11] As Bogle recalls in *Common Sense on Mutual Funds*: "Dr. Samuelson had laid down an implicit challenge for *somebody, somewhere*, to launch an index fund."

It's probably clear by now that Bogle is not one to let a challenge go unanswered. He prepared for battle, and for war. Vanguard's index portfolio was simple, straight and revolutionary—just how Bogle likes things—and priced to sell. Its annual expense ratio then was 0.50 percent, or 50 basis points. The fund wasn't no-load—it had to be sold—but Bogle set about fixing that problem in his own efficient way: Vanguard cut out the middleman and highlighted the absence of a sales charge as a selling point.

The index fund was not exactly an overnight sensation. But that's all changed. Ridiculed for years as "Bogle's Folly," the 500 Index at the end of April 2000 was the biggest U.S. mutual fund, with total net assets of roughly $105 billion—just edging behemoth Fidelity Magellan for the title. In all, Vanguard's stock and bond funds controlled more than $550 billion in shareholder assets at the end of March 2000; about two-thirds of which was indexed.

For Bogle, the value of an index fund is not that it can beat the market—it can't—or even match it. Indexing, he explains, is a proven way to realize considerably all of the market's pretax gains. Additionally, index funds eliminate much of the guesswork and specific sector and company risk involved with investing. And that, Bogle contends, is worth every penny:

There's no point in being contrarian about something that doesn't make sense. An index fund always wins. It wins every single, solitary day, and there's no way around it. The fact that everybody criticized it made me all the more sure.

All Index Funds Are Not Created Equal

Once investors decide to index all or part of their investment portfolio, they still must deal with a crucial question: Which index? A generation ago, there was just one choice—Vanguard's S&P 500 clone. Today, fund families offer close to 300 products that track myriad benchmarks and industries. From large-cap to micro-cap and growth to value, the fund business has tried to fashion something for everyone. Investors can index the 30 large stocks of the Dow Jones Industrial Average or the entire U.S. market; they can index the performance of real estate investment trusts, foreign stocks—even Internet companies.

Additionally, dozens of so-called exchange-traded funds, or ETFs, are low-cost alternatives to traditional funds. ETFs are baskets of securities, listed on a major stock exchange, that track the net asset value of an underlying stock index like the Standard & Poor's 500. Most have cheaper annual management fees and greater tax efficiency than even the cheapest index funds. Unlike other open-end funds, ETFs can be bought and sold continuously through a brokerage account. They can also be sold short— meaning that a shareholder profits when the value of the security declines—and so used as a hedge against a market correction.

Much of the interest in ETFs has focused on Standard & Poor's Depositary Receipts (SPDR), or Spiders—the first of the breed, launched in 1993 to mirror the S&P 500—and more recently, the Nasdaq-100 Tracking Stock. This technology-laden proxy for the high-flying Nasdaq-100 Index has been dubbed "Cubes," for its "QQQ" ticker. The Spider is the biggest ETF, with assets of $19.8 billion at the end of 1999. It's also practically given away, with an annual expense ratio of 0.12 percent—or 12 bucks on a $10,000 investment—fully one-third less than the 500 Index. The wildly successful Cubes, which levies a 0.18 percent yearly fee, garnered nearly $11 billion in assets in the year after its March 1999 debut.

Besides Spiders and Cubes, Mid-Cap Spiders follow the S&P 400 Mid-Cap index; "Diamonds" reflect the 30 stocks in the Dow

Jones Industrial Average, and nine concentrated Select Sector Spiders track leading S&P sectors, including technology, financial services and consumer services. Additionally, international iShares MSCI country funds from Barclays Global Investors offer market exposure to 21 countries including France, Germany, Great Britain, Singapore, Mexico and Brazil.

Barclays Global Investors, the world's biggest manager of index funds, offers its own S&P 500–based ETF, priced to sell at just 0.0945 percent of assets—or $9.45 on every $10,000 in assets. Other Barclays ETFs include funds that track the S&P Mid-Cap 400, S&P SmallCap 600, and the Russell 1000-, 2000- and 3000-stock indices. Barclays enhances its lineup with sector funds such as an Internet index, a telecommunications sector fund and a technology portfolio

ETFs have expense advantages, but you do pay a brokerage commission on every trade. The American Stock Exchange posts extensive background about these products on its Web site (www.amex.com). Click on "Index Shares" for a closer look at the performance and portfolios of the ETF universe. Another useful online research source is the iShares investment data Web site (www.ishares.com).

For Bogle, the choice of an index is a crucial determinant of future returns. His top index-fund pick is a one-size-fits-all portfolio. It's not the 500 Index or any other S&P 500 fund, but an all-stock-market index fund. This portfolio is designed to track the performance of the Wilshire 5000 index, and captures the return and risk characteristics of the entire U.S. market of about 7,200 stocks. As a comprehensive benchmark that covers large-, mid- and small-cap stocks in virtually every industry, the Wilshire 5000 is a much better diversification tool than its S&P 500 counterpart. Still, the influential securities in the S&P 500 accounted for about 75 percent of the total market fund's investment return. Says Bogle:

Which index you use is the number-one factor. The Standard & Poor's 500 is not an index of the total U.S. stock market. You're

taking a large-cap risk that over time is almost certain to revert to the mean. The idea of indexing is to own the market, and therefore beat participants in the market who operate at high costs. If the S&P is not the market, then what is? The Wilshire 5000. The right way is to index the total stock market, particularly for taxable accounts.

How does indexing the total U.S. stock market stack up against the S&P 500? Fairly well, according to a comparison of the Vanguard 500 Index Fund with the Vanguard Total Stock Market Index Fund. For the five years through 1999, the 500 Index averaged 28.49 percent annual gains, a whisper under the S&P 500's 28.54 percent yearly return. Total Stock Market over that same period returned 26.8 percent annually, versus 27.1 percent for the Wilshire 5000.[12]

The S&P 500 index is more concentrated. In the late 1990s, the largest companies in the S&P 500 based on market value began to take on increasingly greater prominence. The index's top 10 companies represented nearly 26 percent of its market capitalization at the end of February 2000. At the end of 1998, the top 10 accounted for about 21 percent of this total. And in December 1995, the top-10 concentration was 17.7 percent.[13]

Narrow leadership gives each stock in the index an outsized weight, adding to the benchmark's volatility and rendering it more vulnerable to erratic price swings. In February 2000, for instance, four stocks—Microsoft, Cisco Systems, General Electric and Intel—alone accounted for 15 percent of the S&P 500's market capitalization.[14]

By definition, S&P 500 index funds carry market risk—but such heavy concentration completely alters that concept. The S&P 500 is supposed to reflect a broad market; at the beginning of 2000, it was far from that objective. Investors in S&P 500 index funds at that time were buying not another "Nifty Fifty," as happened in 1972, but rather a "Terrific Ten" or even a "Fantastic Four." At the same time, they were missing out on relative bargains hidden among the indicator's several hundred other names.

Concentration gave the S&P 500 a higher risk-profile, but surprisingly, the market risk of an S&P 500 index fund apparently was *lower* than the average risk of a U.S. stock fund. Consider that the 500 Index provided a higher return than about 90 percent of all managed domestic equity funds in the five years through 1999, with only about 80 percent of the average risk.[15] This suggests that active managers were taking bigger chances with their buys and sells in an attempt to hurdle their benchmark—something Charles Ellis had warned against 25 years before.

None of this is news to Bogle. He sees the fund business as a clash of two personality types: hedgehogs and foxes. Hedgehogs are patient, long-term investors, while foxes are quick, wily marketers. Bogle draws the analogy from the sixth-century B.C. writings of the Greek philosopher Archilochus, who surmised: "The fox knows many things, but the hedgehog knows one great thing."

And with investing, what is that great thing? Independence, says Bogle. But foxes dominate the fund business today, he notes with alarm. Fund companies try to make investing complicated, he contends, so that individual investors feel they must buy professionally managed funds in order to build financial security and wealth.[16] Indeed, "Enjoy work and family, and leave investing to us" is a universal theme that fund companies pitch to potential shareholders. These presentations usually are accompanied by impressive-looking charts showing funds that outperformed a benchmark index over a predetermined investment horizon.

To say that the foxes' strategy has succeeded would be an understatement, given the trillions of dollars under active management. But Vanguard's "can't-beat-'em, join-'em" appeal also has won a tremendous following. Schisms between opposing philosophies is age-old—hedgehog and fox, tortoise and hare, Apple Computer and Microsoft. But defending the virtues of indexing against the powerful forces of costly active management has been Bogle's lifelong fight—his crusade, really—and when spurred he rallies to the ramparts, contending:

The foxes are trying to manipulate people; they're trying to manipulate investing. Foxes charge a premium for their services, because it's supposedly so complicated and mere mortals can't do it. But the hedgehog says, "Of course mere mortals can do it. Just understand the one great thing: Own the market, and own it at a very low cost. And you will demonstrably get 98 or 99 percent of the market return."

The mutual fund industry has seen many changes in the past decade, some surprising, others frustrating. Certainly the next decade will have its fair share of the unexpected. With so many unresolved issues, are mutual funds still the best vehicle for individual investors? "Good mutual funds are," Bogle replies. "But I don't think we've designed the best mutual fund yet."

Leave that task to the hedgehogs—those fundamental investors who see stock ownership as having one-share, one-vote in an ongoing business. Hedgehogs hold that position, preferably forever unless the company's prospects change. The fox, in contrast, buys pieces of paper and trades greedily. Says Bogle:

Owning versus trading. Businesses versus stock. That's what makes the difference in investment. The smart hedgehog is Warren Buffett. What is he doing? Buying large-cap stocks, selecting a few he thinks are good, and holding them in his favorite holding period—forever. That's the secret.

Putting Active Management in Its Place

Indexing or active management? It doesn't have to be all or none. Many investors will find that it makes sense to blend the two approaches. In this so-called "core and explore" strategy, most of a portfolio is indexed across several investment categories—the core—while the remainder is given to favorite fund managers who have demonstrated an ability to beat the odds and outperform their benchmark average. Even Bogle admits that active fund management has its place in a portfolio. He explains:

> **I don't want to push my argument too far, because I think there is room for professional managers who don't feel bound by style boxes.**

Jack Bogle, defending active management? Don't drop the book; he doesn't mean all active managers—only trailblazers who are sensitive to shareholder costs and taxes. Look for dynamos who stick to Vanguard's top money-management rules: minimal trading and a portfolio that is fully invested in the market. Bogle explains:

> **The chances of beating a fairly measured market starts with having your expenses as low as possible. The active managers who will succeed are those with low costs, relatively low turnover and relatively low cash positions.**

Though Vanguard is best known for indexing, it contracts with outside investment management companies like Wellington for nearly two dozen actively managed offerings, while running its indexed portfolios in-house. Vanguard has a reputation for carefully vetting managers before hiring them and then closely monitoring their performance. Notes Bogle:

> **You don't abandon active management. If investors believe in active management, we give them investments and active management that take advantage of every single attribute that indexing does.**

Bogle outlines some of the most important factors that Vanguard considers in the elaborate process of selecting and retaining active managers, including:

- **Low cost.** Vanguard's 22 actively managed equity funds carried an average expense ratio of 0.47 percent at the end of 1999.[17]
- **Low portfolio turnover.** Half of the industry average is ideal, says Bogle.
- **Minimal style drift.** Funds stick to their stated investment objectives, or style. A large-cap value fund, for instance, should fill its portfolio with the stocks of large, underappreciated companies. A mid-cap blend fund would buy stocks of mid-sized companies and tilt the portfolio between growth and value. Often, managers lack consistency and drift toward whatever types of stocks happen to be popular.
- **Low manager turnover.** Vanguard tries to identify managers who are likely to captain their ships for many years. Edward Owens has managed topflight Vanguard Health Care since its 1984 inception. The legendary John Neff retired from Vanguard Windsor at the end of 1995 after 31 years. As is true of most relationships, longevity in fund managers contributes to consistency and predictability. Newly appointed managers, in contrast, can feel compelled to put their own stamp on a portfolio, even if it requires major buys and sells that can impact performance and incur capital gains taxes.

Bogle himself doesn't trade common stocks—not anymore, at least. He confesses:

I'm afraid I don't know how to make quick money. I might want to, but I don't have any talent that way. I used to do brokerage accounts, but finally found, maybe after 15 years, that it's not a very good game to win anything at. It's a terrible diversion. My broker would call up and try to get me to do something. I really didn't want to spend the time and effort, and I wasn't getting anywhere.

Much of his net worth, Bogle explains, is tied to his Vanguard retirement plan, and this tax-exempt account does contain actively managed stock funds. Of course, tax efficiency is not a concern here, since capital gains are reinvested on a deferred basis until the money is needed. But most of Bogle's money is in relatively secure fixed-income funds—taxable bonds in the retirement account and tax-exempt bonds in the taxable account. As Bogle explains:

It gets tougher and tougher to recommend other than index funds to a taxable investor. There aren't many tax-efficient funds in this industry. You've got to get fund turnover down below 15 percent to have a significant tax advantage.

Searching for a Few Good Funds

Still, most investors enjoy the hunt for talented stock-pickers—paying particular attention to the current headliners. And though many shareholders are aware that fund performance over the past six months or year says nothing about future return, they continue to take a flier on the manager with the hottest hands. With investing, as in basketball, a high-scoring player on a "hot streak" tends to be given the ball more often.

In fact, "hot hands" is an illusion. People see skill in short-term performance where there is none, as we'll learn in Chapter 6 about the psychology of investing. Here's a famous example of how "hot hands" can get out of hand: Suppose you're playing a game with a roomful of people. You toss a series of coins, and everybody predicts whether the coin will show heads or tails. Everyone stands up and raises their hand if they think the coin is going to come up heads. Guess wrong, and you sit down.

After the first toss, half of the players are out. The second toss leaves one quarter of the group in the game. After a dozen or so of these flips, only one person remains standing, and he will be absolutely convinced of his genius. In reality, he just defied the odds. And the chances of his repeating this feat are quite small.

The problem with active stock-fund management, Bogle explains, is not that it has no value. It's that, like the coin-flip champion, winners usually don't repeat. Investing magazines are full of stories about "21 Funds for the 21st Century." In truth, the top funds of the past five years are unlikely to be the best investments for the next five—particularly expensive funds. This concept may be difficult to grasp; investors tend toward optimism—otherwise they wouldn't hand over their money to brokers and funds in the first place. So it's important to be aware that investment returns are subject over time to a gravitational force called *reversion to the mean*.

As reality checks go, reversion to the mean is sobering. What happens is that the market average is ratcheted higher each year by a handful of hot stocks, leaving most other stocks to trail behind. Fund managers smart or lucky enough to hold these supernovas can earn terrific returns, while the rest of the pack can't keep up.

But over time, most of today's superior-performing funds will not maintain their edge. Success brings more assets, and the larger size makes it tougher for even the best manager to buy undiscovered gems in any meaningful quantity without the market noticing and driving up the price. Giant funds especially tend to lose their youthful sprite and begin to resemble their more staid benchmarks. To be sure, this decline can take a decade or longer to develop, but eventually, Bogle observes, funds that go up, come down:

> Surveys tell us that most equity fund investors expect 14 percent annual returns on stocks in the years ahead. Who are we to say they won't get it? But I'd be darned skeptical. Powerful forces call for a reversion to the mean, and expenses would take even a 14 percent market return down to 12 percent for the average fund. I'd rather that shareholders be psychologically and

financially prepared for problems. Time is your friend; emotion is your foe. If you're ready for anything in the financial markets and focus on the long term, you'll earn much better returns.

Bogle values independence and straight shooting, so he also takes umbrage with managers who hope to get away with an all-too-common transgression called "closet indexing." Some fund managers don't like taking risks—with their jobs. Their portfolios are virtual indexes disguised as actively managed funds. They hug an index, fearful of falling behind and unwilling to lead. So performance tends not to deviate from their benchmark. These funds won't usually suffer outsized losses or realize big market-beating gains. The trouble with this strategy is that a group of funds already deliver market performance with market risk—they're called index funds. Says Bogle:

There are three kinds of risk that every investor takes. One is market risk. Two is style risk: large-cap or small-cap, or growth or value or international. And three is manager risk; once you decide where you want to be in the style or objective categories, the manager can either add to or detract from that return. The index fund eliminates two of those three risks. But the most serious risk remains: market risk.

Row Your Boat

Vanguard's seeds were planted on that December day at Princeton in 1949 when Bogle picked up that copy of *Fortune*. In fact, that year would prove to be pivotal for U.S. investors. Americans were healing from the wounds and losses of World War II. They were marrying, getting jobs, buying homes and forging ahead with lives that had been drastically interrupted. A baby boom was only natural, and birth rates remained high for nearly 20 years after the war's end. Another natural result: nesters building nest eggs.

Demand for U.S. stocks boomed in the 1950s along with babies and suburbs. The mutual fund industry in 1949 had fewer than 1 million shareholders who had $1.5 billion invested. By May 1959, nearly 3.9 million shareholders had spread $14 billion among more than 200 different funds.[18]

Those figures seem quaint now, given the U.S. fund industry's phenomenal growth over the past four decades. By June 2000, 88 million shareholders—about half of all U.S. households—had committed $7.1 trillion to roughly 7,900 funds.[19]

To be sure, with so many investors trying to make sense of so many fund choices, Bogle's lone voice in the wilderness has become a plea for investors to build their portfolios on strong, but simple, foundations. "Simplicity is the master key to financial success. The more complex the world around us becomes, the more simplicity we must seek in order to realize our financial goals." This was Bogle's message to an individual investor group on a 1998 visit to Australia. It's part of the advice he gives investors the world over, and can be found online at Vanguard's Web site (www.vanguard.com). His basic approach to investing involves a few clear-cut beliefs:

- Investing is not as difficult as it seems.
- Consider index funds first.
- Own stocks, but hold bonds as well. Build a broadly diversified stock portfolio with mutual funds. This will help mitigate the specific risk of owning just a handful of stocks. Better still, buy the entire stock market through a total stock-market fund.
- Don't own too many funds, and don't trade them. Fund managers within a particular category tend to own many of the same stocks, so it's easy to pay twice for a similar portfolio. Says Bogle, "Buy right and hold tight."
- Think long-term. Markets fluctuate, and these short-term ups and downs usually are just noise. So don't lose sight of bigger goals. If stocks provide annual returns of 10 percent,

Bogle points out, a portfolio will double in seven years, redouble in 14, and redouble again in 21 years—an eightfold increase. Fixed-income securities at, say, 6 percent will double in 12 years and redouble in 24. Over 25 years, $10,000 in stocks would grow to $117,000, while $10,000 in bonds would grow to $42,000.

- **Past performance can only predict a fund's consistency and risk—not returns.**
- **Stay the course, no matter the obstacles.** "There's a point when investors should exit the market," Bogle has said. "The problem is that we never know when it is."

Bogle's almost-Messianic evangelism for indexing and his enthusiastic embrace of the small investor has won him a wide following among fans who shower him with adoration. A dramatic example of their dedication was played out in 1999 when Vanguard's board of directors decided that a company policy requiring directors step down at age 70 also applied to a recalcitrant Bogle, then Vanguard's senior chairman.

The board was stung by a backlash of opposition from investors who felt that the founder was getting a raw deal. Some shareholders even threatened to dump their Vanguard funds in protest. Then, in what seems a face-saving arrangement, the board voted to waive the rule, and Bogle agreed to step down to run Vanguard's specially created Bogle Research Center.

For a tangible sense of how deep devotion to Bogle runs among some Vanguard investors, go to Morningstar's Web site (www.morningstar.com) and visit a hugely popular message board found under the heading "Vanguard Diehards." These Bogle groupies—"Bogleheads," they've dubbed themselves—can't praise the man enough. They call him "Saint Jack," the patron saint of investors. In post after post, they revel in tales of his candor and can-do spirit, such as the time in March 2000 when he fielded questions for two hours after a speech to individual investors in Miami. As one admiring Boglehead wrote in an online love note:

"Jack Bogle should at least be the People's Choice for the equivalent of the Nobel Prize in economics for all the good and substantial benefits we've derived from his life's work."

As for Bogle, he insists that he's done nothing remarkable—and is certainly no saint. He's just being himself, he claims modestly—his everyday, brash, earthy self:

> I don't think I'm anything like a folk hero. But there aren't a lot of people like me in this business. Most keep a lower profile, are much more guarded in the way they speak and much less strident in their advocacy of shareholders' values and rights. If this industry had one fox and 1,000 hedgehogs, maybe I wouldn't stand out. But if it has 1,000 foxes and one hedgehog, you're going to be more distinctive. You carry a different set of values and investment ideas. If it's unusual—even unique—you will stand out.

Uncommon Value, Hidden Growth: Josef Lakonishok

"The attractiveness of value stocks is that because they've had relatively poor performance, investors to some extent have given up. Yet the stocks might not be as bad as the market thinks they are."

To a value investor, what goes down must come up. Value investing is the stock-market equivalent of holding season tickets to a hapless baseball team that for years has done nothing but disappoint. Friends can't fathom your unwavering loyalty. At the darkest times, even you wonder if they may be right. Then the impossible happens. A new manager is hired, changes are made to the lineup, and over the following season a championship contender emerges. Your friends are skeptical at first—just luck, they say—but soon they, too, become believers. And those season tickets—your "shares"—are now a hot item.

Value investors search for situations where they strongly believe that others have the picture wrong. Unlike investors who gladly fork over premium prices for popular "growth" stocks, shareholders of value stocks refuse to pay homage and dollars to Wall Street's darlings. Instead they are devoted to Wall Street's dogs.

Out-of-favor value stocks typically are cheaper than their high-octane growth rivals. The market does not have great expectations for these underachievers; in fact, they're not well-liked at all—and typically not without reason. These companies usually have made big mistakes. They have been plodding, wasteful, rudderless. But sometimes these fallen angels make the tough choices necessary to regain their footing and start anew on the road to recovery.

Nobody loves you when you're down and out, as the old blues song goes—except value investors. Where most others see straw, they see gold. Let index-fund boosters believe in an efficient market of few mistakes. Let growth-oriented investors have no doubt that corporate earnings will reach to the sky. Value investors will have none of that. These contrarians are convinced that the market routinely overreacts to negative developments at otherwise strong companies and overlooks the earnings potential of others.

Unlocking value before it's widely recognized requires doing homework about a company's current financial condition, along with confidence that better days lie ahead and a stubborn conviction to stand tough against the herd. At first sight, this is often not a pretty picture. But in time, if and when a firm's fortunes do improve, depressed shares shine again and shower true believers with a handsome reward.

As a service to readers of this book, Josef Lakonishok, a value-focused portfolio manager, has agreed to divulge the top secret of his trade. It is not for the faint of heart—but here it is nonetheless; just one word:

Patience. Patience? Lakonishok explains:

Value investors should be patient. If you demand that your investments pay off in a short time, this is not for you. To be a value investor, you need "emotional contrarianism." You have to not mind opening the newspaper and seeing bad news.

Lakonishok is one of three principals in Chicago-based investment firm LSV Asset Management, which handles more than $6 billion in pension and endowment assets for institutional clients such as Stanford University, Sears Roebuck and Bank of America. He is also a finance professor at the University of Illinois in Champaign, Illinois, and author of several watershed research studies extolling the superiority of value over growth.

As money managers, Lakonishok and colleagues Andrei Shleifer of the University of Chicago and Harvard University's Robert Vishny—hence the name LSV—buy shares of troubled companies that are out of favor, have below-average past performance and offer little hope for positive change. Why would anyone invest like that? Because such a classic value strategy—rooted in several important valuation methods that we will review later in this chapter—is frequently a hands-down winner.

A Penny Saved

All good things may come to those who wait—but first you need something worth waiting for. Naturally, you spy the most attractive stocks. What could be more worthwhile to have and to hold than the stocks everyone wants to own? To a growth investor, not much. You expect top companies to keep firing on all cylinders. You have faith that management will continue to post impressive gains in quarterly earnings and revenues. Your portfolio is a thing of beauty.

But beauty is in the eye of the shareholder. Stocks that a growth investor feels are reasonably priced, a value investor finds exorbitant. And what looks like a tulip bulb to a value buyer is nothing but a garlic bulb to a growth player. Like the blind men who each describe the elephant differently, perspective about what makes a "good buy" depends on which part of the animal you're touching.

Be careful about chasing performance. Good companies don't always make good stocks. Think about this: If you and I each know it's a good company, then everybody knows. When a story is so well covered, all the good news is likely priced into the stock. Yet buyers pour in, dreaming of riches. These new investors don't want managers; they want magicians. Performance expectations—and the chance for disappointment—are both extremely high. At this point, there is no middle ground; there is only have or have not.

You aren't likely to hear this from Wall Street, however. On Wall Street, beauty is more than skin deep. If any investor can dance with the homecoming queen or king, then we'll all buy tickets to the stock-market prom. That's one reason why you don't see many "sell" opinions from equity analysts. Positive surprises are warmly received; they keep hope alive. But let a company surprise the Street with even a hint of disappointment, and retribution is swift. Investors will sell first and ask questions later—even if the bad news is only temporary.

No one wants to be left standing when the music stops. We all know that stock prices don't reach to the sky—even as we pretend they do. Sure, the magic can dazzle many appreciative audiences, but ultimately, investment returns regress to the mean. Studies show that over longer time horizons, standout investment performance invariably reverts to a market average. A company becomes larger and more mature; earnings growth and stock price appreciation slows to a more sustainable rate. Now the stock has a wide following of knowledgeable investors who have a reasonable idea of what to expect from it. Consistency is normal; surprises are rare. But remember, the market only rewards uncertainty. Says Lakonishok:

> **Individuals put so much weight on past performance. Everybody loves a winner. Now a winner can be a winner for a couple of years, but that doesn't mean it will continue. Microsoft is an unbelievable company. But does its price really reflect what will happen to it in the next five years? No. People are rewarding past success.**

Balancing Value and Risk

Because a value strategy does not lend itself to immediate gains, value is often perceived as a riskier investment course over growth. But really, other than bankruptcy, how much worse can things get? Value stocks are not beautiful, so no one brags about owning them. Their shares are cheap relative to earnings, so no one expects much from them. These companies just don't have many choices left: either they scrape along, go out of business, get acquired or maybe, just maybe, dust themselves off and get back in the game. That's a scary proposition, to be sure, but is it blatantly riskier? Not really. These stocks are so beaten already, there isn't much downside remaining in them. The more acute risk, Lakonishok points out, is that these distressed situations deteriorate further and the stock never goes up.

> **I like to think about value stocks as companies that are under-appreciated by the market. They don't have to be terrible, just on a skid. The attractiveness of value stocks is that because they've had a relatively poor performance, investors to some extent have given up. Yet the stocks might not be as bad as the market thinks they are. The danger is that you are actually buying dying companies. So you would like to find some catalyst; maybe just get involved with companies that are showing signs of recovery.**

Buying quality companies at a cheap price is the fundamental principle of value investing that Benjamin Graham and collaborator David Dodd first espoused in their pioneering 1934 book *Security Analysis*. Graham refined the message for individuals in his 1949 classic *The Intelligent Investor*.

The dismal period following the 1929 stock-market crash nearly wiped out Graham, a New York investment manager, and his clients. *Security Analysis* was his clarion call. He had learned the hard way that investors should greatly diminish their expectations about what the stock market could give, and therefore would be pleasantly surprised when they actually did get something in return. Now he would give them a strategy for success.

Graham felt that finding growth stocks that could beat the market average is difficult for most investors; you'd have better luck going against the crowd. And even if you did manage to pick a high-performance growth stock, its blistering pace could sputter and fickle investors would flock elsewhere.

So he focused on strong companies whose stocks traded at prices near or below intrinsic value—current assets minus total liabilities—the price a rational buyer might pay. Graham wanted to own shares of companies that had fallen on hard times but at their core were good operations with a substantial record of earning money, paying their bills and issuing regular dividends to shareholders. If you could buy into these companies at a discount to intrinsic value, he proposed, you could be assured a "margin of safety" to cushion harmful blows—three words, he said, that "distill the secret of sound investing."

For a stock to be a true bargain, Graham reasoned, its share price should be two-thirds or less of the net current asset value—the margin of safety. Astute buyers could scoop up stocks below net current asset value when skittish investors overreacted to bad news or overlooked diamonds in the rough, he believed. Most of these stock-specific shocks, he asserted, were temporary. As he chided in *The Intelligent Investor*: "When an individual company begins to lose ground in the economy, Wall Street is quick to assume that its future is hopeless and that it should be avoided at any price."[1]

Intelligent investors are not fools to rush into a stock when it's been largely abandoned, Graham argued—if the company's fiscal picture has been carefully and correctly ascertained. Look first for a low price relative to assets—what professionals call "price-to-book value"—and a low price compared to earnings. Ideally, the stock has also suffered a significant decline in share value. Target secondary companies, he advised: small stocks in top industries, leading stocks in unimportant industries and mid-sized firms without much of a following.

But it takes courage to stay the course and resist the often intense pressure to bail out. "You are neither right nor wrong because the crowd disagrees with you," Graham wrote. "You are right because your data and reasoning are right. Similarly, in the world of securities courage becomes a surprise virtue after adequate knowledge and a tested judgment are at hand."[2]

If you buy a stock with a high margin of safety, then mistakes tend to be of lost time more than lost money. Suppose you buy a stock at 50 cents on the dollar and you badly misjudge its value. Over the next five years, the shares return a few percent annually—about what you'd get from risk-free cash. That's tough, but nowhere near as painful as holding a stock that loses 50 percent of its value because high expectations for it fail to materialize. Graham's margin of safety may cause investors to miss spectacular winners, but their odds are skewed in favor of steady, positive total returns.

Becoming a Valuable Investor

Graham eventually would mentor a young, homespun Nebraska native by the name of Warren Buffett, who took the basic principles of value investing he learned at the master's knee and tailored them to his own particular disciplines. Buffett, as many people know, would become one of the greatest stock-market investors of all time. But here's something to ponder: Would Buffett be a multibillionaire if he'd been a growth investor?

It's hard to say. Buffett has a gift for the market that most mortals do not—not least the courage of conviction and a willingness to sink a large percentage of his portfolio into a few specialized companies. But courting value—investing with a margin of safety—probably gave him an edge, for the long-term results of value strategies don't lie: Diversified portfolios of both large- and small-capitalization value stocks have delivered superior returns over a comparable basket of growth stocks while taking less risk. Over a 25-year period between January 1975 and March 2000, the Barra Large Cap Value Index of large-capitalization S&P 500 stocks outdid the comparable Barra Large Cap Growth Index, 17.1 percent versus 15.8 percent, according to mutual fund research firm Morningstar. Risk, as measured by three-year standard deviation (a range of potential outcomes compared to return), was 21.4 for the value index and 24.3 for the growth benchmark.

Value investing has been even more effective with smaller stocks. In the 20 years ending in April 2000, the value segment of the Russell 2000 index of small stocks posted an average annual return of 15.6 percent, against 12.8 percent for the growth component, Morningstar data show. Three-year standard deviation was 18.1 for value and 38.1 for growth. Mid-sized value stocks also fared better than growth on a risk-return basis, Morningstar reports.

Lakonishok's own work corroborates this evidence. A landmark 1994 study, "Contrarian Investment, Extrapolation, and Risk," coauthored with Shleifer and Vishny and published in *The Journal of Finance*, ranked all the companies listed on the New York Stock Exchange and the American Stock Exchange by price-earnings ratios and sorted the stocks into 10 groups. Then the researchers looked at stock performance between April 1968 and April 1990, and assumed that an investor held a portfolio for five years. The result? Stocks with the highest price-earnings ratios returned an average of 11.4 percent annually during the study period, while the lowest P/E stocks averaged 19 percent annual gains.[3]

But what gives value the upper hand? Is it a behavioral story, as Graham suggested—an irrational market overreacting to bad news and pricing stocks too low? Or could it be that the stocks of these troubled companies are downright riskier, so an efficient market compensates investors for playing a more dangerous game?

Efficient-market theorists play the risk card. According to this view, value stocks carry risk that cannot be diversified away, and so command sizable premiums over more reliable growth stocks. Two respected economists, Eugene Fama of the University of Chicago and Kenneth French of Yale University, caused a sensation in the investment world in 1992 with this very argument. But Lakonishok strongly disagrees:

If you listen to Fama and French, value stocks outperform growth stocks because they are more risky. By Fama-French's definition, a variable like book-to-market (price-to-book value) would be a proxy for risk. Now Internet stocks have very little book value and a lot of market price. Those are prime examples of growth companies. Most of us would think those companies are very risky. They have a lot of price volatility and high market sensitivity—high beta. On the other side of the spectrum you'll probably find utilities and machinery stocks. But based on Fama and French, a utility is more risky than Yahoo! because a utility has a high book-to-market.

For Lakonishok, behavior explains it all. The stock market is a market of people, and people are not always logical. Human frailties influence the market's direction and discipline, he relates, giving rise to mispricings and unrealistic expectations:

Inefficiencies are driven by behavioral biases. People extrapolate past performance too far into the future. There is greed, fear, excitement. People are too optimistic about growth stocks and too pessimistic about value stocks. We found little predictability and little persistence in growth rates; companies with very high growth in the past don't necessarily have high growth in the future.

Lakonishok, Shleifer and Vishny responded to the risk argument in what proved to be the most controversial aspect of the Contrarian paper. They charged that value stocks outperform growth—which they fittingly called "glamour" stocks—not because these unloved securities are riskier, but *because investors don't expect much from them*. They observed: "Value strategies yield higher returns because these strategies exploit the suboptimal behavior of the typical investor, and not because these strategies are fundamentally riskier." They continued: "Some investors tend to get overly excited about stocks that have done very well in the past and buy them up, so that these 'glamour' stocks become overpriced. Similarly, they overreact to stocks that have done very badly, oversell them, and these out-of-favor 'value' stocks become underpriced. Because contrarian strategies invest disproportionately in stocks that are underpriced and underinvest in stocks that are overpriced, they outperform the market."[4]

In conversation, Lakonishok illuminates the subject:

> **We tried to see if contrarian strategies are more risky, not by using convoluted measures of risk, but with commonsense examples. People look at volatility—we didn't find that value stocks are more volatile than growth stocks. People look at sensitivity to market movements like beta—we didn't find that value stocks have higher betas. And then it's important to see how value strategies do in down markets, because people are concerned with down-market risk. We found that value strategies do very well, a sign that they are actually defensive. Then we tried to see how value does in recessions, when all of us have less money and an extra dollar is more important. Once more we found that value strategies, contrary to what some people believe, do all right.**

The behavior argument was revisited in a 1997 report, "Good News for Value Stocks: Further Evidence on Market Efficiency," which Lakonishok, Shleifer and Vishny, along with Harvard University professor Rafael La Porta, published in *The Journal of Finance*. Remember how the market tends to reward positive surprises and recoil at negative ones? Lakonishok and his colleagues wanted to see if earnings surprises played a significant role in the difference in performance between value and growth stocks. So they studied the price movement of value and growth stocks on the NYSE, the Amex and Nasdaq stock exchanges, focusing specifically on the three days before and after earnings announcements. The result, says Lakonishok, was remarkable:

We found that value stocks around earnings announcements outperform growth stocks, or glamour stocks, by four percentage points.

Four percentage points of outperformance is a wide gap by any stretch. "A significant amount of the return difference between value and glamour stocks is attributable to earnings surprises that are systematically more positive for value stocks," the researchers reported. "Value stocks provide superior returns because the market slowly realizes that earnings growth rates for value stocks are higher than it initially expected and conversely for glamour stocks."[5] Lakonishok elaborates:

People are too optimistic about growth stocks when earnings are announced. So on average the market should be disappointed with growth stocks. When the earnings of value stocks are announced, people don't expect much, so on average investors should be pleasantly surprised.

Value at a Reasonable Price

Writing more than two centuries ago in *The Wealth of Nations*, the Scottish economist Adam Smith neatly collated the growth-versus-value question—though it was not stocks that caught his attention, but rather how people value what comes easily and what does not. He said: "Nothing is more useful than water: but it will purchase scarce anything; scarce anything can be had in exchange for it. A diamond, on the contrary, has scarce any value in use; but a very great quantity of other goods may frequently be had in exchange for it."[6]

Here's the bottom line: In the stock market, with few exceptions, corporate earnings are everything. Are earnings higher today than they were a year ago, and by how much? From this information, investors set a price to pay for future earnings. Predictability is highly regarded in uncertain times—but uncertainty is rewarded in stable times. Investors are compensated for taking risk, but they don't always like to take chances.

Business conditions fluctuate; growth and value strategies go in and out of style. Investors in U.S. stocks must understand where the economy is in its cycle. Put simply, when the economy is slowing and corporate profits are scarce, the market prices earnings growth like diamonds. In buoyant times, when opportunities abound and earnings growth is plentiful, the market prices it like water. It's like anything else. When you want something that's rare, you pay a higher price. If something is abundant and not precious, you pay less.

What's true for jewelry also is true for stocks. As a rule, a flagging economy favors growth stocks while a robust economy supports value. When growth is elusive, investors run for shelter and security in the biggest, most reliable companies, bidding up their shares. Lower-quality stocks with questionable earnings tend to sag miserably—sometimes more than deserved.

As economic conditions brighten and corporate profitability accelerates, people become more confident about the ability of all companies—not just the safest and soundest—to generate consistent earnings. They get more comfortable with the idea of buying lower-quality stocks—which, indeed, may be improving—and search for bargains among the value bins. The increased demand drives up the prices of these laggard issues, helping value to outperform. Says Lakonishok:

> **Everything goes in cycles. Markets are high and then you see a correction. Prices usually are not going from overpriced to equilibrium. In many cases prices go too low, which presents investors with a buying opportunity.**

How can you find attractive value stocks? Several keys help investors like Lakonishok unlock value in the stock market. The most important comparisons, or ratios, are *price-to-earnings, price-*

to-sales, *price-to-book* and *price-to-cash flow*. Value investors attach "low" to each of these measures. They're relatively easy to grasp with the help of a calculator and a target company's most recent financial statement. Better yet, many Internet Web sites do the math for you. We'll look at each of these four ratios.

In Earnings We Trust

There are many techniques to value a stock, but you don't have to get fancy. Experienced investors like Lakonishok use low price-earnings ratio as an initial screen for value. P/E is a straightforward measure—just divide a stock's price by its last 12 months' earnings per share. A $10 stock with $1-per-share of earnings sports a P/E of 10. A simple equation, to be sure, but it's only a starting point.

Current P/E indicates the level of confidence investors have in a company's future. What do buyers think the stock will be worth a year from now, or five years from now? What are people willing to pay for a share of that expected growth? On the surface, a low P/E stock suggests that investors have little faith in the company's business or management. Popular stocks—trendier companies that everyone wants to own—tend to command higher earnings multiples and generate greater optimism.

As a value investor, you want to rub elbows with the potential superstars before the Wall Street tabloids discover them. Screening for low price-earnings is one proven way to notice a neglected stock. But limiting that search to low-P/E stocks alone could give you nothing more than a list of downtrodden companies with dismal growth potential.

Quality of earnings is what really counts. Many people assume that low P/E is evidence enough that a stock is temporarily out of favor—a perfect buy candidate. Not so. Low P/E is only a first step in a peek behind the numbers. Just because a stock seems like a value doesn't automatically make it so. Stocks usually are cheap for good reasons, like poor management or high debt, and can stay cheap for a long time. Low P/E only holds out the remote chance that the market has made a mistake. It isn't confirmation.

If you choose to be contrary, be confident—at least that will blunt the criticism you'll undoubtedly endure for your boldness. What you see as a gem will look rough-cut to others—and you won't make any money until their minds change. So before you buy, compare the stock with the P/Es of rival stocks in its sector. Are the company's shares trading at a lower multiple than its peers? Has the stock's historical P/E been higher than it is now? That's another sign of an undervalued security. The best way to delve into historical ratios and current comparisons is to go online. Easy-to-use Web sites include Yahoo! Finance (www.quote .yahoo.com) and Market Guide (www.marketguide.com). Earnings estimates for companies also are available on the Web without charge from Zack's Investment Research (www.zacks.com).

Georgia-Pacific Group in May 2000 seemed like a tailor-made value proposition. The stocks of paper companies had been suffering mightily from pricing and inventory concerns, and Georgia-Pacific was hardly immune. By late August 2000, its shares had tumbled below $26 from a 52-week high of $52.

Clearly, Georgia-Pacific had some current problems. But did Wall Street doubt its future growth? Apparently not. Analysts at the time were anticipating earnings-per-share growth of 26 percent for the year 2001. Yet the stock price reflected far less confidence. Georgia-Pacific's trailing P/E of 5.7 contrasted sharply with the paper and paper products sector average of 16.5.

Had investors overreacted? A helpful way to understand if the market has become too pessimistic or too euphoric about a stock is to figure its P/E-to-growth ratio, or PEG ratio. To calculate this, divide a stock's P/E by analysts' estimated earnings-per-share growth rate for the company. Stocks that trade at lower PEG ratios than their peers or the market are potential value plays. Investors use 1.0 as a baseline. If the ratio is less than 1.0, the stock is considered undervalued. Stocks with ratios above 1.0 are thought overvalued.

Georgia-Pacific's P/E of 5.7 divided by its projected 26 percent growth gave it a PEG of 0.22. By that light, the company's stock looked cheap—less than six times earnings for 26 percent annual growth sure seems a bargain.

Full Sales

Price-earnings ratio isn't effective for companies with erratic earnings—or no earnings at all. For those stocks, and as a complement to P/E analysis, Lakonishok employs a useful valuation measure called the price-sales ratio. Essentially, this ratio reflects what a shareholder will pay for a dollar of a company's revenue.

Unlike earnings, sales figures are difficult for management to manipulate, making price-sales a more consistent barometer. And firms with declining earnings and a flat stock price will have inflated P/Es that paint a misleading picture of health. The price-sales ratio can steer you around these obstacles. Says Lakonishok:

> Growth in earnings is a problematic measure when companies are losing money. You might have a cheap company whose earnings are depressed, so the price-earnings ratio is very high. If you go by P/E, it will seem like a growth stock when in essence it may be a deep-value stock. Growth in sales is an indication of performance. If growth in sales is high, you know the company has been doing well.

There are two ways to determine the price-sales ratio:

- Calculate annual sales per share—total revenue divided by shares outstanding. Then divide the current stock price by sales per share. In August 2000, Georgia-Pacific, for instance, was working from annual sales of $21.5 billion and had 170.6 million shares outstanding, making its sales-per-share ratio equal to roughly $126 (21.5/0.1706). Georgia-Pacifc then was trading at about $26, for a price-sales ratio of roughly 0.21—just 21 cents of market value for every dollar of revenue.

- Compute market capitalization—total shares times the stock price. Georgia-Pacific's 170.6 million shares times $26 gives a market cap of about $4.4 billion. Divide that result by annual revenue—$21.5 billion—and you'll get the same deep-value price-sales ratio of 0.21.

Defining "low" price-sales depends on the business, so the measure is best seen against a company's rivals in the same sector or industry. For Georgia-Pacific, a report from stock research firm Market Guide (www.marketguide.com) indicated that the sector average for the paper and paper products business was 1.6 times sales, giving Georgia-Pacific quite an attractive valuation by comparison.

The price-sales ratio also works well in judging Internet and other technology companies where sales growth is high and P/Es often are either stratospheric—the way shares of popular Web site Yahoo! orbited with a P/E ratio of 363 in late August 2000—or nonexistent. Most Internet stocks have scant sales, zero earnings, and negative cash flow. These and other technology companies tend to carry high price-sales ratios, partly because their products and services have high sales margins, and because optimistic investors will pay far more than a dollar for the dream of owning them.

Yahoo! carried a price-sales ratio of 85.7 in August 2000—meaning investors were paying a hefty $85.70 for every dollar of the company's top-line earnings. At the time, you could have bought the revenue stream of established software giant Microsoft for 17.1 times sales—and Microsoft boasted 41 percent net profit margins, versus 24 percent for Yahoo!.

Many other companies typically have low price-sales ratios because they have to churn out lots of sales to offset low-margin pricing. Grocery stores are a good example of a low-margin business and also illustrate why P/E is only one part of the picture in any valuation. Consider supermarket chain Safeway. In August 2000, the company sported a low price-sales ratio of 0.82, reflecting a thin 3.4 percent net margin. In fact, Safeway's price-sales ratio at the time suggested that the stock was a good value. But bottom-fishing value investors would have been put off by its P/E of 24.1. It goes to show that if you look at P/E alone, you might miss some real sales.

Hitting the Books

Lakonishok relies on another stable measure of value called the price-to-book ratio. A stock's book-value per share is the true net worth of a company's tangible assets, also known as net shareholders' equity. This is the price the company realistically could command if the entire operation was sold.

To determine book value, subtract a company's total liabilities from its total assets. Then divide by the number of shares outstanding. Value investors generally shun stocks trading at prices much higher than book value. Instead, they wrap themselves around low price-to-book stocks. Ideally, value investors like to find shares trading below book value, meaning they are buying into the company for less than its breakup value. Assuming the company's fortune is recovering and the value of its assets is increasing, it won't be long, value investors reckon, before growth-oriented investors scent opportunity.

Value investors have good reason to be confident. Studies show that over time, investments in stocks that sell below book value have outperformed their high price-to-book counterparts.

In "Contrarian Investment, Extrapolation, and Risk," Lakonishok and his colleagues compared the performance of low and high price-to-book stocks between April 1968 and April 1990—again slicing the companies into 10 groups. They found that stocks with the highest price-to-book returned 9.3 percent annually on average, while the lowest price-to-book stocks posted an average yearly gain of 19.8 percent.

Is the advantage of a value-oriented, low price-to-book strategy due to value investors taking higher risk? Lakonishok, Vishny and Shleifer measured average returns in the 25 worst months for the stock market over their study period, and in 88 other months in which the market declined. They also looked at the 25 best months for the market, and 122 additional months in which stock prices increased.

Here's what they found: Low price-to-book beat high in every instance. "While the value strategy did disproportionately well in extreme good times, its performance in extreme bad times was also quite impressive," the researchers reported. "Overall," they added, "the value strategy performed somewhat better than the glamour strategy in all states and significantly better in some states. If anything, the superior performance of the value strategy was skewed toward negative market return months rather than positive market return months. The evidence indicates that the value strategy did not expose investors to greater downside risk."[7]

Buy stuff, and buy cheaply. That's not glib advice to "buy low, sell high." Sophisticated institutional investors like Lakonishok show how value strategies can be used effectively. They employ powerful computers to buy and sell value stocks and maintain efficient portfolios. Less-endowed investors also can build a sound array of companies selling at or below book value with the help of online stock-screening tools, combining the results with a search for low-P/E stocks.

It's worth noting a variation on book-value screens, courtesy of legendary value investor Benjamin Graham. He searched for stocks selling at two-thirds of net current asset value—how much a company would be worth in liquidation. Here, current liabilities, long-term debt and other claims ahead of a company's common stock are subtracted from current assets such as cash, receivables and inventory. So if a company's current assets are worth $100 a share and liabilities total $25 a share, then net current assets would be $75 a share. Graham would have refused to pay more than 66 percent of $75, or roughly $50, for the stock. In *The Intelligent Investor*, Graham wrote: "It always seemed, and still seems, ridiculously simple to say that if one can acquire a diversified group of common stocks at a price less than the applicable net current assets alone—after deducting all prior claims, and counting as zero the fixed and other assets—the results should be quite satisfactory."[8]

Cashing In on Cash Flow

Another clue to corporate health is cash flow—money to fuel a company's growth after paying its fixed expenses. You can search far and wide for low P/Es and high estimated growth rates, but truth is, cash is king. A company with plenty of cash on its books can build a strong business in boom times and still cover its bills during economic downturns when sales can sag. The market rewards such quality management. But to find well-run enterprises on the cheap, Lakonishok and other value investors look for companies that are trading at discounts to cash flow per share.

Don't mistake cash flow—net cash provided by operations— for net earnings. While clever accounting tricks can manipulate earnings, cash flow is less pliable, making it a more stable measure than P/E. Commonly, cash flow is defined as earnings before interest, taxes, depreciation and amortization, or EBITDA.

To calculate cash flow, you figure total net income plus depreciation and other non-cash charges. When more cash comes in than goes out, a company has positive cash flow. Companies that spend more than they take in have negative cash flow. Companies report this activity on the Statement of Cash Flows found in quarterly and annual reports. The cash-flow statement is divided into three sections: Operating Activities looks at the ability of a company to generate cash from its day-to-day business; Investing Activities focuses on the future: capital expenditures, invest-

ment or sale of securities and the acquisition or sale of sub-
sidiaries, and Financing Activities discusses the sources and uses
of the cash. The net increase or decrease in cash is the sum of
these activities, plus any exchange-rate impact from foreign currency revenue.

In the best case, a company will generate more cash than it
needs to run its business day-to-day. This surplus is called free
cash flow, and is derived by subtracting capital spending and dividend payments from cash flow.

Free cash flow makes life easier for companies. If your rich
uncle hands you $10,000, you might decide to spend it on a lav-
ish week in Las Vegas. But many people would use the windfall
to pay off credit card bills, put a new roof on the house or invest
in the stock market. A company with extra cash will face similar
choices. It can use the money to retire debt, increase dividends,
develop new products or repurchase stock. All of this improvement can be covered internally—management doesn't have to go
begging by issuing new stock or debt. For obvious reasons, companies that are throwing off lots of cash make attractive acquisition targets.

Value and growth investors alike use cash flow to gauge the
viability of companies that must invest heavily in technology and
equipment before seeing any return for the effort. Broadcasters,
cable television providers, publishers and some high-tech and
Internet companies are good examples of businesses that report
little or no earnings but can still generate positive cash flow.
Stocks selling at a low price-to-cash flow often trade below their
buyout value, and for an accurate picture should be compared to
rival companies in the same industry.

As they did with other standard value measures, Lakonishok
and his colleagues showed in the Contrarian paper that low price-
to-cash flow also outperformed its higher-priced peers. Over the
same 22-year span between 1968 and 1990, the highest price-to-
cash flow stocks posted five-year annualized gains of 9.1 percent,
while shares of the lowest price-to-cash flow companies returned

20.1 percent. Moreover, low price-to-cash flow was a consistent winner, landing on top in 17 of the 22 years, or 77 percent of the time. And for five-year holding periods, low price-to-cash flow won in every case.

Research and Development

What is a fair price to pay for a company when traditional valuation measures don't measure up? Investors in technology and health care are keenly aware of this problem. In this case, price-to-cash flow is a useful barometer; so is research and development spending—a company's investment in the discoveries and designs that will fuel its future growth.

R&D is listed separately only if it represents a significant expense, which for most companies it isn't. But innovative industries, including computers, software, electronics, pharmaceuticals and biotechnology, are heavily dependent on R&D. Lakonishok often unearths valuable clues about a company's viability from this line on a company's income statement. Today's embryonic research can be tomorrow's high-margin best-seller.

In his quest for value, Lakonishok often notices laggard technology stocks. Technology companies typically are anything but value plays, so when a potential buy does come up, Lakonishok becomes more than a little intrigued. Apple Computer was one tired candidate that appeared on his radar screen. By 1998, Apple's stock price had taken a tremendous hit on a seemingly endless stream of disappointments, and most growth-oriented investors had given up. But there were clues that Apple was polishing its act.

Perusing Apple's financial statements, Lakonishok realized that through all the adversity, management had continued to spend substantially on R&D. What, he wondered, could be possessing these executives? R&D expenses cut right into the bottom line. Reducing R&D could boost short-term profits and burnish the computer maker's image on Wall Street. But management was willing to sacrifice immediate fiscal improvements for a potentially greater payoff later—a bold gamble when Wall Street demands that companies report every dollar they can as earnings per share.

Apple's determination was a bullish signal to a value investor like Lakonishok. Apple was investing in R&D when it seemed it could least afford to, but wasn't throwing good money after bad. Apple has boasted a large band of loyal followers from the day it launched its revolutionary Macintosh computer. The company understood the need to pour cash back into R&D to defend its market niche and to keep customers plied with new products.

Calculate R&D as a percentage of sales to help ferret out bargains. Dividing R&D by annual sales gives the amount in percentage terms. Most technology companies spend between 5 percent and 15 percent of total annual revenues on research projects. Make sure R&D is stable or growing quarter-over-quarter on the back of increasing sales. Cisco Systems, a computer networking leader, reported revenues of $12.2 billion in the fiscal year that ended in July 1999. R&D during that time was $1.6 billion, or 13.1 percent of sales. The year before, revenues of $8.5 billion and R&D of $1.03 billion equaled 12.1 percent of sales. And in the year ending in July 1997, Cisco reported revenues of nearly $6.5 billion and R&D of $702 million, or roughly 10.8 percent of sales.[9]

In situations such as Apple's where sales tumble, an increase in R&D as a percentage of sales indicates that management is trying to put growth back on track. At the height of its troubles, Apple reported revenues of $5.5 billion in its June 1997 third quarter, and R&D of $391 million, or 7.1 percent of sales. The year before, sales were $7.5 billion and R&D was $458 million, or 6 percent of sales.[10] Lakonishok explains:

Companies that do a lot of R&D relative to sales are ones that we found are, on average, good investments. Beaten-down technology stocks that have faith in their future are still investing a

lot of money in R&D. It's a signal by company insiders that something positive might happen. At least management believes there is hope.

Company financial reports, which outline research-and-development spending, are available free of charge from a Web site called Free Edgar (www.freeedgar.com). Increasing R&D is a sign that a company is aiming to build a bigger intellectual and sales barrier between itself and its competition. Wall Street, with its obsessive focus on short-term earnings, will likely penalize big R&D spenders. But these outlays eventually come back to a company many times over in the form of new products that improve sales and earnings. Then Wall Street analysts wake up, hike earnings estimates and recommendations, and new buyers send the stock higher. By that time, you've established a comfortable position and are more than happy to sell to them.

The View from the Inside

Company executives and directors are a stock's best shareholders. Insiders know their business more intimately than any Wall Street analyst. They know when a new product is flying out the door or if inventories are piling up. They know whether profit margins are expanding or if production costs are rising. Watch insiders closely. Lakonishok does. His and other in-depth studies show that the insiders' edge is real. Both insider buyers and sellers enjoy significantly above-average returns for their own portfolios.

Lakonishok and colleague Immoo Lee published "Are Insiders' Trades Informative?" as a National Bureau of Economic Research working paper in July 1998. They studied the insider trading actions between 1975 and 1995 at all companies listed on the New York, American and Nasdaq stock exchanges.

Their conclusion? Insider trading activity offers outside

investors real potential for gain, particularly for shareholders of smaller firms. "Insiders in aggregate are contrarian investors," Lakonishok and Lee reported. "However, they predict market movements better than simple contrarian strategies." For example, insiders were heavy sellers just prior to the market crash of October 1987, and became heavy buyers following the crash.

The two researchers found that companies with extensive insider purchases during any six-month period had a return of 22.2 percent over the subsequent year, compared with a return of 14.7 percent for companies with large amounts of insider selling.[11] But when reading insiders' tea leaves, they add, pay particular attention to buyers. Unlike insider selling, which may involve personal matters and other reasons unrelated to the health of the business, insider buying traditionally has been a strongly favorable indicator. Says Lakonishok:

> **When insiders are buying shares, it seems to be a positive signal, especially when they buy shares of smaller companies. The markets for larger companies are, in general, more efficient. But when you see insiders at smaller companies buying shares, it is definitely a positive sign.**

Still, look closely at the motivations and the structure behind insider purchases. It's no secret that investors break into cheers when management increases its stock ownership. And corporations aim to please. Many boards of directors even have institutionalized the share-buying process, loaning money to insiders for purchases and requiring that officers own shares valued at a specific multiple to their annual salary. Sure, it's important that management incentives are aligned with shareholder interests. Direct personal stakes put that issue front and center. But for some corporations, insider buying has become a calculated marketing ploy.

Yet more often than not, when insiders are buying, it means the executive suite is becoming the executives' sweet. You can find insider information in many places. *The Wall Street Journal* and *Barron's* report large insider transactions weekly. Helpful Web sites include Insider SCORES (www.insiderscores.com), and the aptly named Insider Trader (www.insidertrader.com).

When Value Becomes Growth

Stock investors are often challenged to choose between the virtues of value and growth, as if the market weren't big enough for them both. In truth, a well-diversified portfolio will have a mix of value and growth styles. Markets are cyclical; value becomes growth, and growth turns into value. Having representation in both camps assures that at least some of your holdings will always be in favor. And as a risk-control measure, the conservative value stocks will temper the volatile growth stocks. The real advantage is to be disciplined in whatever approach you choose. Tune out noise as much as possible, Lakonishok advises, and focus on achieving the investment horizon that you've set:

> The typical mistake that individual investors make is trying to do too much with their investments instead of looking for simple solutions—buying some stocks, diversifying and holding those stocks, or going to a low-fee mutual fund. Individuals should buy and hold stocks for longer periods of time; they should have a strategic asset allocation. They should decide, "I want to be X percent in equities," and not do excessive buying and selling. This isn't exactly what the brokerage industry advocates. You are constantly bombarded with new ideas, and they make money when you trade.

Lakonishok, as might be expected, would tilt an investment portfolio toward value, since the strategy has delivered higher returns over long periods with less risk. At the same time, he cautions investors to keep their sights low:

> I don't think people should expect to get rich in the stock market. You invest for the long run, and you should at some point get a premium for the risk you are taking. But you should give up the idea that you're going to be 100 percent right. It's not simple to outperform the market. Markets are not so stupid; they're actually quite efficient. There are opportunities, but easy money is not lying on the table. The only thing you can do is try to beat the odds by making smarter decisions.

Yet "smarter" decisions can be difficult ones. Does a plummeting stock price signal that investors have overreacted to bad news about a fundamentally sound company, or is the company really in trouble? Companies can stay flat on their backs for a long, long time. Some never get up. As a contrarian, you want to see concern about a company from other investors, not mourning. How do you recognize the difference? Lakonishok, as you might imagine, has more than a little experience in this area. His advice? Again, be patient:

> Wait. Don't buy such a company while it is going down. Wait for tangible signs of recovery: for earnings to improve, for analysts to become more optimistic, for the stock price to start to move. Find situations where insiders are starting to buy those shares or a company announces a share buyback—which is also a positive sign.

Here's another interesting idea: Patience breeds success. How so? Because big institutions and other sophisticated, knowledgeable players—your competition—aren't going to sit idly while struggling value companies get their acts together. Even if they wanted to, most money managers can't load their portfolios with deadweight stocks that might bear fruit in a few years. Investors by and large are too impatient; they demand results yesterday, and vote with their wallets if gift-wrapped presents aren't delivered every year. In a business where talent is paid on annual performance and assets under management, most portfolio managers simply don't stand a chance supporting ugly, scary, value stocks. Notes Lakonishok:

> **Value stocks in the long run are very attractive. One then might expect to find more money managers who would take extreme value positions. But you don't. It's difficult to defend, and the stocks are not so pretty. People are sticking to their guns; it is how they got their clients. Money managers know they cannot afford to underperform.**

If much of the "smart money" is looking elsewhere in the market to generate high performance and to justify fees, then in theory it should be relatively easier for individuals to build viable positions in the value camp. Of course, the remaining value players are still formidable foes. And since value stocks are not going to do well all of the time, you should expect pain and anguish over your decision to buy the unloved—especially in bull markets when growth stocks are raging. But if you bought well—heeding Graham's margin of safety—the dry spells will be easier to bear.

A wide margin of safety will also help you when it comes time to sell an investment. Graham advocated selling a stock once its share price reached the company's intrinsic value per share. Lakonishok also maintains his own strict approach to selling:

> **Maybe we bought a value stock that became expensive over time—America Online might fit this bill; it was a value stock but then became much more expensive. Or maybe the stock was somewhat of a value stock, but we bought it because momentum was very strong. Then momentum deteriorated and the stock became less attractive. Those are, for us, the two main reasons for selling. The best situation is if we bought a value stock and it became a growth stock; that means we did something right.**

**CHAPTER
6**

It's All in the Mind:
Richard Thaler

*"People exaggerate their own skills.
They are optimistic about their prospects
and overconfident about their guesses,
including which managers to pick."*

Yᴏᴜ ᴀʀᴇ ɢɪᴠᴇɴ $1,000. Choose between (a) a sure gain of $500, or (b) a 50 percent chance to gain $1,000 and a 50 percent chance to gain nothing.

Now consider another scenario. You're given $2,000. Choose between (a) a sure loss of $500, or (b) a 50 percent chance to lose $1,000 and a 50 percent chance to lose nothing.

Did you take the sure thing, or take the chance? Look closely at this problem. The possible outcome from each situation is the same. But how the question is phrased will influence your decision.

In the first example, most people will choose the certain $500 gain and walk away with $1,500. But in the second instance, most respondents will select option b. They will gamble, though it ultimately could cost them even more money.[1]

Such reasoning is irrational. In the second example, pick (b) and you could be left with $1,000 instead of $2,000. Pick (a) and you're guaranteed $1,500. But when it means protecting what we have, in this case $2,000, most of us feel there's no alternative but to take the chance. Better to lose trying than to go down without a fight.

The above example offers a keen insight into a hard-wired personality trait that most people share: We tend to avoid risk to capture additional gain, but will take risks to avoid a loss. The rational individual would choose option (a) in both situations and pocket $1,500. But honestly, how many of us are so rational? Which begs the question: If people are not always rational, how then can the stock market—composed of imperfect investors—be efficient?

Welcome to the paradoxical field of behavioral finance, where investing literally is a state of mind. Defenders of efficient markets claim that investors act rationally and make decisions after carefully reviewing all the available information. Behavioral finance dismisses that notion. Behaviorists combine psychology and finance—contending that preconceptions and cognitive errors lead investors to misinterpret events and to overlook opportunities. They believe that securities markets are ruled by heated, helter-skelter emotion, not cold, calculated reason. In the behavioral realm, psychology matters; emotion matters. And not incidentally, perceptive investors can profit from understanding others' foibles and limitations—as well as their own.

At the forefront of this debate is Richard Thaler, a University of Chicago professor of behavioral science and economics, who has devoted nearly three decades to identifying and understanding beliefs and preferences that can influence investment decisions. These systematic errors of judgment are called "heuristic biases"—mental rules of thumb—and they show up in uniquely expressive ways. These include:

- Overconfidence
- Optimism
- Confusing chance with skill
- Aversion to loss
- Decision regret
- Anchoring
- Ignoring the big picture

While behavioral finance is relatively new to most investors, its basic premise is not. In fact, fundamentals of behavioral finance are as old as mankind itself. The dynamics of human nature—the ingrained switches that trigger powerful emotions of love, hate, greed, courage, fear—are largely unchanged; only the settings in which we play them out are different.

Before Markowitz, Sharpe and other leading proponents of a

rational stock market came along, sages like economist John Maynard Keynes and investor Benjamin Graham routinely factored human nature into their investment strategies. They understood how other people's perceptions can influence stock prices. A famous insight into investor psychology and stock-market behavior is Lord Keynes's "beauty contest" example. A newspaper contest in the 1930s featured photographs of 100 women. The object was to pick the six that would receive the most votes as being the prettiest. The key to increasing your odds, Keynes observed, was not to choose the six you thought were prettiest, or even the ones that other people thought were prettiest. Instead, you should anticipate what other people would expect other people to choose.

In this way, behavioral finance is important for what it can teach us about ourselves. If we take the time to look seriously at investment mistakes that people tend to make, we may see our own reflection. Then, by realistic examination, we can learn how to end a cycle of costly snap decisions that all of us fall victim to at times. It might help to think about behavioral finance in the following manner: Understanding risk tolerance can give us a strong baseline about the type of investments we can handle comfortably; understanding ourselves can make us better investors when buying and selling those investments.

Knowing how to avoid the mental traps that you constantly encounter as an investor can be more valuable than picking a winning stock. Humility—accepting the fact that the stock market owes you nothing—is a good place to begin. If investors today were more aware of how the mind can move stocks, Thaler believes, they would be more likely to make better investment decisions. As he explains:

The most common mistake investors make is not thinking about everybody else. Look at the Internet stocks. Everybody thought they alone discovered the Internet. They failed to realize that lots of people had the same insight yesterday and had already bid prices up to ridiculous levels.

Overcoming Overconfidence

Just behind the left-field bleachers at Pacific Bell Park, the new home of the San Francisco Giants baseball team, a miniature replica of the redbrick stadium has been built for children to get a chance to swing for the fences—even if that's only 30 feet away. At every home game, kids under eight years old wait their turn to smack a white plastic ball mounted on a tee, while older kids cover the bases and the outfield.

One sunny Sunday afternoon, a sandy-haired boy of about six strides determinedly to home plate. He looks at the rubber tee with disgust. "I don't need that," he announces, scooping up a plastic bat. But since this is a T-ball game, the stand stays. The boy grips the bat, grimaces and swings with all his might—and the ball dribbles slowly toward third base.

He just might have a bright future in money management. But overconfidence—he was too good for the tee—unfortunately does not end with six-year-olds. Adults stage frequent displays of over-confidence, and investing is fertile ground. People are prone to con-fuse accidental success with investment know-how. "Everybody's a genius in a bull market," goes an old saying on Wall Street. When stock prices are rising, many investors get swept up in an exhilarat-ing sense of omnipotence. Conversations turn to how much money they've made in the market—even if it's only on paper. Those who haven't shared in the new wealth often become envious and are given to investment risks they might otherwise avoid.

But when the stock market becomes a money machine, why not pull the handle? For good reason. When investing seems a sure thing and novice players are convinced that they can beat experienced veterans, the risk of a fall is actually greatest.

Overconfidence fosters this false sense of empowerment. We tend to revel in our successes and forget the failures. And the level of stock-market revelry in the United States was noisy and boisterous during the late 1990s and into the new century. Amer-icans developed a love affair with stocks, and the new equity culture blended seamlessly with the popular culture. Buying stocks became a kind of adrenaline-filled spectator sport. At Pacific Bell Park, an electronic stock ticker near the left-field foul pole prominently displayed current Nasdaq prices, so fans could keep score of both the home team and their investments. CNBC, the closely watched financial news network, offered a "pregame" outlook before the New York Stock Exchange's opening bell. Then a "half-time report" aired midday, followed by "postgame" highlights after the close. Corporate chief executives, especially heads of dot.com companies, became overnight celebrities.

And if you couldn't be a CEO, you at least could make the same money. "Who Wants to Be a Millionaire?"—a quiz show where the winner goes home with $1 million—was the highest-rated U.S. television program. Topping the best-seller lists at the time was *The Millionaire Mind*, by Thomas Stanley, a sequel to his hugely popular *The Millionaire Next Door*. Who wants to be a millionaire? Who doesn't? Pink Floyd had it right: Money. It's a hit.[2]

People who exhibit overconfidence believe they are skilled hitters and moneymakers, and moreover, that they have an uncanny ability to choose others with similarly remarkable talents. In truth, overconfidence leads people to overestimate their knowledge and abilities. For example, rate your own driving skills. Are you above average, average, or below average? Most people would measure their abilities against other drivers and conclude that they are above average. But unlike the unique children of Lake Wobegon, it's mathematically impossible for a majority of a group to be above average. Half will be average or higher, and half will be average or lower.

When people believe they know more than they actually do, they often make statements they can't substantiate. Overconfident stock buyers similarly make investments they can't justify. Evidence points to overconfidence as a leading cause of excessive trading among individuals. After a few winning hands, people become convinced that they have a knack for investing, and they act on it.

Yet active trading exacts an enormous toll on performance.

Investors who continuously buy and sell set themselves up for lower total returns. A groundbreaking study looked at the stock-trading activity of 66,465 U.S. households with accounts at an unnamed discount brokerage over a six-year period ending in January 1997. The results showed that annualized portfolio returns before costs averaged 11.4 percent for individuals who made frequent trades—monthly turnover in excess of 8.8 percent—while those who traded infrequently earned 18.5 percent. On average, households turned over roughly 75 percent of their stockholdings each year, incurring transaction costs, brokerage commissions and capital gains taxes with every trade. In reporting the findings, Terrance Odean, an economist at the University of California at Davis who coauthored the study, quipped that "trading is hazardous to your wealth."[3]

Just to break even on these trades, a replacement stock has to perform strongly enough to cover trading costs. But Odean found that the stocks investors bought actually fared worse over the following year. On average, the new stock underperformed the old one by 2.3 percentage points. Once trading costs are factored in, this shortfall more than doubles.[4] By their reasoning, investors might think they're getting rid of losers and replacing them with winners. But in fact, they're doing just the opposite, as Thaler observes:

> **People exaggerate their own skills. They are optimistic about their prospects and overconfident about their guesses, including which managers to pick. If you ask people a question like "How do you rate your ability to get along with people?" ninety percent think they're above average. 90 percent of all investors also think they're above average at picking money managers, which is why they think they can find the one-third who can beat the index, and why they're willing to pay money to get that chance.**

Overconfidence is particularly acute in the independent-minded world of online investing, where investors can tap into great quantities of information and buy or sell with just one click. But information is not knowledge. Odean studied the investment habits of 1,607 people who switched to Internet-based trading from telephone-based trading between 1991 and 1996. Before making the change, these investors outperformed the market by 2.4 percentage points on average. After going online, they traded more speculatively and less profitably—underperforming the market by 3.5 percentage points a year.[5]

Investors would be better off to own the stocks of quality companies and hold them, instead of trying to sample everything in the store. As Pogo Possum, the classic comic strip character, might have noted wryly about active stock traders: "We have met the enemy and he is us." Trading is not investing. Many overconfident investors are convinced they have "hot hands," in the way a basketball player on a shooting streak will keep racking up points.

But in fact, statistics on professional basketball players fail to support the hot hand theory; neither does the idea hold up when it comes to investing. Psychologist Daniel Kahneman and investment researcher Mark Riepe, writing in their illuminating *Journal of Portfolio Management* commentary "Aspects of Investor Psychology," said: "The hot hand fallacy is ubiquitous in the world of finance, where it lends credibility to the claims of fund managers who have been successful for a few years. The tendency to attribute causal significance to chance fluctuations also leads investors to overreact to any information to which their attention is drawn."[6] If you are easily given to overconfidence, one solution is to trade less, particularly in taxable accounts.

You might reasonably expect professional investors to show greater restraint than individuals. Not necessarily. Money managers and investment advisers are routinely overconfident in their ability to outperform an index, though most fail to hurdle that benchmark. Overconfidence causes people to underreact to news and information. Wall Street brokerage analysts often are too confident or overly pessimistic about a company's business prospects. As we will see later in this chapter, astute investors can exploit these biases.

Optimal Illusions

To be sure, biases and preferences are familiar and reassuring. People don't like uncertainty. When balancing risk against reward, investors will dig through layer upon layer of soul-searching in an effort to engineer a successful outcome. We want to know that our future is secure, but of course, this is unknowable. Ultimately we all face the same bottom-line question: "Should I or shouldn't I?"

Investing is a responsibility that can impact your quality of life. Too often, though, we rationalize these important decisions instead of acting rationally. People see opportunities where in fact there are none. We act hastily, then devise tidy ways to justify our actions.

Rationalization makes us feel better about our choices and commitments. We're convinced that we possess superior knowledge and skill. This is especially true in a long-running bull market, when the quest for long-term security can give way to a lust for quick-gain speculation. How convenient it is to believe that we've dotted our *i*'s and crossed our *t*'s, when in fact we've merely closed our eyes and crossed our fingers.

Excessively optimistic investors also tend to get too excited about winners and too depressed about losers. Thaler and colleague Werner DeBondt studied such emotional swings and published their results in a groundbreaking paper, "Does the Stock Market Overreact?"[7] The authors ranked the 35 best-performing and 35 worst-performing New York Stock Exchange issues over a five-year period, then held them as a group for another five years. Looking back, they found that the worst-performing stocks over the initial five years—value stocks—had beaten the best-performing growth stocks by 32 percentage points. Against a market index, value stocks outperformed by 12 percentage points, while growth stocks trailed the index by more than 4 percentage points.[7] Recalls Thaler:

Our research predicted that winners would subsequently underperform, since investors were overly optimistic about

their prospects, and that losers would subsequently outper-form because these battered stocks had little downside risk. That shouldn't happen in an efficient market. In an efficient market, you can't predict future price movements from past price movements. Stock prices are supposed to have no memory. We found that they do.

Hold up that mirror again. It's helpful to come to terms with the errors you are prone to make, and to recognize situations in which these mistakes occur. If you tend to act on intuition, try to reflect more. Ask for advice. Have doubts. Be skeptical. Give yourself reasons not to buy or sell *right now*.

Sometimes, that's easier said than done. Most of us are predisposed toward optimism. Indeed, a positive outlook is extremely important for good mental health. Yet being overly optimistic probably is not the best way to manage your finances. Optimists tend to inflate their abilities, and to discount the likelihood that they will suffer bad fortune. Optimists also tend to believe they have more control over events than they really do.

In a recent study of overconfidence and optimism in asset-allocation decisions, Thaler and fellow behavioral finance colleagues Kahneman and Shlomo Benartzi asked about the investing habits of subscribers to Morningstar.com, the fund-ranking company's informational Web site. About 1,000 people responded, and their answers were striking. Asked if they spend more time thinking about an investment's potential gain or its possible loss, 74 percent of the participants thought about winning and just 7 percent considered losing. On average, the respondents believed there was an 85 percent chance that stocks would outperform bonds over the "long run"—say, 20 years. Fully one-third expected a 100 percent success rate from stocks—no chance at all that stocks would underperform bonds. With obvious understatement, the researchers reported, "There's no doubt that people tend to be overly optimistic."[8]

Don't Lose Yourself

You and a coworker have decided to invest some retirement money into the stock market. As a guide, you are each given charts displaying the 30-year return for a portfolio of selected equity mutual funds. The charts are identical except in how they show historical performance. You review the first chart; a smooth ascending line from beginning to end highlights the funds' impressive long-term result. Your colleague receives the other chart—a bar chart of annualized returns that bares the often extreme ups and downs of year-to-year volatility.

In each case, it's important to realize that the outcome is the same, only the presentation is different. Does that influence your decision? Thaler and co-researcher Benartzi, now at the University of California at Los Angeles, found that asset allocation varied greatly depending on which of the two charts investors studied.

If the market were indeed completely efficient, Thaler claims, investors should react similarly to both charts, since both produced ultimately positive returns. Instead, investors shown the smoother rise said they would commit 90 percent of their retirement funds to stocks, while those who saw the more jagged progression allocated stocks just 40 percent of their money.[9]

The reason for this discrepancy, Thaler believes, involves a bias that behaviorists call "loss aversion." Put simply, the pain of short-term loss overpowers the pleasure of long-term gain. Recall the scenario presented at the beginning of this chapter. It's a famous experiment in Prospect Theory, in which Kahneman and his colleague, the late Amos Tversky, found that individuals are more distressed about the prospect of certain loss than they are elated by a sure gain. Loss aversion explores the great lengths to which people will go to avoid the pain of loss, even if it means bearing additional risk.

Tversky and Kahneman determined that a loss hurts about twice as much as a gain elicits joy. More to the point, investors routinely demand that any potential winning be at least twice the potential loss. So if you propose a gamble on the toss of a coin and people have to put $50 of their own money at stake, they would need to win at least $100 for the gamble to be worthwhile. Economist Paul Samuelson noticed this disparity in the early 1960s, describing an encounter with a university colleague in which Samuelson offered a bet: heads, you win $200, and tails, you lose $100. The colleague refused, saying, "I won't bet because I would feel the $100 loss more than the $200 gain."[10]

Thaler and Benartzi derived the term "myopic loss aversion" to describe the combination of loss aversion with the fact that even long-term investors will tend to monitor their portfolios closely. In a 1995 research paper, they raised the important idea that loss aversion influences the valuation of stocks and bonds. It's well-documented that the difference in long-term returns between stocks and bonds is quite significant. At the time of Thaler and Benartzi's study, the annualized real rate of return on stocks over the previous 60 years was about 7 percent, while the return on bonds was less than 1 percent. Why is the equity premium so large? The authors venture that a possible solution to this so-called "equity-premium puzzle" is that investors' fear of short-term loss, coupled with their frequent portfolio checkups, impels stockholders to demand an excess rate of return over bonds.[11]

Loss aversion coupled with a myopic perspective makes the pain of losing even greater. If investors are overly concerned with short-term losses, stocks will present an uncomfortably high risk. Investors would tend to allocate too little to stocks, or perhaps not at all. A counter to loss aversion is lengthening your investment time horizon—the period over which you measure gains and losses. Says Thaler:

Loss aversion isn't as great if you take a long enough view. However, the chance for losing money on a quarterly basis is quite high. Losing hurts. It's an instinct. It probably goes back to living at subsistence levels. When you're at subsistence, any reduction is life-threatening. Most of us can afford to lose a little. But our bodies are still hardwired to be very sensitive to any loss.

Fear and Regret

People tend to feel pained and regretful after making an error in judgment. And as we have seen, people will go to great lengths to avoid pain. This defense against "decision regret" is noticeable in how investors treat the sale of winning and losing positions.

When deciding to sell a security, evidence suggests that people are more likely to sell winners too soon and are reluctant to part with losers. This turns out to be a costly strategy, because winners are likely to do better in the short run than losers.[12] They take this action even though a more optimal tax-avoidance strategy is to let winners ride and get rid of losers, since the government shares your losses with you but makes you share your gains. Thaler offers an explanation:

> Say I have two stocks, each selling at $100. One I bought at $50 and one at $200. I can sell the one that's gone up and declare victory. But if I sell the one that's gone down, I have to declare defeat. As long as I'm still holding it on the books, I can wait for it to go back up and convince myself that I'm really an OK stock-picker after all.
>
> People are reluctant to close an account with red ink. They'd rather leave it open. The losers in a poker game always want to keep playing. The winners are ready to go home.

Anticipation of regret, combined with apprehension about being the greater fool—the rube who bought at the top—exercises tremendous control over investor behavior. For instance, investors live in fear of investing money in a stock and then seeing the stock immediately take a dive. Suppose that shares of a stock you bought at $50 recently traded at $100. Understandably pleased, you mention this good fortune to a close associate at the office. Your coworker then buys the stock at $100 a share. Two days later, the share price plummets to $80. Who is more stricken—you or your colleague? Most people would agree that our coworker would be the more anguished. After all, we're still enjoying a $30 gain—though chances are we would begin to worry about the stock dropping past our own purchase point. Notes Thaler:

I tell people that a good way of asking whether you should keep a stock—ignoring tax considerations—is whether you'd be willing to buy it. If we would never dream of buying it at the current price, then, again, neglecting taxes for the moment, we probably should be selling it.

What if you consider selling a stock but decide against it, and the stock plummets? Now what if the stock drops and you cash out, but then turns around and goes even higher than before? How might you feel? Consider the following example: Mr. Paul owns shares in company A. During the past year, he thought about switching to the stock of company B, but didn't. He now finds that had he switched, he would be better off by $20,000. Ms. George owned shares in company B. During the past year, she switched to the stock of company A. She now finds that she would have been better off if she had stayed with company B. Who is more upset?[13]

Most of us would concur that Ms. George was more upset, although in financial terms the results are the same. The difference is that Ms. George is feeling the regret of commission; she wishes she hadn't done something she did. Mr. Paul suffers from the weaker regret of omission; he laments failing to act in a way that, in hindsight, would have benefited him.[14]

Thaler and Kahneman, in an unpublished survey, asked more than 100 wealthy individual investors to recall the financial decisions they most regretted. Was the decision something they did or did not do? Most people said their worst regret was about some action they had taken. A minority said they regretted an omission. Strikingly, people who reported a regret of omission had a much higher proportion of their portfolio in stocks. Kahneman and

Thaler concluded that people who regret missed opportunities take more risks than those who regret attempts that failed.

As you will read in the next section, one way to avoid regret is to spread investment over a specific time period rather than all at once. Incrementally investing a set amount monthly or quarterly is not optimal, for it may leave you less exposed to the market on its best days, but conversely you won't regret as much if valuations go against you. Another effective tactic is to take a broad view of a portfolio. For instance, if your net worth is $500,000 and a stock you own loses $5,000 in value, the pain of that loss will be mitigated if you view the downturn in percentage terms. It seems more palatable to suffer a 1 percent drop in your wealth than to lose $5,000.

Picture Frames

The famous essay that pioneered modern decision theory—why and how people make certain choices—was written by Daniel Bernoulli, the Swiss mathematician, and delivered in 1738 to the St. Petersburg Academy of Sciences. Among other points in this work, Bernoulli was trying to understand why people buy insurance. He considered a merchant's decision about whether or not to send a ship from Amsterdam to St. Petersburg. The ship is loaded with spice and it's winter, and the probability of a total loss, Bernoulli said, is 5 percent. He analyzed the decision as if the merchant were reasoning with his overall state of wealth in mind. The merchant would say to himself: This will be my net worth if my ship makes it to St. Petersburg, if it sinks or if I avoid the transaction.

Three possible outcomes; three distinct states of wealth—as if overall net worth is what people really think about when making decisions. Bernoulli assumed that people think in broader terms than they actually do. This is sound in theory, but not usual in practice. People are prone to look at individual gains and losses one frame at a time rather than see the big picture. Indeed, a global view would give them greater comfort with their decisions and help them to make better ones.

In behavioral terms, a tendency to compartmentalize decisions is known as "mental accounting." Among investors, this narrow view becomes an issue when portfolio goals are divided into specific boxes: There's money for retirement, for a kid's college education, for current income, for speculation.

Except it's one pie, no matter how you slice it. Yogi Berra summed this up succinctly when he ordered a pizza and was asked how many pieces he wanted. "I'm hungry," the baseball legend is said to have replied. "Cut it into eighths."

Yet mental accounting must serve a purpose, or else why would we favor it? Indeed, we take comfort in the little things. It's less overwhelming to keep important parts of our life in tidy corners of the mind. Thaler observes:

Mental accounting is set up to solve self-control problems. People will set aside a certain amount of money that they're willing to gamble. They set that up as their gambling account so that they won't go and invade the rest of their money. And that serves a function. It's a fiction, but it will prevent them from losing the money for their house or their children's education. So these boundaries can serve useful budgeting purposes.

In one noteworthy experiment, Tversky and Kahneman posed the following two options: You pay $40 for a theater ticket, but as you enter the theater you realize that you've lost the ticket. Would you buy another? Now suppose you arrive at the theater to buy a $40 ticket and discover that you've lost $40. You have enough cash to buy another ticket—would you?

Most people would not buy a replacement ticket, but would spend another $40. Their decision is due to the way the choices are framed, Tversky and Kahneman reasoned. People establish a mental account for the theater tickets, and they've budgeted $40 for it. If they buy another ticket, that's $80—twice what they had planned to spend. In the other example, the lost $40 is charged to a different mental account, like a special dinner or a new shirt.

Perhaps mental accounting is good for self-discipline, but these fragmented decisions can limit an investor's horizon. A better attitude is to see life as a series of repeated gambles in which you make many risky decisions. Some work, and others don't. If you dwell over every failure, you'll have a lot of dark days—and might not fully appreciate the joyful times. But if instead you occasionally review your progress in life—the highs and lows of career, family, health, finances—then you will tend to be more rational and matter-of-fact because you're now seeing the world through a broader, less emotional lens.

For instance, consider this gamble: With the toss of a coin, you will either win $15,000 or lose $10,000. Do you accept? Most people wouldn't. Now imagine that your entire net worth is $1 million. The same bet is offered, but this time you're told that with one coin flip, you will be worth $990,000 or $1.015 million.

Somehow, this bet seems more bearable—even attractive. When you think in terms of overall wealth, as Bernoulli suggested, you have a different take on risk. Gains become less exciting, and losses are less painful. Every bump doesn't become an earthquake. You'll play again another day.

Anchors Aweigh

Ask someone from New York City to estimate the population of San Francisco. What might they say? Presumably they know the population of New York because they live there. And they know that San Francisco is a smaller city. A natural way to come to an answer is to start with the number you know—in this case, the population of New York City—and then adjust for the second part—the population of San Francisco. But most people will anchor on the number they already know. So it's likely that someone from New York will overestimate the population of San Francisco—choosing a number that's smaller, but not small enough. In contrast, a resident of San Francisco will underestimate the population of New York City—picking a higher population number, but still short of the mark.

Anchoring is a reference point, a mental shortcut that people routinely use to answer a complex problem or question. Up until now, we've looked at the emotional side of investor psychology, areas where people can recognize poor judgment and appropriately modify their behavior. Anchoring is different. It's hardware—you can't reprogram it.

On Wall Street, where news and information obeys no speed limit, anchoring is frequently apparent. You just can't judge a stock by its coverage. Securities analysts can be biased, tethered to their opinions and reluctant to admit when they're wrong. Sharp-eyed stock buyers can occasionally profit from others' short-term myopia. As Thaler claims:

Anchoring can cause investors to think things haven't changed when they have. Anchors are useful, but people end up giving too much weight to the anchor and not going far enough from it.

Say you want to sell your house. You estimate its value and study the sale prices of comparable homes in the neighborhood. That sales history becomes your anchor. Then, just as you list the property, the housing market softens and prices begin to decline. You're forced to change your estimate of the house's value—but most likely not enough.

Anchoring causes people to underreact to recent developments. This shows up when shareholders are reluctant to sell top stocks and mutual funds that have lost their edge, or to buy laggards that seem to have turned a corner.

When a company's management reports better-than-expected earnings, Wall Street often is too tepid with its praise. Sometimes analysts simply don't believe their eyes. Suppose a company earned

25 cents per share in the last quarter, and one covering analyst fore-casts EPS of 30 cents for the current quarter. But the company actually reports per-share earnings of 40 cents. What happens?

The company's stock price will jump as pleasantly surprised investors react to the positive news. Our analyst, however, still thinks that his 30-cents-a-share prediction is reasonable. Maybe he bumps up estimates for the next quarter to 35 cents. Then the company reports a 50-cents-a-share quarter, and the analyst is surprised again. It usually takes a couple of more quarters before he gets the picture straight that this company is firing on all cylin-ders. Says Thaler:

Analysts are overconfident and anchored to their beliefs. Then they get surprised. Once analysts believe the surprises, they raise earnings estimates. People take notice, and the stock price goes up.

A related heuristic to anchoring is called "representativeness." Studies show that when people are exposed to a long sequence of outcomes, they tend to assume that the future will represent the past.

In the stock market, shareholders who experience repeated earnings disappointments, for example, believe that the consis-tently bad news will persist indefinitely. The stock price gets beaten down, and eventually many investors give up on the com-pany—perhaps unfairly. Should the company's fortunes begin to turn for the better, the market often will ignore the improvement.

At the same time, everybody loves a winner. People are prone to see top-performing stocks as being able to grow to the sky, even when early warnings—such as declining profit margins—point to a slowdown in business.

Contrarian and value investors will attempt to go against the herd mentality and profit from this frequent error. Look for stocks with a long history of negative earnings surprises. Then try to notice some signal that the firm's luck is changing.

Insider buying can be a good indicator. If you can't be a corporate executive, then invest like one. High-ranking executives and directors are the first to know about changing conditions for their business and industry. Insiders—chairman of the board, chief executive, president, chief financial officer, vice presidents—are among the earliest to spot value or excess within a company and to act on it. These internal factors will be reflected in the stock price long before investors read about them in the quarterly report.

Another clue is when management increases the quarterly dividend at the same time it announces better-than-expected earnings. A dividend hike usually is the underpinning of a fundamental earnings change, because management doesn't tend to toss around cash dividends unless they think the ongoing earnings stream of the company is going to be higher.

When they feel their stock is either well above or well below fair value, insiders will respond accordingly with regard to their shareholdings. Insider buying tends to confirm that some extraordinary development is happening to the business. And corporate insiders who acquire shares in the open market, as any individual investor would, send a more powerful signal than executives who increase their ownership through stock options, which are exercised at below-market prices.

Insider selling, on the other hand, is harder to pin down. Usually there are about twice as many sellers as buyers, as executives make routine adjustments for tax planning and portfolio diversification purposes.

But when insider selling is at extremes—as was true in mid-2000—it's generally a bearish sign. Thaler advises:

Find companies where insider buying seems to provide a strong signal that the company has turned itself around, and yet the market hasn't reacted yet. Management often knows things about the company that they announce and the public doesn't listen to. So when key insiders are buying, one reason can be that the stock is too cheap.

Company stock repurchases, coupled with earnings improvement, can offer yet another clue that a business is brightening. When management views its stock as undervalued, it often buys back shares. Through this action, management is wordlessly and strongly suggesting that the company's prospects are buoyant.

But share repurchases cannot be taken at face value. For starters, companies frequently don't even buy all the shares they say they will. Before buying shares yourself, contact the company's investor relations department and determine why the shares are being retired. Maybe the activity is unconnected to day-to-day operations. Sometimes a firm will buy back its shares to offset dilution from employee stock-option programs. Be careful: Share buybacks are also used as a clever accounting gimmick. Eliminating shares from the market reduces a company's total shares outstanding. Net earnings are then spread across a smaller share base, effectively boosting earnings per share without management actually improving sales and costs.

It's far more meaningful when a company buys back shares with excess cash flow, not debt. But for many investors, a buyback is a nonevent that doesn't change their opinion of the stock; expectations are low and they don't believe the company has a chance. Yet if management is on target, investors will start to notice this stock is a value—only there won't be as many shares around to buy, further boosting the stock price.

To steer clear of anchoring and representativeness in these and other decisions, try to be aware of your own preconceptions and prejudices. Take a step back and see the entire playing field. Winners don't always repeat; losers often come from behind.

Getting In with the In Crowd

Thaler first took notice of irrational economic behavior in the 1970s when he was a Ph.D. candidate in economics at the University of Rochester. One financial decision that struck him as odd was that most of his colleagues on the faculty chose to be paid over 12 months instead of 9 months, even though it made more economic sense to take a fatter paycheck in fewer installments. In 1977, Thaler met Tversky and Kahneman, two great pioneers of cognitive psychology, and joined an inner circle of free thinkers who would dare to challenge the finance establishment's Efficient Market Theory.

Since 1992, Thaler has collaborated with money manager Russell Fuller on developing practical investment strategies using behavioral finance principles. Fuller & Thaler Asset Management (www.fullerthaler.com), based in San Mateo, California, handles investment accounts for large pension funds and other institutions. They map strategy for the three behaviorally based mutual funds that Fuller & Thaler is aiming at investment advisers and their clients: Undiscovered Managers Behavioral Growth, Behavioral Value and Behavioral Long/Short.

Thaler doesn't manage investments. He and his partners at the firm search for stocks with a positive change in earnings that is well above Wall Street analysts' forecasts. All three funds generally buy a stock after its initial earnings surprise—even if there's already been an enthusiastic reaction. A traditional manager will be reluctant to move into a stock that has jumped several points in a day on good earnings news alone. But behaviorists like Thaler and Fuller, in contrast, are encouraged. They reason that if the earnings change is lasting and the turnaround story becomes known, then even though the stock may be up a lot, it isn't coming back down.

To measure the impact of an earnings surprise on a stock's price, go online at Yahoo! Finance (www.quote.yahoo.com). At the homepage, go to "Research: Earnings" and click on "Surprises." Another good resource is Thomson Investors Network (www.thomsoninvest.net). Find the tab marked "Earnings," then, under the "First Call" table, click on "Surprises." You'll see a link for both the 50 biggest positive and the 50 biggest negative surprises of the past 30 days.

Early results for the Fuller & Thaler funds have been mostly positive: Behavioral Growth gained 39.4 percent in the 12 months ended July 2000—an impressive 30.4 percentage points better than the Standard & Poor's 500-stock index. Over the same period, Behavioral Value posted a formidable 20.8 percent return, beating the S&P 500 by 11.8 percent during a ferocious bear market for value stocks. Only the Long/Short fund has lagged, down 2 percent in the period—11 percent below the S&P 500. This was a time when the long-short strategy, which attempts to profit from both rising and falling stock prices, was hampered by intermittent rallies in technology stocks.

For Thaler and his colleagues, a rich source of information and insight can be found in the quarterly earnings conference calls that take place between management and Wall Street analysts. Conference calls have a language and life all their own. At these frank exchanges between management and Wall Street analysts, listening can be far more valuable than speaking.

Expectations and preconceptions were prominently displayed at Microsoft's call in April 2000, for example. The software giant was under fire from both Wall Street and the U.S. government, and investors were looking for Microsoft executives to speak glowingly about their company's strong future. Microsoft's chief financial officer attempted to strike an upbeat tone, and normally such bullishness would spike the stock higher. But he conceded that the company remained "guarded" about near-term prospects for revenue growth.

The Street's reaction was swift. A spirited question-and-answer session followed management's presentation, as analysts tried to digest their disappointment. The next trading day, amid three brokerage downgrades and published reports that federal regulators would split the company, Microsoft shares tumbled nearly 16 percent.

Such candidness about current and future business operations traditionally has been a perk for influential Wall Street professionals. While everyone else was forced to settle for a honey-coated earnings release, the Street's heavy hitters got to hear management's intimate tale directly and could buy or sell the stock on the news.

No longer. Many companies are allowing individual investors access to these once-closed conferences, increasingly via the Internet. Several independent investment Web sites now allow anyone to listen to a live "webcast" of a call or to review the complete proceedings later at their convenience.

You can learn a lot by listening, but first you have to understand what is being said. A conference call may seem smooth and polished on the outside, but below the surface is a subtext of verbal nuances and cues. In essence, two calls are occurring simultaneously: management's view of the future and Wall Street's interpretation. At stake: the value of a stock.

Frequently, both sides will see eye to eye. But when confusion and disagreement are evident, these calls become interesting. And a sharp listener just might catch positive information before it's fully reflected in the stock price.

Conference calls generally are held either before the U.S. markets open at 9:30 A.M. EST or after the 4 P.M. close. Companies release earnings over the business wires, and the call begins about 30 minutes later. Senior executives, usually the chief executive and the chief financial officer, discuss corporate developments and fundamentals in a colloquial but scripted presentation that usually lasts no more than 25 minutes. In their statements, the CEO gives a colorful overview and the CFO digs into the numbers. Then the floor is opened to questions from Wall Street analysts and big shareholders. This give-and-take continues for another half hour or so, after which everyone goes back to business.

Before the call, though, it's anything but business as usual. Prior to the announcement, the company's investor relations and legal staff pore over facts and figures, attempting to put the right spin on the ball. This doesn't involve lies or even half-truths— misleading the investment community can have serious legal repercussions and destroy reputations. So you can reasonably assume you're hearing an honest, real-world appraisal, albeit from the company's vantage. Remember that in this context, investors are the buyers and management is a seller. While executives will provide full disclosure, they also want to show their property in the best possible light.

Breaking the Code

To interpret a conference call like an analyst, you'll first need to do some homework. Webcasters make it simple to sift through company reports and breaking news during the live call. While convenient, this could be distracting. Prior to the call, use these sites for due diligence. BestCalls (www.bestcalls.com) is a best bet with a comprehensive portal that links to sites of other webcasters, investment news and research services, message boards, SEC reports and financial publications. Jot down both the consensus earnings estimate and the covering brokerage firms. You can find this information quickly at Yahoo! Finance. Type in a ticker symbol and hit "Get Quotes." Under "More Info," click on "Research" to find the Street forecast. Click on "Covering Brokers" for a list of Wall Street firms that publish estimates. Now you're ready for an insider's tip: If an analyst who does not follow the company asks a solid, forward-looking question, it's a clue that a "buy" recommendation on the stock might be coming soon.

During the first minutes of the call, the spotlight is on management. What executives say is important, but pay close attention to how they say it. They will choose words carefully, for they know that hanging on every syllable is an attuned audience with their own agendas. This includes friendly covering analysts, curious analysts, long-term investors, momentum players, short-sellers, arbitrageurs, analysts that are bullish about a competitor and the hungry rivals themselves.

The question-and-answer period is the second act of this dramatic production. Here's where the fun begins. Now you're listening to experts who follow the company for a living and hearing management's off-the-cuff answers. Response from both sides can be enlightening. When analysts are troubled, they tend to hammer on the prickly point that's nagging them. On the Microsoft call, for example, analysts repeatedly quizzed management for further clarity about revenues, a sign that the company's message wasn't getting completely across. "I'm trying to stitch together all the puzzle pieces," one participant confessed. Such broad uncertainty could be a catalyst for analyst downgrades, as happened to Microsoft.

Honestly, it's difficult to outmaneuver the pros when a company stumbles on earnings. Microsoft's stock promptly fell five points in after-hours trading following its April bombshell. Your chances of beating the Street are much better when companies surprise to the upside.

When company news is good, discount those analysts who preface a question with congratulatory fluff such as "great quarter," because they're probably long the stock or angling for an investment banking gig. Rather, you want to hear an analyst beginning a query with statements such as "I can't believe you got to these numbers; my numbers were nowhere near this," or "That was stronger than we expected. Why are you doing so well?"

That's the sound of an analyst who has not yet recognized that a fundamental change is transforming the company, and it's a good bet that estimates will have to be raised. This analyst is still locked in the past—though not without good reason. Analysts construct sophisticated revenue and valuation models in an effort to predict a company's performance. Being wrong can cost their firm and its clients plenty of money. When management says things the analysts can't quite agree with because it's inconsistent with their earnings model, that's your best shot at latching onto a winner, even though you don't know the true value of the information. Observes Thaler:

Sometimes you will hear analysts resisting. Say the analyst was predicting the company will earn $2 a share and it earns $2.50. He wants the firm to be wrong, not him. When we hear analysts

stubbornly failing to recognize that something has happened, that's our kind of firm.

On occasion, analysts in fact might know more than management does about general industry trends, since they continuously tap a broad range of key players for investment insight. But it's highly unlikely that an outside analyst will know more about a company's inner workings than will management. If insistent analysts refuse to believe the company's optimistic guidance, either they aren't up-to-date or they haven't been listening to management—characteristics of overconfidence and anchoring.

Analysts do say the darndest things. Several years ago, for instance, a manufacturing company in which Fuller & Thaler Asset Management owned stock reported a change in earnings that beat all expectations. Fuller was listening to the conference call that followed when he heard the company's chief financial officer tell an analyst pointedly that his earnings estimate for the next quarter was too low. After a pause, the analyst retorted: "No, it's not." Such blatant anchoring doesn't show itself every day. An elated Fuller couldn't write a "buy" ticket fast enough.

CHAPTER 7

Passport to Wealth: Gary Brinson

"Why limit yourself to companies in the United States? Why not include all global pharmaceutical companies, all global auto companies, all global energy companies? I can't think of a good, sound reason."

Given the spectacular performance that many people have come to expect from the U.S. stock market, investing anywhere else seems downright un-American. So if an investment adviser suggests that you earmark 20 percent of your stock portfolio to markets outside of the United States, you might understandably wonder why. The Standard & Poor's 500 stock index returned 23.7 percent each year on average for the five years through April 2000, while British stocks, for example, averaged a 12.4 percent annualized gain and Japanese stocks eked out a 1.1 percent finish. Even the benchmark Morgan Stanley Capital International All-Country World Index, excluding the United States, managed just a 9.7 percent return.

Now suppose your investment adviser recommends dividing this 20 percent among the following companies: cellular telephone leader Nokia, telecommunications giant Vodafone AirTouch, high-fashion designer Gucci Group, automaker DaimlerChrysler, food conglomerate Nestlé and entertainment and electronics titan Sony.

That sounds better. In fact, you probably know most of these businesses by name and may even buy their products—a comforting thought—except that none of them are U.S. firms. Nokia is based in Finland. Vodafone combined with U.S. wireless telephone firm AirTouch Communications but kept its British address. Gucci is the venerable Italian fashion house, based in the Netherlands. DaimlerChrysler was formed when Stuttgart's Daimler-Benz took over Detroit's Chrysler. Nestlé is an old-line Swiss confectioner. Sony is a Japanese icon.

Still unconvinced? You're not alone. Many Americans would rather travel the world than invest in it. Shares of non-U.S. companies do not figure prominently in individuals' portfolios. In part, there's a tendency for investors worldwide to remain close to camp, a behavior known as "home-country bias." What's more, U.S. investors especially can be blasé about opportunities abroad since domestic companies dominate such a large and wealthy indigenous marketplace.

But staying on the farm—even one as large as the United States—is narrow-minded. In particular, it keeps you from investing in leading multinational companies based outside of the United States that are benefiting from increasingly open world markets. Indeed, with so much business being conducted across borders and time zones, it's even hard to say anymore what exactly a U.S. company is. Is a BMW made in South Carolina a German car or an American car? Does it matter that Sony is Japanese if it makes the high-quality stereo system you want?

To Gary Brinson, the chairman of influential Chicago-based investment manager UBS Asset Management, stocks should be chosen according to business, not borders. Where a company is based doesn't much matter—as long as management knows where it's going. Astute investors want to find industry leaders, regardless of where they are.

In the global investment arena that Brinson envisions, borders and barriers are obsolete and stocks trade around the clock. "Capital markets of the future will be borderless," he asserts. Country-specific issues will not completely disappear, only the myopia of looking at the industry from a single-country perspective.[1] Investors no longer would diversify portfolios according to a set amount of U.S., European, Asian and Latin American exposure, or even make distinctions between "developed" and "emerging" markets. Geography would be an investing footnote, not a guide. Instead, people would structure their portfolios by industries and sectors. They would pick the best possible stocks for diversification across business lines, regardless of where the companies happen to call home. Portfolio allocations by country, as investors are strongly advised to practice now, would make as much sense as a U.S. investor divvying up stock holdings among each of the 50 states. Says Brinson:

> The world is becoming a single, big, global equity market. Regional distinctions will become anachronistic. I wouldn't define a U.S. portfolio in terms of how much money was invested in California, New York, Florida and Illinois. If I showed you a U.S. portfolio broken down by states—37 percent in New York, 12 percent in California, 19 percent in Washington and so forth—you'd wonder "Why is that relevant?" On a global scale, it's not useful to say, "You have X percent in Switzerland, Y percent in Germany and Z percent in Finland." What you want to know is, "What industries am I represented in?"

Will borderless investing really span the globe, as Brinson claims? After all, throughout history people have been living—for better or worse—inside of regions and borders that have both united and divided them. The growth of investment and business within individual economies has been framed largely by such geographic and cultural constraints. But the increasing pace of cross-border corporate mergers and alliances, particularly between Europe and the United States, is creating unprecedented change, Brinson contends. The seeds, he adds, were planted in the 1970s when intrepid non-U.S. companies gained a foothold on U.S. soil and started to profoundly impact American companies and workers. Recalls Brinson:

> You went to buy a car, and you were no longer just looking at General Motors, Ford and Chrysler. There were German and Japanese imports. If you went to buy a television set, it wasn't just RCA and Zenith—there was this company called Sony. At the same time, more and more U.S. companies would talk about competition in a global sense. Coca-Cola in the 1970s

reported strong growth coming not in the United States, but in Europe and Latin America.

Today, the world of business is more interwoven than ever. Many people don't think twice about the lightning speed of communications and commerce. The Internet, always accessible, is dismantling corporate hierarchies. Business increasingly is cooperative *and* competitive, so that rival companies will work together to build a marketplace and then battle for the biggest share. There's even a management term to describe this trend: "co-opetition."[2] For instance, if you have a popular hamburger stand and another stand opens just down the street, the increased foot traffic can benefit both businesses. How much benefit depends on you.

Such friendly struggle has long been an accepted practice in Japan, where companies and suppliers are linked through clubby networks called *keiretsu*. In the United States, reciprocation is prominent among fast-growing Internet Web sites that gain visibility through co-marketing and co-branding relationships with other sites and traditional offline companies.

Of course, every business still wants to capture the most market share it can for its product or service—competition is alive and well. But as technology gives ordinary people extraordinary access to information and ideas, consumer markets and corporate productivity should continue to explode. For many companies, there's more than enough work to go around; they can barely keep up with their order book.

Such an open-minded environment doesn't support the old management strategy of command and control. Wiser managers understand the value of turning enemies into allies. While not sharing state secrets, companies establish networks to trade products and help each other thrive. The Internet is playing a major role in this evolution. For example, giant chemical companies, energy conglomerates and manufacturers are establishing electronic marketplaces and joining existing Web-based exchanges in an effort to cut costs and speed transactions.

Still, competitive barriers don't fall without resistance. Nationalistic opposition to corporate cross-pollination and free trade has and will continue to produce hiccups and headlines, but the momentum for cross-border mergers and acquisitions is growing. Major trans-Atlantic activity since 1998, for example, has brought the combination of Daimler-Benz and Chrysler, British energy producer British Petroleum and U.S. oil refiner Amoco and German financial services leader Deutschebank and U.S. counterpart Bankers Trust. Just think about the Daimler-Chrysler linkup for a moment. Who could have envisioned at the beginning of the 1990s that a German automobile manufacturer would gobble up one of Detroit's Big Three—an American name-plate—without angry protest from U.S. labor groups and politicians? Certainly not anyone who vividly recalls the backlash in the 1980s against Japanese-made cars.

Perhaps this remarkable transformation from clashing cultures to connected ones really began when the first sledgehammer hit the Berlin Wall that momentous October day in 1989. Since then, a bull market for democracy has matured, not only in Europe but also in much of Latin America and Asia. In many countries, street fighters have matured into straight fighters—defending the rule of law, encouraging competition and foreign investment, and embracing the technology and innovation that promises to improve business and living conditions.

The Internet has accelerated these changes dramatically. At the end of 1999, an estimated 100 million people in the United States were connected to the Web, and a total of 177 million are expected to crowd online by 2003.[3] Worldwide, the number of Internet users is expected to swell to 502 million by 2003 from 142 million in 1998.[4] By giving different cultures a way to relate and communicate, the Internet is helping to break down boundaries and to create common bonds. A smaller, more connected world is familiar and less threatening, in the way small-town life is friendlier and less harried than the pace of a city. The amiable cross-border corporate mergers of the 1990s have helped to knit this fabric tighter. Brinson himself took a pioneering step in 1997 when he merged Brinson Partners with giant Union Bank of Switzerland. For Brinson, blending operations with UBS was a logical way to extend his money-management firm's scope, reach and return on investment.

Brinson explains the motivation that is encouraging multinational companies to focus squarely on what they do best and not try to be all things to all customers:

> **Companies want to do business with a size and scope that allow them to operate all over the world. DaimlerChrysler is saying, "We're not German; we're not American. We're a global automobile company generating revenues and profits from around the world." It's the same with Deutschebank and Bankers Trust, which creates a global financial services business, or British Petroleum and Amoco, which is a global energy company. But although these companies are diversifying globally, they are sticking to the business they know—automobiles, banking, energy. There are economies of scale from that.**

Stocks Without Frontiers

Multinational companies are bred to compete on a global landscape. Everything about their branded products and services, from design and creation to marketing and distribution, is aimed at reaching the most people in the most efficient and economical way. They understand how to focus on many diverse markets while tailoring products to local tastes. The ability to spread costs and revenues across regions blunts the impact from unfavorable developments in any single economy or country, creating a healthier, leaner operation.

For investors in any language, what should matter most about a multinational enterprise is not the native tongue of its key executives, but how innately those officials can articulate and execute a vision that will create a more dynamic, responsive organization. Don't limit yourself when it comes to investments; the best companies certainly aren't.

Novartis, for instance, is a giant pharmaceutical company based in Switzerland. But for all its rivals care, Novartis could be headquartered at Disneyland. Competitors rightly are more concerned that Novartis operates in nearly 150 countries worldwide. Indeed, Novartis in 1999 sold just 2 percent of its products in Switzerland and 37 percent in the United States.[5] If geographic origin is incidental to executives at Merck, Pfizer, Pharmacia & Upjohn (itself a merger of Swedish and U.S. firms) and other huge drugmakers, should it matter to investors? Absolutely not, Brinson asserts:

Novartis is not Swiss; ask the people at Merck or Pfizer. Novartis is just a big, global pharmaceutical company. It's the same with DaimlerChrysler. People say, "Should we call this a German company or an American company?" Call it what it is—a big, global automobile company. The fact that it's headquartered in some particular region is irrelevant.

This global prism—the sense that the world is my office—is also true of U.S.-based multinational companies. Unlike their peers in Europe and Asia, U.S. firms enjoy the luxury of a large and wealthy marketplace right in their backyard. Yet selling abroad has become an essential element of corporate life for many U.S. businesses. Coca-Cola is based in Atlanta, Georgia, but nearly two-thirds of its 1999 sales of $19.8 billion came from outside of the United States.[6] Globalization also has been particularly critical to the growth of U.S. technology companies. At International Business Machines, nondomestic revenue in 1999 accounted for 57 percent of sales. Computer chip manufacturer Intel also registered 57 percent of its sales abroad.[7] In addition to pharmaceuticals and technology, other industries reaping the benefits of global consolidation and competition include automobiles, banking, communications, insurance, retailing, energy and oil.

U.S. multinationals often encourage employees to obtain over-seas work experience as a fast track to upper management. In Brinson's mind, professional and individual U.S. investors also are becoming more familiar with the ways of the world, and will use their global perspective to diversify portfolios more broadly. Allocating assets by industries will be the first criterion; geography will be a secondary aspect—especially when investing in widely followed large-capitalization stocks. Novartis, for instance, collected 36 percent of its 1999 revenues from European operations, and another 37 percent of sales in the United States; that same year, rival Pharmacia & Upjohn garnered 29 percent of its revenue from Europe, and 40 percent from the United States.[8] From those figures, it's a toss-up as to which company is European and which is American—Novartis of Basel, Switzerland, or Pharmacia & Upjohn of Peapack, New Jersey?

Viewed through this window, it makes perfect sense to over-come home-country bias and pick the biggest and best of a breed. You would own Novartis for representation in the global pharmaceutical sector—but only after comparing its products, valuation and other investment merits to Pharmacia & Upjohn, Merck, Pfizer and other competitors. In the same vein, DaimlerChrysler is a global auto play; BP is a worldwide energy stake; Coca-Cola and McDonald's are bets on rising worldwide living standards.

To really know where a company's fortunes may be heading, you should understand how it is handling current growth and competing against sometimes better-equipped rivals. A multinational that markets itself correctly to foreign consumers will integrate with local culture. Den Fujita, the dynamic Japanese entrepreneur who in the early 1970s made McDonald's a household name in Japan, tells of being in a Chicago hotel room some years ago and watching a television interview with a group of visiting Japanese Boy Scouts. One of the boys was asked what surprised him most about the United States. "I was amazed to see McDonald's here, too," he answered.[9] The visitor's wonder is understandable. McDonald's caught on

quickly after it entered the Japanese market. Asia-Pacific operations accounted for $6.4 billion, or 16.6 percent, of McDonald's
$38.5 billion in 1999 systemwide sales. In fact, only about half of
the Golden Arches' sales that year came from the United States.[10]

Equity-market investors who doubt the lasting effects of globalization can learn a lot from their own routine buying habits.
Americans generally are not overly sensitive about where an item is
made. While "Buy American" commands strong support in places,
Americans generally are discriminate shoppers who want the best
product at the best possible price. And because the United States
has made it relatively easy for foreign companies to establish
factories and operations, "Buy American" is no longer so clear-cut.
If we don't make geographic distinctions in buying goods and
services, why do so when buying stocks? Brinson says he believes
that U.S. investors are beginning to embrace this interdependent
world of business and trade:

**Increasingly investors will define a portfolio of worldwide
opportunities. This will be like international investing was
years ago. In 1983, we gave a conference on international investing, and virtually nobody showed up. Today, if you talk about
international investing, you don't get any argument. Five years
from today, this discussion will be "Of course. These are big,
global companies; it's silly to categorize them by geographic
region." And if individuals look at the way they behave, their
consumption is already consistent with investing this way. You
don't mind using a Sony tape recorder. You probably don't even
pay attention to the fact that the recorder is a Sony. You don't
care. All you want is a good recorder.**

Rule #1: Allocation, Allocation, Allocation

Brinson has never shied from controversy. He dropped a bombshell on the investment business in 1986 when he and two col-

leagues claimed that asset allocation—the amount of money you earmark to stocks, bonds and cash—was more crucial to investment returns than either the specific stocks you picked or market timing. To be precise, their study showed that on average over time, asset mix could account for 93.6 percent—basically all—of a portfolio's return. Stock selection and market-timing determined the rest.[11] The study was repeated in 1991, with similar results.[12] Says Brinson:

> **We were trying to explain how much of returns over time was explained by asset mix. As we showed in the study, on average—and that's important—it's roughly 90 percent. When we did a second study, we got a similar result. Conceptually, people do have a decent understanding of the importance of asset allocation. If your grandmother has a desired asset mix of 20 percent stocks and 80 percent bonds, and your nephew has just the reciprocal—80 percent stocks and 20 percent bonds—those two decisions are going to create portfolios that look and perform very differently over time.**

Grandma could put the entire 20 percent share of her portfolio allocated to stocks in volatile Internet-related bets like Amazon.com and eBay, while your nephew keeps an 80 percent equity allocation in relatively conservative blue-chip stalwarts such as Wal-Mart and General Electric. According to Brinson, investment *discipline*—choosing how much money you're willing to put into stocks and sticking to it—says more about the return you can expect than investment *strategy*—the stocks you ultimately pick.

Nowadays, asset allocation is widely viewed as the basic foundation of a properly positioned portfolio. The importance of maintaining the allocation has been loudly drummed into individual investors. Conventional wisdom encourages people to set an allocation and then rebalance their holdings periodically—say, every six months or a year—to return to base. Say you put half of a $200,000 portfolio into stocks and leave the rest in bonds and cash. Now suppose your $100,000 in stocks gains 15 percent in a year, bringing the value to $115,000. The bonds and cash grow by 5 percent, or $5,000, giving your portfolio a total value of $220,000.

To maintain your stated allocation, you then would need to sell $5,000 worth of stocks, easing the value of your equity portion to $110,000—or 50 percent of the portfolio. Conversely, if your stocks dropped 15 percent in a year, the value of those holdings would be $85,000. If the bonds and cash portion returned 5 percent, then the portfolio would be worth $190,000. This time, you'd have to buy $10,000 worth of stocks to keep your allocation steady.

In theory, asset allocation disciplines you to buy stocks when prices are low and sell at high points. Except in a bull market especially, there's a tendency to put on a few extra pounds of equity. Who has the courage to sell when stock prices look certain to head higher?

The additional weight in equities is probably tolerable for skilled investors who have stronger stomachs for major market swings. In Chapter 9, William Sharpe discusses the importance of properly assessing your ability to withstand market risk. Brinson and his research partners were focused more on the danger of trading too much, too often—an impulse that comes when we focus myopically on individual stocks. They conducted their study in response to a disturbing behavior they observed in the early 1980s among many experienced institutional investors. These pension funds and other powerful players were spending a vast amount of energy and cash on hiring and firing portfolio managers, and worrying about minute details like how much stock to own in General Motors relative to Ford. To Brinson, all this second-guessing was eating into their investment returns and preventing them from building optimal portfolios. He recalls:

In discussions with clients, we found that asset allocation was really—if I could use the term—accidental. They'd hire Manager

X and then somebody would say, "What about Manager Y?" So they'd hire these different managers, and the resulting asset mix would be just a by-product of those microdecisions.

Brinson and his colleagues suggested that the most important variable affecting long-run performance wasn't Ford versus General Motors. Rather, it was how much money a client had in the stock and bond markets, and then how those assets were distributed among various styles and segments.

Stock selection does factor in when comparing two portfolios of equal allocations. Say Grandma has 80 percent of a $250,000 portfolio in stocks, and your nephew has a $250,000 portfolio, also with 80 percent in stocks. It matters a great deal to the overall return and risk of each if one owns $25,000 worth of Amazon.com shares and the other holds $25,000 worth of Wal-Mart. Attempts at market-timing—trying to buy low and sell high—will also have a role in the performance outcome.

Money managers understandably did not take kindly to the suggestion that allocation mattered more than strategy, and their carefully researched stock picks weren't so valuable after all. But Brinson—an active manager himself—wasn't condemning active management. Still, many people interpreted the results in just that way.

In an attempt to shed some objective light on the Brinson work, Roger Ibbotson and colleague Paul Kaplan of investment research firm Ibbotson Associates produced a much-debated report in December 1998 titled "Does Asset Allocation Policy Explain 40%, 90%, or 100% of Performance?" Their study included 10 years of monthly returns on 94 balanced mutual funds through March 31, 1998.

Ibbotson and Kaplan asked three key questions relevant to building the best portfolio possible. The first—How much of the variability of a single fund's investment return is due to asset allocation?—is actually the only issue that Brinson and his partners specifically addressed. The second and third questions came from Ibbotson and Kaplan: How much of the variation in performance *between* funds is due to asset mix? And what percentage of total return comes from a fund's investment policy—its asset allocation?

The Ibbotson and Kaplan study corroborated Brinson's findings. Roughly 90 percent of the variability of a single fund's return *across* time hinges on investment policy. Over many years, the most important factor in portfolio return is just staying invested in the market—though consistent, skillful stock-picking does bring some added value.

Stock-picking is far more crucial when considering the second question. Allocation determines just 40 percent of the returns between funds, Ibbotson and Kaplan concluded. Asset allocation from one fund to another does not seem to influence performance, because most portfolios tend to hold similar blends of securities. It's what funds do with their allocations—the active part of money management—that differentiates them. In fact, when there are differences between funds, the study showed, more than half of the discrepancy is attributable to timing and selection.

For the third question, Ibbotson and Kaplan surmised that 100 percent of a single fund's return is explained by investment policy. They claim that active stock selection and timing, on average, do not normally provide returns above a benchmark.

So fill a portfolio with Warren Buffett clones—if you can find them. The point is to decide to hold stocks, bonds and cash, and then figure out the blend of each that best reflects your risk tolerance. At its essence, the Brinson study reiterated a crucial and often-quoted key to investment success: Be in the stock market at all times, at a level that's comfortable to you, and you won't miss its best days or panic on its worst.

All Together Now

Once you come to terms with the portion of your assets that should be invested in stocks, you'd do well to put some of that money to work in shares of non-U.S. companies. International investing offers potentially high returns, portfolio diversification and participation in the rapidly evolving global economy.

Efficient frontier charts—and the investment advisers who adhere to them—typically claim that putting 20 percent of equity assets into non-U.S. stocks, traditionally represented by the Morgan Stanley Capital International EAFE (Europe, Australasia, Far East) index, can significantly offset the risk of an all–Standard & Poor's 500 portfolio. Why? Because stocks in developed markets, such as Europe, frequently do not move in tandem with U.S. stocks; the correlation is even less evident in the emerging markets of Asia and Latin America. Remember how Harry Markowitz laid out the virtues of a diversified portfolio? Holding securities that move independently tends to create a portfolio with more of the stability and security that investors seek.

Yet international investing produced mostly disappointing returns in the 1990s. With few exceptions, U.S. shareholders did much better staying at home. U.S. stocks posted a 15.6 percent average annual gain in the decade through November 1999, for example, while British stocks averaged 11 percent and long-suffering Japanese equities stumbled to a negative 2.1 percent finish. EAFE itself also fared dismally, with a 5 percent average annualized return over that period, in large part due to an unfortunate outsized stake in Japan.[13]

Indeed, more than a few sophisticated investors dispel the international investment premise. For them, going global doesn't measure up as an effective way to diversify risk. Prominent investment manager Rex Sinquefield, a vocal proponent of portfolio diversification and investing by asset class, has cast doubt on the risk-reward benefits of large-cap world indices like EAFE. In a 1996 research paper, he showed that from 1970 to 1994, a globally diversified portfolio of large stocks was less risky than a U.S.-only portfolio—but not measurably so.[14] "EAFE and other foreign-market-like portfolios fail" as diversifiers, he concluded, noting that international value and international small stocks diversify U.S. portfolios better than EAFE.

The stay-at-home crowd adds that a strong U.S. economy makes international stocks less appealing, and many attractive choices can be found among streamlined U.S. companies that have become world leaders in their industries. Critics contend, moreover, that markets outside of the United States don't hold up any better during major market downturns—toppling another pillar of support from the global diversification strategy.

If that's the case, then isn't international investment just throwing good money after bad? No, because it's unrealistic to assume that U.S. companies will always dominate their global competitors. True, many U.S. companies are lean and profitable, but Novartis could produce a world-class drug that decimates a top-selling Merck product. Aging, affluent baby boomers in the United States might decide that Toyota's Lexus is the hands-down choice over Ford's Lincoln Continental. Investing outside of the U.S. allows you to diversify specific, or unsystematic, risk—the risk that a company's fortunes might sour—and to buy into companies that don't operate in the United States. For instance, if you're bullish on Mexico's growth prospects, the country's telecommunications powerhouse Teléfonos de México is the prime beneficiary—not U.S. counterparts AT&T or MCI WorldCom.

And while companies certainly are more global in their outlook, actually getting goods and capital across world markets isn't so well integrated. Business cycles, economic policies and consumer spending are highly variable, and greatly influence stock-market returns. So it's misguided to believe that U.S. markets always will perform better than markets abroad. For example, Wall Street between 1983 and 1987 was a friendly venue for investors; U.S. stocks averaged a 16.3 percent annual return during that time—well above their historical norm. But over the same five-year span, Japanese stocks surged 28.2 percent annually on average and U.K. equities rose 22.1 percent.[15] More recently, U.S. stock-market performance has lagged many foreign counterparts. The S&P 500 rose 12.4 percent in the 12 months through April 2000, while French stocks gained 29.5 percent,

German stocks rose 25.5 percent and Japanese stocks soared 38.8 percent.[16]

For investors who choose to venture beyond U.S. stocks, market forces and trends at the century's turn are largely favorable no matter which direction you look. Healthy consumer demand for goods and services is benefiting many companies in the developed markets of Europe and Asia, including Japan. The erratic markets of Latin and South America are maturing. Deregulation, corporate restructuring, and mergers and acquisitions are each playing major roles, particularly among utilities and telecommunications providers, banks and brokerages, and technology firms. Cross-border transactions, such as the DaimlerChrysler link, reflect a strong desire among competitors to expand market share, to boost productivity and to take advantage of new technology that is driving truly revolutionary changes in manufacturing, sales and distribution. Brinson observes:

> **The investment business follows how businesses conduct themselves. To the extent that Merck sees itself as a global pharmaceutical company, and so does Novartis, then by definition that means you can't analyze one or the other without analyzing both, because they're both competing on the same global playing field. And that's going to force investors to do analysis and build portfolios from a global perspective.**

The world is becoming more global every day. Soon, trading stocks around the clock, around the world, could be commonplace. In December 1999, for example, seven popular Nasdaq-traded U.S. companies were approved for listing on the Stock Exchange of Hong Kong. These pioneers included five technology names: Microsoft, Intel, Cisco Systems, Dell Computer and Applied Materials. The two others: biotechnology leader Amgen and coffee retailer Starbucks. In return, some Hong Kong companies will list on Nasdaq. Eventually, all the stocks in the Nasdaq-100 index could trade in Hong Kong. At the same time, the New York Stock Exchange was looking to forge alliances with leading bourses around the world, including Toronto, London, Paris and Frankfurt.

With more people doing business beyond their own borders, the number of firms that can be called multinational is growing. In fact, there's a sense that multinational companies should be seen as a separate asset class, like energy, transportation or technology. Building global stock portfolios country by country currently follows a more traditional framework. A portfolio manager would decide to keep 10 percent of assets in French equities, for example, and so might hold shares of luxury goods retailer LVMH Moët Hennessy, insurer AXA Group, pharmaceutical giant Rhône-Poulenc, oil producer Total-Fina and semiconductor leader STMicroelectronics. But these multinationals have nothing in common other than a French address. It makes more sense, in Brinson's view, for investors to include LVMH as part of their global consumer exposure, Total-Fina as a global energy play and STMicroelectronics as a global technology holding.

As more investors do begin to look at the world with a broader view, asset allocation will still be crucial, but the nature of the assets will change. Expect EAFE—the international investment standard—to see tough competition from new indices that allocate large-cap stocks according to industries, not countries. So, for example, a U.S. restaurant chain would no longer be part of your domestic component; it would belong to a global services segment. Brinson explains:

> **People will begin to see that optimal risk-return configurations come from this kind of global perspective. They'll categorize the playing field not by country, but by industries and sectors. If they're investing stock by stock, then they make those decisions in terms of "How much do I want in pharmaceuticals? In energy? In autos? In financial services?" If they're buying mutual funds, they'll have to look for funds that tell shareholders, "We're going to invest on this global basis."**

Travel Advisories

Investing abroad has never been for homebodies. Global investors pack some unique baggage. The first is currency risk. Investments outside of the United States are made in local currency, not good old American greenbacks. This can be problematic, depending on which side of the ocean you're on. As every globetrotter knows, when the U.S. dollar is weak, it costs more dollars to buy things overseas. If you visit Japan and the exchange rate is 100 yen to the dollar, a 200-yen cup of coffee is more expensive than if you received 125 yen on the dollar.

Accordingly, a Japanese stock trading at 1,000 yen per share will cost a U.S. investor $10 at 100 yen to the dollar. If the stock price doesn't move, but the yen weakens to 125 on the dollar, your shares are now worth just $8. Suppose the exchange rate is 125 yen to $1 and the stock gains 10 percent, to 1,100 yen. You've got appreciation in the stock in yen, but your shares in dollars are worth just $8.80— or $1.20 less than you initially paid. Currency swings can work to your advantage as well. If the yen is at 125 to the dollar, you can buy that 1,100-yen stock for $8.80 per share. Say the share price of the stock moves to 1,200 yen and a dollar buys 100 yen. Now that stock fetches $12 per share if you sell it—a $3.20-per-share profit.

Some international fund managers will deflect currency risk through hedging, which renders a portfolio currency-neutral, as if it were denominated in dollars. Hedging not only carries a cost, it eliminates the positive effect of favorable currency fluctuations— one reason why it's not universally done. Alternately, currency risk can be mitigated through diversification among different countries and by investing long-term, as the impact of currency swings tends to cancel out over several years. For his part, Brinson acknowledges currency risk, but contends that it ought not to drive investment decisions:

An investor might say, "I invest in Novartis in Swiss francs, and I invest in Merck in U.S. dollars." That is confusing. The proper

way to think about it is that I can invest in Novartis and hedge Swiss francs into U.S. dollars. Or I could invest in Merck and hedge dollars into Swiss francs. Currency exposure needs to be controlled separately from my underlying investments.

Another fundamental concern for the international investor is political and economic risk. Suppose an ambitious government decides to nationalize its industries or force foreigners to pay an investment tax. Or maybe a circus of politicians has trouble getting its economic show under the big top. You think things in Washington are bad? You could have been a shareholder of Japanese stocks in the 1990s—"Japanese investor" then was practically an oxymoron. While anxious shareholders waited—and waited—for a government-led rescue, the Japanese stock market tanked—and tanked.

Investors can be forgiven a desire to keep their money in the United States. People are most comfortable with familiar faces and places. Even Warren Buffett has said that foreign exposure in his portfolio comes from U.S.-based multinational holdings like Coca-Cola and Gillette. If it's good enough for Buffett, then why not for everyone? Brinson sharply disagrees:

Warren's myopic. He gets foreign exposure, but it's like saying, "We're going to play golf, but only holes 1, 7, 13 and 18." Why limit yourself to companies in the United States? Why not include all global pharmaceutical companies, all global automobile companies, all global energy companies? I can't think of a good, sound reason.

A World to the Wise

International investing hasn't been a big lure for most Americans. But Brinson's empathic arguments recall a quote about the evolution of the Internet and e-commerce that is attributed to Andrew Grove, the founder of semiconductor giant Intel. In the near future, Grove said, we won't speak of Internet companies and non-Internet companies, because *every* company will be an Internet company. Not that every firm will sell its products online or become the Amazon.com of its field, but every company will use the Net because it's an easy, straightforward way to deal with customers and to facilitate operations. Even if you own a corner deli, the Internet can be a tremendous asset. Maybe you won't launch itsmydeli.com, but you can shop online for better and cheaper suppliers to grow your bottom line.

Brinson is saying much the same: All companies will be global. Even U.S. industries with little foreign exposure, such as banks and telephone companies, can't escape international concerns. For example, Itasca, Illinois–based First Midwest Bancorp has a niche business serving the Chicago suburbs, but it now has to contend with Dutch banking giant ABN AMRO, which has a broad retail branch-banking network in the Midwest through its LaSalle Group subsidiary. First Midwest also face competition from U.S.-based rivals with more of an international scope, such as Citigroup and Bank of America Corp.

A company like First Midwest doesn't have to open branches overseas in order to think globally. The effects of globalization ring loudly any time a potential First Midwest customer opens an account with LaSalle. But the paradox is that to scale global heights in business nowadays, you have to act locally. Time and again, well-intentioned companies that tried to enter a foreign marketplace without adapting to local culture and tastes have failed miserably. Chevrolet's attempt to sell the Nova in Latin America is a classic example. To English speakers, "nova" might bring to mind an exploding star, but in Spanish the word literally translates to "doesn't go."

In that regard, a well-respected local firm might have a unique advantage over a foreign buyer of a popular crosstown rival. It's easy to buy your way into an overseas market—just fork over the cash. The hard part is blending your way of doing business and theirs without a culture clash. Even a powerhouse like America

Online, which "gets" the Net so skillfully and has gained tremendous operating leverage as a result, has had difficulty transporting its business model to Europe. Its flat-rate pricing hasn't gone over with Europeans, and early efforts to dominate European countries in the way it does the United States have fallen short.

The lesson bears repeating: Think globally, act locally. If a leading company enters a market abroad and stumbles, home-market players can benefit. Indeed, if these smaller companies can outmaneuver a formidable Goliath, perhaps they belong in a global investment portfolio right alongside the major multinationals of their industry. Such democracy is what globalization ultimately is all about.

So when should investors board this globalization train? Brinson, not surprisingly, already is waving you out of the station:

They have to start thinking about it now. It needs to be on their radar screen. For the individual investor, the choices will be to put together U.S. and non-U.S. funds and look at them as a totality, or to take an industry and sector approach. I don't know how fast this will continue, but we might be surprised by how rapidly change takes place. But it's not a smooth road. There are going to be potholes. At times, you won't be able to see the trend. But that's true historically of economic change. It's easy to look back and see trends; if you lived through that time, you dealt with fluctuation.

Brinson is circumspect about his own investments, other than to say that his portfolio is diversified globally across both developed and emerging markets. As you might expect from a money manager and stock-picker, he's no fan of the theory that markets are efficient, and his investments are actively managed. Still, he says he understands why many people are drawn to the simplicity of indexing a portfolio against a specific benchmark, although he isn't about to sing its praises:

Indexation represents low-friction trading and gives a predictable return. By definition, you know what the relative performance is going to be because you're virtually replicating a particular market. Whatever that market is—U.S., international, global—you know what you're going to get. The vices of indexation are that it gets you into very large capitalization companies, for it tends to drive money toward what has done well.

The predictability of index strategies is, to Brinson, a liability. He points out that in the early 1980s, with inflation soaring past 10 percent annually, energy stocks represented more than one-quarter of the S&P 500's total market capitalization. By comparison, at the end of 1999, with inflation low, energy stocks accounted for just 6 percent of the S&P while the fast-track technology sector commanded a 28 percent weighting. Yet indexed investors have no say in this allocation, whether they like it or not. Brinson says that he always prefers to have a choice about what goes in and out of his portfolio. Being forced to keep a disproportionate amount of money in the most popular market sector is not always the most sensible strategy, he claims.

Indeed, suppose you believe that technology is overvalued and health care is due to rebound. As an index-fund investor, you would have little chance of catching any sentiment shift early, when the most value exists. For that reason alone, Brinson encourages people not to take the daily special. A portfolio layered with carefully chosen, well-researched stocks can lead skilled active managers to beat the average and earn their fees, he contends. To be sure, he admits, such outperformance is not easy—especially year after year—but it is possible, particularly when investing in less-developed stock markets:

With emerging markets, there are very good reasons to think that active management should provide added value. Information is hard to get; it's expensive, and the markets themselves

are probably not reflecting true equilibrium because you simply don't have enough participants. Truly efficient markets—which is what makes indexation work—involve many participants with a lot of knowledge and nobody having a smarter advantage than somebody else.

Spanning the Globe

Having a global perspective means focusing on the bottom-up fundamentals of a specific company and placing less emphasis on the top-down economic factors of a particular country. In today's new, global economy, when you evaluate a company as a potential investment, you must look hard at its international rivals. For it's no longer American versus French, or German versus Japanese. It's Nokia against Motorola and Qualcomm. It's Toshiba, the Japan-based computer maker, going keyboard to keyboard with Dell and Compaq. It's DaimlerChrysler driving customers into a Mercedes instead of a Lexus or a Lincoln.

Yet for all of the progress and convenience that globalization has fostered, it's been difficult for U.S. investors to obtain trustworthy financial information about non-U.S. companies. But the gap in GAAP, or generally accepted accounting principles, is being bridged. Increasingly, companies from around the world are listing on U.S. exchanges in a specialized format called American Depository Receipts, or ADRs. In this way, U.S. investors can purchase non-U.S. securities without the high transaction costs that are often typical of international trading.

To create an ADR, non-U.S. companies bundle a set amount of their home-market shares—called ordinary shares—into a single unit that trades like common stock. The ADR price of Novartis, for instance, is quoted on the New York Stock Exchange in U.S. dollars, just like Merck or Pfizer. But it's important to understand that although ADRs trade in the United States, they are actually non-U.S. shares and so do not eliminate currency risk.

ADRs do alleviate accounting concerns that often loom over non-U.S. companies. A firm can list its ADR shares in one of four ways. Level I is the most basic, with the stock price quoted on the Over-the-Counter Bulletin Board, and on the thinly traded "pink sheets." But reporting requirements in this case are minimal, and issuers do not have to divulge too much about their business to investors. For companies that don't wish to raise capital in the United States, a Level I ADR is a common option. Nestlé is a prominent example of a Level I ADR.

Companies that want to trade on major U.S. exchanges, such as the New York Stock Exchange, will issue Level II and Level III ADRs. But first they must adhere to stricter reporting standards—namely, filing a comprehensive form 20-F with federal Securities and Exchange Commission regulators. The 20-F is similar to a U.S. company's form 10-K, the annual report that divulges key financial results and business information. Level III companies must meet these Level II requirements and are also permitted to tap the U.S. public markets for capital. For some multinationals, a fourth option is to issue Global Depositary Receipts, or GDRs, which allow companies to raise capital in two or more markets at the same time.

The Internet is a tremendous tool for researching non-U.S. companies. Many firms post financial statements and shareholder material in English on their company Web sites. You can also find 20-F and other reports without charge through an online search engine called FreeEdgar (www.freedgar.com).

Extensive information about ADRs also is online at Yahoo! Finance (www.finance.yahoo.com). Type in a ticker symbol to retrieve a company profile, financials, Wall Street estimates, recent insider shareholders' buys and sells and institutional ownership figures. Worldly Investor (www.worldlyinvestor.com), a virtual tour guide for the global investment landscape, offers an ADR stock-screener to help make investment decisions. ADR.com (www.adr.com) provides research and analysis, earnings estimates, stock-price charts, institutional holdings, and links to company Web sites. The Bank of New York's resource center (www.adrbny.com) is strong on education and insight, especially its *Global Equity Investment Guide*. And Wright Investors Service (www.wisi.com) gives unbiased in-depth information on hundreds of non-U.S. companies.

Selecting Sectors

Where do you put your money outside of the United States to take advantage of this brave new world? Investment sectors that promise above-average growth over the next decade include technology, the Internet, telecommunications, media, entertainment, financial services, health care and pharmaceuticals.

Why these sectors? Because they will be key beneficiaries of the Information Age. Information is power, as despots and dictators have long understood. But today, information is empowering. Demand is increasing worldwide for innovative technology and communications that make life easier and more enjoyable. The aging, wealthy populations that dominate developed Europe and Japan will thrive on information, education and entertainment—"info-tainment," really. They want active leisure time that expands their horizons and their minds. They will seek advice about personal finance and learn how to become better investors. And not only will people live better, they will live longer as a result of advancements in preventative and restorative medicine.

At the same time, the relatively youthful populations of emerging markets in Asia and Latin America are ready to shake the status quo and begin to build their own wealth. Joining them will be the youth of Europe and the United States, who have ideas about what the future should hold and will work toward them. People 30 and under at the beginning of the twenty-first century represent the first truly wired generation. Not only do they "get" the Internet—they *are* the Internet. They will create and adopt the innovations that the rest of us will follow.

Younger generations have time and energy; older generations have experience and wealth. It's always been that way—trades, skills and standards pass from one hand to another. Technology speeds the transfer of knowledge and extends its value worldwide. A tailor in London makes a suit for a customer in San Francisco for the same price as an off-the-rack item at a local department store. Experts in New York and Moscow diagnose a patient in Cairo with a rare disease as if they all were face-to-face in the hospital. With the help of a digital camera and a personalized Web page, you're able to "attend" your nephew's birthday party even though he's 3,000 miles away.

New ways of relating to each other change how we view the world, and the greater understanding and perspective influences how we invest. "What's good for the country is good for General Motors, and vice versa," former General Motors CEO Charles E. Wilson said in the early 1950s. Today, what's good for General Motors, Toyota or BMW is still good for the country—but which country? The United States? Japan? Germany? The fact that we're asking the question at all is remarkable. Today, the only passport you need to invest in the world around you is a modem and some tightly packed Web sites. So don't box yourself in; go for the globe.

**CHAPTER
8**

Widows, Orphans and Other Risk-Takers: Peter Bernstein

"Love affairs are the wrong way to manage your assets. Stocks should probably be the largest asset class that you own. The case is strong enough that you probably place most of your bet in that direction. But if you bet 100 percent and you're wrong, you're going to mismanage the situation."

INVESTING HAS NEVER been the same since a young graduate student named Harry Markowitz drew a line between investment risk and reward. Yet for all the remarkable advancements that have been made in how to handle a portfolio wisely, investors are still tussling with the thorny matter of how much to venture in the hope of achieving above-average gain.

Where do we go from here? Peter Bernstein has long pondered that question. As a chronicler of investing and its guiding theories, Bernstein is a one-man Greek chorus for the events, people and principles that have shaped finance and investment over the past half-century. He's been an eyewitness to an astounding revolution that has created new ways for individuals and institutions to gauge investment risk. But investors today are looking at a new century. When the history of investing is told a generation from now, which ideas and theories will have remained crucial to success?

Few observers of market behavior are better qualified to predict what might lie ahead for investing than Bernstein, a gentlemanly financial philosopher and scholar who began his Wall Street career in the 1950s when he took over his father's investment management firm. He has authored two best-selling books: *Against the Gods: The Remarkable Story of Risk*, published in 1996, and 1992's *Capital Ideas: The Improbable Origins of Modern Wall Street*. Bernstein understands that risk and reward are symbiotic; one cannot exist without the other. The irony is not lost on him that many investors are willing to load a portfolio with greater risk—especially in bull markets—convinced they have the power to control adversity:

A good investor avoids being greedy—avoids thinking that a bull market is equivalent to brilliance. The better an investment has treated you, the more you should think about distancing yourself. The stock doesn't know you own it. The stock market doesn't know you're there, and it's not going to be considerate. You don't *deserve* to get anything, really. The market is not an accommodation machine. It owes you nothing.

Seeing the Blind Spots

Bernstein has been described as a master of the "art of holding hands." Indeed, his quiet, knowing manner about stock-market behavior can be quite comforting—words of wisdom from a genteel family doctor. Bernstein is methodical and scientific about the stock market; he seems able to tune out the noise that causes so many investors to act against their best interests.

Yet Bernstein also can appreciate the emotional volatility that investors feel. It's important, he says, to be realistic about what the market can give—and what it can take away. Sure, he'd be the first to agree that the market can be a roller coaster; thrills and chills, he'll remind you, are part of the deal. You can control portfolio volatility, but only to a point. You might, for instance, believe that the market gains of the late 1990s will continue and the Dow Jones Industrial Average will keep humming past thousand-point milestones like a car's odometer. You could be fabulously right—or terribly wrong. For his own peace of mind, Bernstein leaves no stone unturned, secure in the knowledge that nothing is certain:

I begin every day with the mantra "I don't know." The long-term case for equities is powerful. But we really don't know if it's going to replicate itself. There may be miracles, there may be disasters, but you can't predict them. You have to get up every morning with a clear recognition that you don't know what's

going to happen, and manage your affairs accordingly. Surprises come along, and long-established relationships get out of whack.

The trouble is, we want to know. Understandably, we want to believe that life will be good to us, investment decisions will pan out, intelligence and foresight will bring us comfort and stability. It's also understandable that we are filled with doubts and fears that what we'll end up with is not financial security but financial scarcity. "What's going to happen with the market?" is a question that is constantly asked of Wall Street professionals, pundits and anyone who follows stocks with more than a passing interest. What that query really means is "What will happen to me?"

What can anyone say? A doctor can't guarantee that a patient will respond to treatment. A parent can't completely assure a child's safety. In truth, who knows?

But who wants to hear that? So instead of simply saying "I don't know" when asked for investment advice, you try to fashion a reply. You might first toss off a flip quip like "Buy low. Sell high." Then, feeling a bit sheepish, you take an authoritative stance. If you're bullish, you might trot out the broad historical argument for stocks—it's a compelling and factual claim, after all—and explain how the Standard & Poor's 500-stock index has proved a better inflation-adjusted investment than cash or bonds throughout the twentieth century. If stocks continue to match their historical average since 1926, you would point out, then the value of your investment portfolio would double roughly every seven years. But in fairness, you would pause to caution about the inevitable shocks and blocks along the way.

Depending on your audience, you also might launch into a brief analysis of the current state of the economy, interest rates, technology, worker productivity, consumer confidence and maybe even the demographically influenced spending and savings patterns of the baby boom generation. Bearish investors would address the same issues, but advocate a "duck-and-cover" approach.

Bernstein maintains more objectivity. Visiting his Manhattan office, you won't see market play-by-play from financial news network CNBC or a real-time stock ticker on a television screen. In fact, there's no television. Doesn't Bernstein ever get caught up in the market's day-to-day gyrations? "No," he replies. "What am I going to do about it?" He adds:

> **A good investor is realistic about the nature of the market, which is a bunch of other people making decisions that may or may not be right. The future is unpredictable, and you have to make decisions and choices from that assumption. The "long run" is a very long run; it's not necessarily somebody's adult life.**

We can't possibly know more about the long run than the short run. You don't know as much about next week as you do about today. In his classic book about Hollywood, *Adventures in the Screen Trade*, Academy Award–winning scriptwriter William Goldman shared a key insight about the movie business that investors ought to find relevant. "Nobody knows anything," he asserted. "Not one person in the entire motion picture industry *knows* for a certainty what's going to work. Every time out it's a guess—and, if you're lucky, an educated one."[1]

Stock-market forecasting follows a similar script. Bernstein observes that long-range forecasts fall into two groups. The first type of forecaster looks at market trends over the past few years and extrapolates a potential outcome from this recent past. A second approach is to dispense with history and paint a grand vision of the market's future. Bernstein asserts that of the two choices, extrapolation makes more sense:

> **Important change occurs infrequently, in bursts, not gradually, so that extrapolations at least provide a road map that we can follow to detect when deviations from past experience begin to show up. The total-break-with-the-past forecasts assume that**

we know much more about the future than we can possibly know. Only by luck will the real thing turn out to resemble such a forecast.

The Performance Game

Nobody knows anything. But they certainly can learn. A good place to begin, however difficult, is to acknowledge that in a marketplace that is mostly, but not totally, efficient, anything can still happen. Thinking that you're somehow immune invites complacency.

Clearly, investors overreact and underreact to market and world events. Uncertainty is not inherently bad; it's your enemy when jarring price jolts shake you out of the market, but can be a friend when volatility offers buying opportunities. When bellwether telecommunications giant Lucent Technologies cautioned in early January 2000 that it would miss Wall Street's first-quarter earnings estimates by a wide margin, skittish investors knocked 40 percent off Lucent's share price in a single trading day. Did the warning damage the company's fundamental, long-term outlook? That remains to be seen. Yet 179 million Lucent shares changed hands that chaotic day—eight times average volume. Sellers bailed and buyers sailed. Just eight weeks later, Lucent had recovered every inch of lost ground and was trading at its pre-alarm level.

Which side of this trade would you have been on? Where would you have stood after the crash of October 1987? Or the bear market of 1973–74? Or 1962? Or 1957? Lucent shareholders were alone in feeling the pain of a 40 percent correction. What would you do if the *entire* S&P 500 index suffered a 40 percent decline and stayed flat for several months, not weeks?

These are tough questions that all investors must ask themselves. Start by saying, "It's *no* different this time." Then you'll either be better equipped for adversity, or pleasantly surprised by its absence. Bernstein explains that investors tend to focus on the hole and not the doughnut; they obsess about lost opportunities rather than look at what they've gained.

Such an avaricious mind-set is especially rampant in frothy bull markets. Doubling your money in six months isn't enough when others are tripling theirs. Frustration, jealousy and anger rise to a slow boil. In 1998 and 1999, Internet and other technology growth stocks ruled the market. The Russell 2000 Growth Index of small-capitalization stocks rose 78 percent between January 1999 and March 2000, while the countervailing Russell 2000 Value Index declined 1 percent. Shareholders in value funds pulled money first and asked questions later. Fund managers were often forced to sell stocks that were already down to cover net-asset outflows, which had a snowball effect on prices.

Investors who avoided these hot growth sectors could only watch agape as Internet millionaires, and sometimes billionaires, were created literally overnight. A timely editorial cartoon of the day showed a man and a woman sitting on cheap folding chairs outside their run-down trailer home. The woman is screaming at her hapless mate: "Can't you come up with one 'dot-com' idea?"

What did you do in the Internet revolution? Not enough? When so much money is sloshing about, nothing seems enough. "If only" becomes a call to action—and to your broker. "If only" you had bought Web portal Yahoo! before the world knew about it. "If only" you had grabbed shares of Internet rocket Commerce One at its $21-a-share initial public offering in July 1999. By March 2000, the shares fetched $240 apiece. If only you had sold before they crashed.

Regrets, we all have a few. Regrettably, the impulse to get-rich-quick can destroy the most thoughtful investment plan. "If only" often becomes "Do it." So you leap, then look. If only we could tune out distractions. Says Bernstein:

There are two kinds of risk. The first is the risk that if you do something, you will lose. The other risk is that you fail to do

something and miss out on winning. This anxiety encourages us to take risks that we wouldn't take otherwise because we don't want to miss out. This is a natural kind of greed. In bull markets, it leads to people willing to take greater and greater risks the higher the market goes. They say, "I missed out on this; I want to be sure I don't miss out on the rest."

Shares Not Shared Alike

Envy creates a powerful motivation to invest—just not to invest wisely. "Market risk" assumes an entirely new meaning when investors ignore traditional valuation yardsticks and believe that this time, it really is different.

At these times, in fact, investor behavior really *is* different. The emergence of the Nasdaq stock market as a powerhouse exchange is a good example. In March 2000, the Nasdaq Composite Index, laden with high-flying technology stocks, including mainstays Microsoft, Cisco Systems, Intel and Sun Microsystems, hurdled the 5000 barrier. Investors stampeded into popular Internet and biotechnology stocks that had come to symbolize the "New Economy," and their appetite seemed insatiable. The Nasdaq had blown through 4000 two months before, and 3000 two months before that. On a chart, this explosion resembled a rocket's liftoff; on paper, some lucky investors were making a lot of money.

Many Nasdaq stocks commanded record market capitalizations—stock price multiplied by the number of shares outstanding. For instance, computer networking giant Cisco Systems had a valuation of $478 billion with the Nasdaq at 5000; in July 1998, when the Nasdaq raced past the 2000 level, Cisco was valued at $99 billion. Sun Microsystems, valued at $154 billion at Nasdaq 5000, had a $19 billion market-cap at Nasdaq 2000.

Phenomenal investor demand also lifted the market-cap of smaller Nasdaq-listed companies, particularly during nine dizzying weeks between late December 1999 and early March 2000 when the Nasdaq scaled 5000 from 4000. Some examples: data-storage leader Network Appliance's market-cap soared to $36 billion from $12 billion; computer-chip leader PMC-Sierra's market-cap reached $33 billion from $10 billion, shares of communications equipment upstart Juniper Networks were valued at $42 billion from $16 billion.

While euphoric investors eagerly embraced the New Economy Nasdaq, the 30 stalwart blue-chips of the Dow Jones Industrial Average were being tossed onto the "Old Economy" scrap heap. The venerable Dow tumbled below 10,000—a level first crossed on its way up in April 1999. Beaten-down blue-chips once were considered shelter in the storm, quality companies that would hold up in a bad market. This time, the waves washed over them. Established brand-names like Coca-Cola, Procter & Gamble and McDonald's—regulars on the safest corner of the Street—were ransacked, one by one. In early March 2000, 23 of the Dow 30 stocks were off 20 percent or more from their 52-week highs—the definition of a bear market.[2] Had the Dow enjoyed the same good fortune as the Nasdaq during the first 10 weeks of 2000, the average would have been at 13,000 instead of struggling to keep above 10,000.

Clearly, the U.S. stock market had become bifurcated. On one side were technology stocks. On the other: everything else. And so it was that billionaire Warren Buffett, one of the most successful investors of the twentieth century, felt compelled to apologize to Berkshire Hathaway shareholders in his annual chairman's letter recapping 1999—one of the company's toughest years ever. "We had the worst absolute performance of my tenure," a chagrined Buffett confessed. Holdings in Coke, Gillette, American Express and other hard-hit large consumer and financial stocks contributed to a 50 percent decline in Berkshire's Class A shares between June 1998 and March 2000. It was indeed truly amazing that Buffett, who only two years before was lauded as the "Oracle of Omaha," a quiet sage revered for his Midas touch, should now be penning a self-criticism in which he labeled himself the "guilty party."

How do you describe investing under circumstances like this? "Precarious" and "speculative" are two words that come to mind—right before "bubble." Stocks of companies with no earnings and unproved revenue usually don't streak into outer space while shares of well-known, established, profitable companies become too cheap. And when a small number of stocks swing the market averages, the increasing concentration creates razor-sharp volatility. Stock-market news grabs the nightly headlines. Everyone seems to have a surefire stock, a day trade, a get-rich-quick start-up scheme. Perhaps not surprisingly, the unsettled environment makes many investors feel both giddy and guarded, the way people act in a tense game of musical chairs.

Such a topsy-turvy market calls for a cool head like Bernstein's:

We don't know exactly how to measure risk. And we sure don't know how to measure the market. It's crazy that a small number of stocks can swing the averages. Those stocks are not representative of most people's portfolios. Also, the indices become very risky because they're not diversified. People who are doing spectacularly well don't realize that they're doing it because they took very big risks.

I'm a big believer in diversification, because I'm totally convinced that forecasts will be wrong. Diversification is the guiding principle. That's the only way you can live through the hard times. It's going to cost you in the short run, because not everything will be going through the roof.

Stock buyers find many ways to justify this new investing paradigm: The "next new thing" is here; new technologies are revolutionary; the "new" economy is burying the "old"; inflation is dead; the business cycle is dead; economic recession—dead again.

Unfortunately, this logic is dead wrong. It's true that technological advancements and productivity gains have been remarkable, especially among U.S.-based companies. And it seems that in the United States at least, runaway inflation has become less of an economic threat. But markets have a way of correcting imbalances. You should not expect positive or negative conditions to persist indefinitely. The stocks of young, innovative Internet companies may soar on a promise and a prayer, but not if they fail to produce meaningful earnings.

But investors in early 2000 paid little heed. In fact, they were pricing growth stocks as if the U.S. economy were verging on collapse when all signs pointed to a continuation of the country's Great Boom. Remember that when corporate earnings growth is abundant, the market prices it like water; when growth is scarce, the market prices it like diamonds. If earnings were decelerating, then the high multiples of the technology sector and the "Nifty Fifty" of the S&P 500 would be understandable. But the profit outlook for U.S. companies was bullish, with reasonably optimistic earnings news.

In such a hopeful environment, bargain-hungry investors ought to be scooping up value stocks like those in Buffett's portfolio. Instead, a "bargain" was a knocked-down tech stock. It was a period when many otherwise levelheaded investors became disconnected from value. This was a momentum-driven market, in which successively higher prices were paid in the hope that fast-growing companies would continue their eye-popping upward trajectories. That's the essence of the momentum game: Winners repeat. Be a winner, or watch others win. The choice is yours.

Many investors do sit on the sidelines in feverish markets—but only for a while. Pretty soon they get fed up with losing out simply because they can't justify stocks with triple-digit price-earnings multiples—or no earnings at all. The party and locker-room chatter can be deafening—and demoralizing. You got a 25 percent annual return from a mutual fund? Big deal. Plenty of Internet stocks move that much in a few trading days.

Bragging rights in a bull market can take on an importance not seen since junior high. An uncomfortable feeling starts to develop—it gets worse if you're familiar with these high-flying companies and their technologies. Maybe you access the Internet through America Online, search the Web and track investments through Yahoo!, and order Chinese takeout with your Qualcomm mobile phone. If you followed Peter Lynch's investment formula of buying what you know and use, there's probably a good argument for those stocks to be in your portfolio. But they aren't, and the awful realization sinks in that you've been missing out on some of the biggest gains of the past decade. The car is ready, and you're standing next to the buggy, whip in hand.

A nagging question gnaws at you: If you're so smart, why aren't you rich—or richer? And one day you throw in the towel. If Cisco is soaring, then go long Cisco. If Internet stocks have journeyed to the outer limits, then buckle up and ride with them. You do a bit of soul-searching and rationalization, and decide that you have nothing to lose except your original investment—same as always. And if the Internet really is the greatest innovation since peanut butter, and will improve daily life like the toaster did, then Internet and other technology stocks are undervalued and you can't possibly lose. You start to love the big-game stocks and the big scores they bring. It's so easy; why didn't you do this sooner? Bernstein offers a couple of good reasons:

> **Love affairs are the wrong way to manage your assets. Stocks should probably be the largest asset class that you own. The case is strong enough that you probably place most of your bet in that direction. But if you bet 100 percent and you're wrong, you're going to mismanage the situation. That's the biggest risk of all—that you lose objectivity. Facts matter, but what other people are saying about them is always suspect. A big secret of investment is keeping your ears shut.**

How Are We Doing?

Individuals aren't the only investors who succumb to the moment. Professional investment advisers and money managers who take the plunge and chase performance. Many do so reluctantly, pushed by clients and shareholders who clearly are not in the mood for reality-based investing. For money managers in momentum-driven markets, standing on principle can be shakier than those high-priced stocks they disdain. And investor loyalty is only as good as last year's record; fall too far behind, and clients may vote with their wallets and leave.

The temptation to chase performance in fast-moving markets can be a real problem for money managers, whose compensation is figured as a percentage of the assets in their portfolio. When you manage other people's money, the more you get, the more you get. The dilemma in momentum-driven markets is that investors' impatience and sense of entitlement drive portfolio managers' decisions—except that professionals are supposedly being rewarded for their independence. At such times, more than usual, individual and professional investors both could use some perspective, Bernstein points out:

> When I started in the business in the 1950s and we managed individual portfolios, the Dow Jones Industrial Average was a bogey, but the clients didn't care. They just said, "How are we doing?" If the market went down they wanted to be sure they survived, and when it was going up there was a lot of competition at their cocktail parties. They always had friends who had done better, but essentially the question was "Are we doing all right?"
>
> That's probably the right question. Are you comfortable with how you're doing? If the market is going up, you want to be going up. You'd like to be going up more than the market, but not if it involves risks that you don't want to take. Each of us in our own gut has to decide how we feel about this.

Whatever Happened to the .400 Hitters?

In baseball, attaining a .400 batting average—four hits in every 10 at bats—is a crowning achievement. Most batters are lucky to average even .300 in a season, and the average for all players has hovered right around .260 since record-keeping began in 1870.

At least one batter reached .400 in nine of the 30 seasons between 1901 and 1930. Ty Cobb and Rogers Hornsby did it three times each. Ted Williams of the Boston Red Sox slugged out a .406 average in 1941. But since then, no player has managed to bat .400. Why? Not because hitters are less skilled, but more likely because fielding and defensive strategy have improved greatly.

Bernstein applies this analogy to the investment business and why money managers have such difficulty outperforming their benchmarks. Are today's managers less talented, or has the market become so efficient and informed that even exceptional managers are left swinging at the plate? "Where, Oh Where, Are the .400 Hitters of Yesteryear?" Bernstein wondered aloud in a newsletter he pens regularly for subscribers.[3]

"Few managers are any longer even trying to hit .400," Bernstein observes. "Growing numbers of today's investors are sufficiently educated, sophisticated and informed to block their way."[4] To be sure, in-depth professional research and historical data is available to anyone with a computer and a modem, so access to knowledge alone doesn't provide the competitive advantage it once did. Says Bernstein:

Competition is too tough for somebody to hit .400. The market is full of smart, eager, highly motivated, highly informed people. The top quintile is likely to beat the market, but it gets tougher to beat it by a lot. It's hard to be a winner by enough to matter, or to stay a winner by enough to matter. Even the best— even Warren Buffett—aren't able to beat the market by as much as they did in the past.

If investors want herdlike performance, they can simply buy an inexpensive index fund. Active managers must do more to add value. They should have the freedom to hold cash when they believe that stocks are richly priced, and to be aggressive when they spot value.

But financial advisers and portfolio managers often are dissuaded from acting on any deep conviction. Clients and shareholders want above-average returns—not shoot-the-lights-out showmanship. Accordingly, there's little incentive for investment professionals to attempt to hit .400. You can't beat the market by a lot unless you bet big. But if you fumble, shareholders flee. "Tracking error"—the deviation from that all-important benchmark—is active management's biggest nemesis. It's also a predicament that Bernstein can appreciate:

If you run a high-risk portfolio, there will be a big tracking error since the bets are not going to work out all the time. In the big years the client will say, "That's what we paid you for." In the bad years they'll say, "Get out of here." It's better to be safe than sorry.

The Premium for Risk

Stock investors expect to be compensated for taking additional risk. Shareholders receive an "equity risk premium" for the uncertainty. The equity risk premium hinges on the value of bonds and the level of interest rates. It follows that investors should buy stocks only when they promise a higher expected return than bonds. The difference between the two expected returns is the equity risk premium.

When people perceive equities as less risky—a surer thing—they are willing to pay higher prices for them. One of the most calming, bullish signals for U.S. stocks in the late 1990s was the country's historically low inflation rate. Says Bernstein:

Inflation is terrifying. It obscures the future. You don't know whether you're making a good purchase. Anything that isn't going to last beyond today becomes questionable. So inflation has got to be a very important consideration in what people will pay for stocks.

For investors in a low-inflation environment, something quite striking occurs. The equity risk premium shrinks because there is less risk apparent in the economy. What's more, a balanced portfolio of stocks and bonds looks sensible.

Cash traditionally has been an attractive diversification tool since it holds up against inflation better than bonds. When interest rates are climbing, cash can be invested short-term and reinvested at prevailing yields, while bonds—especially longer-term issues—are locked in at lower rates. But if low inflation is here for an extended stay, due to productivity gains and government policy, then adding bonds to a portfolio is timely, Bernstein says. Most important, with an unwinding of inflation fears, investors could look at bonds as an entity independent from stocks, valued on their own fundamentals. Adds Bernstein:

> **The long run is not relevant all the time. A critically important element that makes me skeptical about the conventional risk-premium approach is that most of it is based on the experience of the last 40 or 50 years—a unique event in the bond market that's not likely to replay. The bond market is a separate consideration. What happens in the bond market is irrelevant to the stock market. You have to think about the stock market as separate from the bond market, and make judgments about it without regard to interest rates.**

So Bernstein recommends that investors seriously consider adding bonds to a portfolio. U.S. Treasuries and top-flight corporate securities offer a high degree of comfort. He explains:

> **Bonds are there so when the stock market goes down, you don't sell out in a panic. That's really why I own bonds. They're the security blanket that enables you to manage your stocks intelligently. A very important part of the equity decision is what you have in bonds. The bond portion enables me, as a risk-averse investor, to own equities without panicking. A bad**

investor is an investor who sells out when the stock market is down. To be a good investor, set yourself up so you won't be a bad investor. Because, believe me, the temptation to sell when it's going down is hard to resist.

On the Trail of the Pioneers

Bernstein was raised in the 1930s during the Great Depression, a watershed event that profoundly influenced his thinking about how people handle personal finances and investments. In 1929, his father had sold his family's business, joined a New York brokerage firm, and invested proceeds from that sale into the stock market. A few months later, in October 1929, the market crashed. Prices finally hit bottom in late 1932—nearly 90 percent below their 1929 highs.

The hardship of those years, Bernstein confides, probably has made him a more conservative investor than was actually necessary. It also likely helped him when he took over his father's investment management business in the early 1950s, for he could empathize with people who in good faith had entrusted their savings to the decisions of complete strangers. What we call "the market," after all, essentially is a giant trust exercise between personalities who might not get along together alone in a room, but cooperate on the trading floor. "I can recall many clients during bull markets who thanked me for the way I was making them richer," Bernstein has noted. "I always reminded them that they were thanking the wrong person. Their gratitude was due instead to all those other nice investors out there who were willing to pay higher prices for their assets than we had paid when we acquired them."

Bernstein has long been fascinated by what drives investors. So it seems natural that he would gravitate to studying the pioneers of finance who fostered theories and ideas that money managers and marketers on Wall Street have turned into investment products and tools.

For Bernstein, the three most important "capital ideas" that have influenced the evolution and maturation of investing are Markowitz's Portfolio Theory, William Sharpe's Capital Asset Pricing Model and Eugene Fama's Efficient Market Hypothesis. Together, they form a holy trinity of investing. "The theories are so basic," Bernstein explains, "they're sort of like the Law of Gravity."

Bernstein credits Markowitz for a concept that is not fancy or complicated—just pure and elegant. Over the decades since Portfolio Theory was introduced, many have tried to gild the thesis with elaborate additions and interpretations, but its powerful original message remains: You don't get a return without taking risk, and you should expect to be proportionately compensated for the level of uncertainty you face. "Harry is the high priest," explains Bernstein. "You have to think about risk as well as return. And if you think about risk, you have to deal with it."

Risk is such an integral aspect of investing—no pain, no profit—it's remarkable that this framework wasn't already part of the liturgy. It's not as if investors in the early 1950s weren't aware of the risk-reward trade-off—both the Depression and World War II had brought a generation face-to-face with loss and victory. But Markowitz quantified market risk. Bernstein is struck by Markowitz's choice of "portfolio" to underpin his work. Diversification is Markowitz's risk-management strategy, and a portfolio by definition involves a collection of various assets. Using "portfolio" to illustrate the theory is a calculated way to encourage investors to judge a stock not in isolation, but in relation to their other assets. Such a global approach to investing had not been seen in finance before, as Bernstein observes:

> **Prior to Markowitz, people were aware of risk, obviously. Widows' and orphans' portfolios were not invested like aggressive businessmen's. There was a sense that different people had different appetites and capacities for risk, and you adjusted a portfolio accordingly. But that there was a systematic relationship between risk and expected return, and that once you**

thought in those terms it set out a portfolio management paradigm for you—that was his idea and it was not there before.

William Sharpe put his own indelible stamp on Markowitz's theory. Bernstein clearly respects the important ways that Sharpe has helped investors to become more aware of how the money game is played. After all, the market may not care about you, but you certainly care a great deal about it. Bernstein praises Sharpe as the "Son of Markowitz"—no small compliment. As we will learn in the next chapter, Sharpe's innovative thinking in the early 1960s led to the introduction of a then-radical concept called the Capital Asset Pricing Model. Sharpe focused his study of risk on the portfolio's "covariance"—the way securities acted and reacted with each other. As Bernstein describes it, Sharpe's work made Portfolio Theory more accessible. Instead of Markowitz's painstaking task of comparing the risk-reward relationship of each stock against every other holding, the Capital Asset Pricing Model reduced the equation to the interaction between an asset and the market as a whole. Notes Bernstein:

The Capital Asset Pricing Model tremendously simplified the method that Markowitz laid out. The model, in its full flower, says the market is efficient, and the optimal portfolio is the market. You can take that or leave that, but it's important because it focuses on diversification and on covariance, which is really the essence of taking risk. Controlling volatility is fundamental if you're going to be a survivor.

The last bold investment theory in the triangle is the Efficient Market Hypothesis, which says that the price of a security reflects all available information known to investors. Stock buyers believe their shares are worth more than what they paid, while sellers assume their shares are worth less than the sale price. But if players in an efficient market buy and sell at the "right" price, then security selection essentially is a waste of time, and superior investment performance is largely due to luck, not skill.

The Efficient Market Hypothesis is the culmination of work that Fama, now a professor at the University of Chicago, conducted in the mid-1960s. Fama claims that current securities prices reflect not only past events, but also events that the market expects will occur in the future. This theory has asserted enormous influence over investors, advisers and portfolio managers who are skeptical about active management. It has created a parallel universe to active management, in which naysayers are able to argue persuasively that the opportunity for even the most skilled investor to outperform the market is so remote, it's not even worth trying. Just buy an index fund, they say, and match the market's return.

Princeton University professor Burton Malkiel helped to evangelize this belief in *A Random Walk Down Wall Street*, published in 1973. He characterizes stock selection as a "random walk" that discounts individual talent and insight. The random walk theory claims that stock prices are unpredictable: You can't forecast where a stock is heading based on where it's been. If Amazon.com drops three points today, for instance, that says nothing about how it will act next week. As Malkiel writes: "The market is so efficient—prices move so quickly when new information does arise—that no one can consistently buy or sell quickly enough to benefit."[5]

Bernstein says he's not completely convinced of that:

I don't think that all information is immediately available. All information doesn't carry the same meaning to all investors. More important, there is an implicit notion that there's a "right price," an equilibrium price, and if the market deviates from that, it will come back. I don't believe there is an equilibrium price. Equilibrium means stability and standing still. Life doesn't stand still.

The market is highly efficient, Bernstein surmises, but not completely. Proponents of behavioral finance like Richard Thaler, the subject of an earlier chapter, claim that the Efficient Market

Hypothesis is flawed because it assumes that every investor is rational, and people are not always so levelheaded. It's difficult to be rational when you don't know the future; rationality and perspective comes easier in hindsight. Says Bernstein:

> The case for active management is much stronger than the efficient-market people would lead us to believe. Active management is extraordinarily difficult, because there are so many knowledgeable investors and information does move so fast. But active management is impossible and not worth doing? That's wrong. The market is hard to beat. There are a lot of smart people trying to do the same thing. Nobody's saying that it's easy. But possible? Yes.

Possible, but probable? The fact that the average is tough to outperform would seem to speak well for an indexed approach. And indeed, Bernstein admits, his "gut sense" is that passive investing—buying an index fund—is the best strategy overall. "My greatest comfort is with the money I have in index funds," he admits. But, he notes, even that approach is flawed:

> What am I going to invest passively in? I'm still making a decision. If I'm going to own an S&P 500 index fund, which I used to think was the answer to all maidens' prayers, I'm buying a very undiversified portfolio in which the greatest weights are the stocks that have gone up the most. Is that really how I want to invest? The passive choice is an active one. There isn't any place to hide.

CHAPTER 9

We're All Investors Now:
William Sharpe

"Concentrate far more on using the market than beating it. Focus on questions of asset allocation, diversification and changes through time. Spend more time on tailoring the portfolio to your needs and circumstances."

William F. Sharpe shared the 1990 Nobel Prize in Economic Sciences for his groundbreaking work on asset allocation and for simplifying the ways that investors measure and control portfolio risk. Most people would consider that a career capper. But Sharpe is constantly retooling the wheel. The prominent economist retired from Stanford University in 1999 after nearly four decades of teaching and research. His current endeavor is no less consuming: collaborating with a Web-based financial advisory company he founded to harness the democratic power of the Internet and bring sophisticated Wall Street portfolio analysis to Main Street.

Nothing simple for Sharpe, who instead tries to make things easy for others. "I like to think of myself as being fairly much a revolutionary," he says. "I try to change the way people look at problems and solve them."

A big problem for individual investors is that just like corporations, pension funds, investment firms and financial advisers, they yearn to achieve the highest investment returns for the least amount of risk. But individuals, unless they have a skilled adviser or broker, don't have access to the computer programs and high-priced consultants that institutional investors rely on to craft winning portfolios.

So Sharpe, a self-described "computer freak" with his own Web site (www.wsharpe.com), conceived of blending professional investment advice and financial planning software into an affordable personal finance service for individuals, delivered via the Web. In 1996, Sharpe founded and became chairman of Financial

Engines (www.financialengines.com), an online service that assists individual investors in retirement and life planning and aims to teach them better personal finance skills. Subscribers create goal-oriented portfolios based on risk tolerance and expected return, updated daily to reflect changing market conditions. Just a couple of computer mouse-clicks tell you whether you're on track to a fulfilling lifestyle after you've stopped working.

Will you have enough money to live comfortably in retirement? The answer to that question matters far more than whether the Dow Jones Industrial Average is up or down 300 points today. Long-run results depend on a portfolio's asset mix and the unique risks of each holding. The right recipe depends on how much income you will need to retire with ease and how rough of a ride you can live with in the meantime.

Except when you're late for work and scrambling to get kids to school, the optimal combination of stocks, bonds, cash and risk isn't exactly a top priority. It's just that employers have made it so. The responsibility to allocate an employer-sponsored 401(k) or other retirement plan is being delegated increasingly to employees. These workers may know a lot about their jobs, but very little about asset allocation. Investing the money wisely is complicated enough, but the challenge is not just handling investments—but managing investment risk. Once these issues were a pension fund's concern—now they're yours. Yet employers typically don't retain investment counselors for their staff, and a mutual fund prospectus won't tell you if its inherent risks match your goals and temperament. This trend troubles Sharpe, who observes:

Investment decisions are moving to individuals who are ill-prepared to make them. These are complicated issues. To say, "Here are 8,000 mutual funds—or even 10—do what's right," is not very helpful. And the advice that people are getting seems to ignore risk. They're bookkeeping schemes in which you earn 9 percent every year like clockwork and die right on schedule. There's no uncertainty at all. Making a decision as to how much to save in

stocks, bonds or cash without acknowledging uncertainty, let alone trying to estimate it, seems to me the height of folly.

All That Glitters

How much investment risk am I willing to take? How much should I save? What investments should I buy? What are the chances that I'll reach my retirement goal? How do I keep income flowing through retirement? All of these concerns are crucial to your financial well-being, but your response to the first question will set the stage for the rest.

Nobody can accurately predict what the future will bring, of course. That's why it's important to reach a level of comfort with both the investment risk of your portfolio and the consequences if things don't go as planned. Perhaps you assume that the stocks in your portfolio will return an average of nearly 29 percent each year, just what the Standard & Poor's 500 index achieved from January 1995 through December 1999. That would be fantastic, but you also must allow that you probably will be sorely disappointed. To begin with, the annual average pretax return from U.S. stocks between 1926 and 1999 was 11.3 percent, and even that result is hardly a given.[1]

Realistic investors must recognize the fact that between now and retirement, their investment results might fare well below average. There's also the chance that market sentiment could take a terrible turn at the worst possible moment. Suppose you're 64 years old, with two-thirds of your investment assets in large-capitalization, blue-chip U.S. stocks. You're looking forward to retirement in less than a year. Investors have been wildly bullish, but the market is looking toppy. After much hand-wringing, you decide to hold your positions. Then the S&P 500 promptly loses 25 percent of its value in a week and treads water for months.

What can you do? Such bad luck would take a big toll on your retirement plans. You wouldn't necessarily have to abandon your dreams, but you would have to adjust your immediate expectations. Until market conditions improved, you could work longer, dip into savings or reduce your income needs.

But if you're 34 years old and most of your retirement wealth will come from future contributions, a 25 percent drop in the market, while mentally jarring, is really a drop in the bucket. Panicked selling and short-term thinking only hurt your chances of getting what you want. Invariably, people sell when prices are falling and buy when confidence returns and prices are higher. This is precisely the opposite of what you should do, though admittedly that's easier said than done. Sharpe says:

If you just take somebody's current investments and project it without any notion of risk, you give a wildly distorted view of what the future might hold. It may be the best estimate if you've done it carefully, but they have no notion of how good or bad it can get. So when and if it gets bad, they're likely to be desperately disappointed if they're already retired, and do the wrong thing if they haven't retired.

Give people a sense of why they should or shouldn't be worried about changing market conditions, and they're inclined to make informed, reasonable decisions. Information is key when stock-market volatility is high and prices come unhinged. But while many computerized financial planning programs offer a glimpse into the future, they often are just one-dimensional snapshots that spotlight return—but not risk.

The retirement planning tool on the Quicken Web site (www .quicken.com/retirement), for example, does a simple and straightforward review of your financial prospects. First, type in your age, salary and personal savings. Say you're 45 years old, a corporate vice president making $75,000 a year, with $180,000 invested in U.S. equities and $70,000 in cash. You'd like to retire at 65 with an income of $60,000 a year—or 80 percent of your preretirement salary.

Will you scale that goal—and how long will the money last? Factor in an annual 10 percent investment return, 3 percent annual inflation rate, Social Security income, and the Quicken program flashes a green light. "Your plan is succeeding!" it cries. At retirement, you'll have a net worth of roughly $823,000, promises the computer, enough to last until you're at least 81.

Congratulations—except the Quicken program doesn't say that you have only a 50 percent chance of reaching this magic number, and an equal chance of falling behind. And the value of your portfolio at retirement will change greatly depending on whether big gains come early, compounding in value for more than a decade, or just a few years before you're handed the gold watch.

Still, the conventional wisdom behind these calculators often assumes that if you invest X dollars now, you'll have Y at retirement. That's misleading, says Sharpe, because it doesn't account for things to go terribly wrong:

We can say with great assurance that you will not have Y. It's like saying, "Tell me what the temperature will be on the day of my retirement ceremony." I can say, "The weather will be 57 degrees." What does that number mean? It means there's a 50 percent chance it will be more than that and a 50 percent chance it will be less. But if you really think it's going to be 57 degrees exactly, then you can be making some disastrous decisions. And you certainly can't make investment decisions, which are inherently risk-and-return trade-offs, if you don't have risk to look at. If you assume there is no risk, then you say, "Let's put all my money in stocks, because they give the highest return."

A more useful tool would be a series of best-case and worst-case outcomes, ranging around a median portfolio value. To design an optimal basket of investments, Financial Engines computes thousands of potential economic scenarios and historical rates of return for 15 distinct asset classes. It analyzes interest and inflation rates, along with the performance of large, medium and small U.S. stocks—in both value and growth investment styles—and the stocks of emerging markets, Europe and the Pacific. Financial Engines tracks 11,000 mutual funds and more than 6,000 stocks. The software also crunches the expected return of long-, intermediate- and short-term government bonds, mortgage bonds, U.S. corporate bonds and international bonds.

Financial Engines estimated that our 45-year-old executive, assuming a level of risk about equal to the market, would have a 47 percent chance of achieving a $60,000-a-year retirement income, with a median portfolio value of $674,000. But it also computes a range of possibilities. In the best of all worlds, income would reach $138,000 a year with a portfolio value of $2.1 million. In half of the scenarios, estimated annual income is at least $58,400. Worst case, the portfolio would generate just $32,000 a year with a total value of just $215,000. To improve your odds, you have a few options: work longer, save more, lower your sights or take more risk.

Planning Ahead

Investors seeking professional help with personal finances traditionally enlist a registered investment adviser or financial planner to establish a savings and investment blueprint, and then prescribe a series of actions. You either pay the adviser to handle the portfolio, or self-manage it.

The financial advice business is split between "fee-only" and "fee-based" planners who often steer clients into mutual funds. Fee-only planners charge clients a percentage of assets under management, on top of fund expenses. In contrast, "fee-based" planners work on commission from fund companies. Fee-only planners generally recommend funds that do not levy a "load," or sales commission. Fee-based planners, including brokerage and bank representatives, ordinarily select load funds.

In choosing an adviser, remember that you are the employer— not the other way around. You're looking for someone to trust. Don't hesitate to ask pointed questions that you would of any potential employee. The expertise of financial planners varies widely, so examine backgrounds closely and request to speak with at least three current clients.

As a resource, the National Association of Personal Financial Planners has a financial planner interview form on its Web site (www.napfa.org/intrview.htm), with a list of "tough questions to ask" of a prospective candidate. Besides inquiring into a planner's education, experience and compensation, you're also encouraged to be explicit. Some suggestions: "Have you ever been cited by a professional or regulatory governing body for disciplinary reasons?", "Do you take possession of, or have access to, my assets?" and "Does any member of your firm act as a general partner, participate in or receive compensation from investments you may recommend to me?" You should also ask an adviser for a copy of his firm's Form ADV Part II registration with the Securities and Exchange Commission, commonly known as an "ADV," which discusses the firm and the background of its officers in greater detail.

Once you've picked an adviser, you can then begin to learn more about your own attitudes toward money and investing. Expect a test of your risk temperature, often with a personality-oriented questionnaire that typecasts you as a conservative, moderate or aggressive investor. From this baseline result, a tailored investment portfolio is allocated accordingly between stocks, mutual funds, bonds and cash. Over the course of your relationship, the adviser will fashion the portfolio to your specific needs, and will be on-call to keep you on track.

Risk-tolerance questionnaires also figure prominently on many financial Web sites, particularly those from leading mutual fund companies and major Wall Street brokerages. Their goal, besides trying to sell their funds and professional investing service, is for you to develop a baseline comfort level with market swings—useful knowledge in building a portfolio. A standard tactic is to ask what you would do if the stock market suffered a sudden 20 percent drop in value: sell everything, do nothing or buy more. Choosing to buy more would indicate a greater ability to withstand investment risk—at least over the short term.

But often these checklists promise more than they deliver, and some are downright unfathomable, like a rambling multiple-choice test from the Safeco family of funds (www.safecofunds .com) that includes the following query: "You happen to be in Las Vegas for business. You would: (a) head straight for the poker tables; (b) play the slot machines; (c) never even think of gambling." Other questions ask what you would do if you won $100 in a lottery—perhaps "(c) go out on the town"—and if you're the kind of soul who gives to charities soliciting at airports.

What do these questions have in common with investment risk and diversification? The Las Vegas reference suggests that the stock market is a casino. But maybe someone who wouldn't dream of gambling at the tables has a steady habit of gobbling up initial stock offerings of technology start-ups.

A questionnaire like this tells you something about your personal behavior, but virtually nothing about your investing behavior, and this sort of time-consuming exercise frustrates Sharpe. To him, whether your risk profile makes you a turtle or a tiger is meaningless. What really matters is that you set realistic investment goals that spring from the amount of portfolio risk you are willing to accept. Sharpe contends that people don't give enough thought to their risk tolerance, so they end up with portfolios that they ordinarily might not choose. He adds:

The way you need to answer the question "How much risk should I take?" is: "If I get more aggressive, will I meet my retirement goals? How bad could it be in a bad year?"

Capital, Assets and Other Comforts

Sharpe's efforts to demystify investing date back to 1960, when Harry Markowitz's Portfolio Theory was not widely known and Sharpe was a 26-year-old researcher at the RAND Corporation, an influential Los Angeles–based think tank. At the time, Sharpe was a Ph.D. candidate at the University of California at Los Angeles in need of a dissertation topic.

A professor suggested he pay a visit to Markowitz, a fellow economist seven years his senior who was just settling in at RAND. Sharpe was well versed with "Portfolio Selection," Markowitz's seminal 1952 introduction of Portfolio Theory, expanded in a 1959 book. In fact, you might even call Sharpe a Markowitz fan, struck as he was by Portfolio Theory's simple but elegant explanation of the inherent relationship between risk, return and diversification.

So Sharpe strode down the hall and introduced himself. Neither of them knew it then, but that casual knock on Markowitz's office door would forever change investing.

Before Markowitz, people intuitively understood the importance of diversifying against market mistakes. But they had no concrete means of interpreting their risk-reward trade-off. Markowitz showed them. His risk-measurement tool allowed investors to fashion stronger portfolios. Markowitz and Portfolio Theory is to investing what Henry Ford and the Model A is to transportation—a pioneering innovator with a disruptive technology that ultimately would set a new standard.

When Sharpe and Markowitz met, the two scholars found they had much in common, notably an appreciation of computers, numbers and the unpredictability of chance. Markowitz agreed to the role of Sharpe's unofficial thesis adviser. Sharpe's official project was to simplify Portfolio Theory and make it more accessible.

Not only would Sharpe streamline and popularize Markowitz's work, he soon would eclipse his mentor with his own revolutionary tool for valuing securities and assessing their risk. The Capital Asset Pricing Model was remarkable on many levels, as we will discover later in this chapter, but what really sets it apart is its practicality and usefulness. Indeed, one of Sharpe's great strengths has been his ability to shape investment theories into substance. Over the past four decades, investors have readily grasped his insights and used them to make better-informed buy-and-sell decisions. Markowitz himself offers glowing praise: "Sharpe is a more gregarious fellow than I am," he confides. "I had left finance and was doing linear programming. Sharpe got around and spoke to people in the business. He's the one who really got this field started."[2]

Puzzling Over Pieces

The meeting of these two uncompromising minds, Sharpe and Markowitz, would lead to breathtaking investment breakthroughs that resonate still. In their conversations, Markowitz conferred with Sharpe about the many ways that various assets in a portfolio will interact, or correlate, and the difficulty in classifying these complex relationships. Markowitz had covered vast theoretical ground on this subject in "Portfolio Selection," advocating diversified portfolios to mitigate risk. But actually building these efficient investment vehicles was a daunting and expensive proposition.

"Portfolio Selection" noted that an investment portfolio contains two elements: expected return and risk. Expected return is how a group of securities might perform based on assumptions about a company's future earnings, cash flow, sales and other relevant business factors—and your confidence in this analysis. Risk is all the things that could go wrong not only with a specific company and the market itself, but also with the *combination* of securities in the portfolio. Just as some people are matched better than others, so it goes with investments. As Sharpe recalls:

Markowitz came along, and there was light. Until Markowitz, no theory even took risk into account. Markowitz's procedures were designed to answer the question "If you've made estimates of a security's risk and correlation, what's the best way to build a portfolio?" But they were silent on where those estimates would come from, and if there was a natural relationship among securities in which higher expected return carried more risk.

Markowitz figured that Portfolio Theory could be made more accessible, useful—and cheaper—giving investors a real-world understanding of how various holdings interact, or *correlate*. For instance, if you knew that the trading activity of General Motors stock was highly consistent with that of Ford, you probably would not own shares in both companies. But how would adding shares of General Electric affect a portfolio that included Ford or GM? Is what's good for General Motors also good for General Electric, or do the stocks of these two industrial giants act independently enough to offer an investor true diversification?

If investors could grasp an elementary understanding of this concept, Markowitz thought, they might avoid the asset concentration and overlap that can saddle a portfolio with unintentional risks and drag down performance. He invited Sharpe to take a shot at creating a populist method to measure portfolio risk and volatility.

Not only did Sharpe take a shot, he hit a bull's-eye. In "A Simplified Model for Portfolio Analysis," his 1961 dissertation, Sharpe streamlined Portfolio Theory with an assumption that one key factor, which he called "systematic risk"—later dubbed "beta"— influenced a portfolio's volatility.

Beta measures the sensitivity of a security to the market that an investor hopes to outperform. For those who buy stocks of larger companies, the usual market benchmark is the S&P 500; investors in smaller stocks often use the Russell 2000 stock index, while international-stock investors frequently compare performance to the Morgan Stanley Capital International Europe, Australasia and Far East Index, commonly known as EAFE. Bondholders benchmark against the Lehman Brothers Aggregate Bond Index. In each case, the market beta is always expressed as 1.0, a reference point from which to sketch the risk profile of other investments. An asset with a beta above 1.0 is considered more volatile than the broad market, while a beta lower than 1.0 indicates below-market risk. Index funds, by definition, carry market risk, so generally have betas of 1.0.

Beta is only a guide, not an absolute, and should be considered along with other performance and valuation measures. Yet as a rule, beta clearly illustrates how adding or removing an asset from a portfolio impacts its overall risk versus the market. It's much easier to determine how, for example, General Electric alters the risk and expected return of your total portfolio compared to the Standard & Poor's 500-stock index than it is to calculate GE's influence on every last portfolio holding.

The Pricing Is Right

The Simplified Model encouraged Sharpe to delve deeper into the workings of investment risk—with striking results. It makes perfect sense that investors will always seek the highest return for the least amount of risk. It's also a given that diversification eliminates some risk, but not all. What part of risk-taking is compensated, Sharpe wondered, and what is not? He recalls:

> I asked the question, "In a simple world, what kind of risks would be rewarded in the long run?" The answer came out that there's no reason to expect reward just for bearing risk. Otherwise you'd make a lot of money in Las Vegas. If prices are sensible and markets are rational, you would expect to be rewarded for the risk of doing badly in bad times. If there's reward for risk, it's got to be special.

When you buy a stock, you expect the shares to perform well in good times, but you also take the chance that the stock price will not hold up during bad times. People naturally don't like to suffer the losses that a market downturn brings; in fact, those dark days are precisely when security and stability are most desired. For standing under this Damoclean sword, investors demand a greater potential payoff—a "risk premium"—to hold assets that can fare poorly when markets turn south. But when the future of a company or the market seems bright and optimism reigns, the premium for owning these shares tends to narrow.

Measuring the relationship of returns and the risk premium to the overall market formed the essence of Sharpe's 1964 paper "Capital Asset Prices: A Theory of Market Equilibrium Under Conditions of Risk." Soon after, economist Eugene Fama referred to the innovative work as the "Capital Asset Pricing Model," or CAPM—pronounced "cap-em." The label stuck. As Sharpe explains:

> **The key insight of the Capital Asset Pricing Model is that higher expected returns go with the greater risk of doing badly in bad times. Beta is a measure of that. Securities or asset classes with high betas tend to do worse in bad times than those with low betas.**

Every investment involves two distinct risks, the CAPM notes. The first is systematic risk, defined by beta. Systematic risk is an asset's sensitivity to conditions that move the entire market. Interest-rate changes, inflation, economic health and political upheaval are all sources of systematic risk. No matter how far and wide you diversify a portfolio, the swings in value that come from capricious events cannot be eliminated. Systematic risk is always present in an investment to a varying degree; it's the price of playing the game.

The second, unsystematic risk, is specific to each firm or industry. Sales slump, a key product fails, a dishonest manager absconds with the company payroll. Unforeseen setbacks happen all the time in business, but investors can smooth out these bumps through careful diversification. By strategically combining uncorrelated securities, for example, or offsetting long positions with short sales—a bet that a stock's price will fall—investors can fine-tune portfolio risk to suit their personal threshold.

Investors expect a sweetener for taking outsized risks, but because investments can be combined to reduce volatility, unsystematic risk should not be rewarded, Sharpe reasoned. Accordingly, he concluded, that leaves beta as the sole determinant of expected return. In that case, only systematic risk, or market risk, should be rewarded.

"Do you beat the market?" investment adviser Peter Bernstein recalls Sharpe asking him when they first met in 1969. Sharpe's bluntness took Bernstein off guard. "No one had ever asked me that question before," Bernstein wrote in *Capital Ideas: The Improbable Origins of Modern Wall Street*, his classic history of finance and investment. "In my world of investment counseling . . . it was unthinkable that any of us would ever deliver below-average returns."[3]

But Sharpe was coming from a CAPM world, where investors can hope to receive more than the market return only by accepting greater volatility in their portfolios. "If you want to have a shot at better-than-market return," Sharpe relates, "you've got to put yourself in a position where you can get really hammered if the market falls." If instead you choose to take less-than-market risk, you should expect below-market returns. A specialized mutual fund that invests in real estate investment trusts, for example, will tend to have a low beta since its performance is tied more tightly to the property market than the stock market. With its low correlation to stocks, it should deliver below-average returns in up markets and outperform high-beta assets in down markets.

Sharpe's elegant but bold argument rattled investment professionals in the 1960s and still reverberates today. Wall Street did not take kindly to the suggestion that investors could beat the market only by adding risk. Money managers at the time weren't accustomed to being so challenged, and "the market" was a nebulous concept, at best. There was no heated debate about efficient markets or any distinction between "active" and "passive" portfolio management. Clients would ask the professionals "How did you do?" and be satisfied with a single number. Today, an investment firm is remiss if it doesn't compare its return to a benchmark index. The bottom-line question is not "How did you do?" but "Did you do better than if I had invested in a passively managed fund?"

Portfolio managers who lament being judged on whether they are shouldering inordinate risk to achieve above-average performance can rail at the CAPM for giving investors the ability to make that call. "I didn't know how important it would be," Sharpe says now about his effort, "but I figured it was probably more important than anything else I was likely to do."

Yet over the years, the CAPM has come under fire for being too simplistic, too reliant on one unrealistic factor, to have any predictive value. By the 1980s, there were loud proclamations about the death of beta. In 1992, Fama and Yale University economist Kenneth French together devised a contentious theory that a stock's market capitalization and price-to-book value matter more than its beta. This "Three-Factor Model" acknowledges Sharpe's conclusion that investors get paid for being in the market—the equity premium—but they also receive an additional bonus for owning both small-cap stocks and "value" stocks that trade below "book," the net value of a company's total assets minus intangible assets and liabilities. Sharpe replies:

I'd be the last to argue that only one factor drives market correlation. There are not as many as some may think, but there's certainly more than one. The CAPM was a simple, strong set of assumptions that got a nice, clean result. Then we said, let's bring more complexity into it to try to get closer to the real

world. People—myself and others—went on to "extended" capital asset pricing models, where expected return is a function of beta, taxes, liquidity, dividend yield and other things people care about. Did the CAPM evolve? Of course. But the fundamental idea remains.

For the Capital Asset Pricing Model, beta and other contributions to finance and investing, Sharpe was awarded the 1990 Nobel Prize in Economic Sciences, a distinction he shared with Markowitz and the late economist Merton Miller. Today, Sharpe still pushes the edge—far out on his own efficient frontier.

The Efficient Investor

The first stock Sharpe bought was also one of his last. This was in the 1950s, when he was a young student with a caseload of classes about economics and markets. He had saved $450 to buy a car, but decided to apply his book learning and invest the money in a promising stock. After digging into financial statements and chatting with a broker, he found a hot buy in an established retailer. But within a few weeks, the $450 became $400 and Sharpe sold out. "I thought, this has proven—although it's a small sample—that I can't find the right securities," he recalls. "That raised my concern as to whether anyone else could."

Though Sharpe may not be an expert stock picker, he does know about constructing efficient portfolios. Since turning his attention to issues that concern individual investors, Sharpe has been trying to simplify the often-daunting process of picking mutual funds. His Sharpe Ratio—discussed in Chapter 1—is a proven, risk-adjusted measure to determine the added value of one fund manager over another. If you are considering two funds with similarly attractive holdings and past returns, the investment with the higher Sharpe Ratio is a better choice, for its manager achieved those favorable results with less risk.

Sharpe's methods don't tell people which funds to buy—that ultimately is an individual's decision—but rather how to blend them together to create a diverse and dynamic portfolio. He says:

Concentrate far more on using the market than beating it. Focus on questions of asset allocation, diversification and changes through time. Spend more time on tailoring the portfolio to your needs and circumstances: "What are the things that I should do because I'm me?" as opposed to "Anybody could do it if they just were smart enough." Even very smart people who not only have a lot of information but process it efficiently and cleverly have trouble beating the market by large amounts with any regularity.

Outside of his Financial Engines shares, Sharpe has followed a conservative investment approach that you might expect of someone who bailed out of a stock after a 10 percent loss. His portfolio consists of mutual funds—mostly index funds—that mix value and growth strategies and that he trades infrequently. There's nothing too exotic, except the Vanguard Emerging Markets Stock Index Fund, which invests in developing countries.

Sharpe also doesn't advocate taking big bets on any one particular investment style. While it's all right to tilt a portfolio in a specific direction—say, small stocks over large, or growth over value—he says investors should temper their enthusiasm. So if you would normally divide an equity portfolio equally between value and growth, but are convinced that growth is a better long-term style, then, Sharpe advises, allocate 60 percent to growth and 40 percent to value. "You want to think very carefully before you make big bets on any strategy that diverges significantly," he says.

Pure value investors learned this lesson the hard way. Although many notable studies show that value strategies outperform growth strategies over holding periods of many years, growth funds decimated their value counterparts in the last two years of the

1990s as technology and biotechnology stocks produced strato-spheric returns. Between February 1998 and February 2000, the high-growth computer and Internet-related stocks that make up the technology component of the S&P 500 tripled in value. With-out them, in fact, the bellwether index actually would have lost roughly 1 percent.[4] One benchmark, two markets; no question, this was an extraordinary period for U.S. equities—and investors.

The performance in 1999 of the small-stock Russell 2000 Growth Index against its Russell 2000 Value counterpart tells a similar story in a few lopsided numbers. According to fund-rating service Morningstar, the Russell growth strategy returned 43.1 percent in 1999 and boasted a three-year average annual gain of 17.8 percent. The value approach lost 1.5 percent in 1999 and limped out a three-year record of 6.7 percent. Large value stocks weren't spared either. The Wilshire Large Growth Index returned 37.3 percent in 1999 and turned in a three-year average perform-ance of 37.7 percent. Its Wilshire Large Value counterpart gained 1.7 percent in 1999 and averaged 14.1 percent annually on a three-year basis.

For an individual investor who has been sold on the suppos-edly superior virtues of value investing, "painful" is a polite and understated description for the torture of watching your portfolio wither each trading day. In the face of such abysmal performance, it became difficult in 1999 and early 2000 for many value funds to retain a strong base of shareholder assets, and more than one value-fund manager who held stubbornly to their convictions wound up true to their beliefs but out of a job.

But an investment or investment strategy doesn't remain over-bought or underloved for long. Smart operators discover the error and exploit it for their own gain, bringing the price of the asset closer to fair value. If you agree with Sharpe that unstable mar-kets eventually return to a more balanced state—and history clearly shows this to be the case—then going forward, the per-formance of momentum-driven growth strategies should revert to the mean while value strategies regain their footing.

Performance is important, to be sure. It's especially important to mutual-fund families, which sell their wares on the basis of recent returns. If results are particularly stellar, the fund companies crow over how many stars or points their various offerings have received from objective outfits like Morningstar and Value Line.

Investors are drawn to these alluring one-year and three-year figures, as one might expect, even though we are also told in the same breath that past performance is no indication of future returns. But there's a widely held perception, nonetheless, that a fund manager who beat the market soundly last year has "hot hands" and so will rack up another market-drumming year. Don't worry, the thinking goes, you haven't missed anything; in fact, the best is yet to come.

Chasing performance is one of the biggest mistakes an investor can make. Sharpe has three words of advice: Don't do it. Selecting funds from top-performance lists assumes either that the same stocks or sectors will keep racing along unusually well, or that the fund manager will continue to display superior investment knowledge. Do you have what it takes to discover the investment managers who have what it takes, and find them before everyone else? Such precision timing is found in watches, not investments.

It may prove more successful to take a contrarian stance and unearth some of those buried funds, stocks and industries that nobody loves—perhaps fortune is about to shine on some of the more worthy candidates. Sure, throwing money at rock-star managers and buying the latest hot fund can make you a lot of money in a short time. Besides, it's fun and gives you bragging rights. But today's fads, like last weekend's parties, are quickly gone and forgotten. Now, maybe for a rock star it's better to burn out than to fade away, as rock legend Neil Young sang, but flashy performance makes a lousy long-term investment strategy. Sharpe, not surprisingly, has some scathing lyrics of his own about this subject. He says:

The "rock-star syndrome," or the hot fund of the year, sells a lot of magazines. They say: "Here's this great manager, he's got these great ideas and really blew out the lights last year. Why don't you put new money in that fund, and maybe take some money out of your old, boring funds, which we recommended as hot last year—but they haven't done so well." This encourages churning. It encourages lack of diversification. It encourages people to follow whatever category has done well recently.

When it comes to mutual funds, the key factors within an investor's control are costs, portfolio risk and tax efficiency. Performance, unfortunately, is not on the list. Still, many investment professionals contend that a fund's total return is more important than its fees, particularly where a skilled manager is involved. But remember that fees directly impact total return. In fact, Sharpe says that a fund's expense ratio is an investor's single most important consideration:

Performance comes and goes, but the expense stays forever. Ask an investor what the expense ratios are for their funds. In most cases, you'll find they don't know. Now, that's the first thing you ought to look at. Every dollar of expenses takes a dollar away from your performance. And if there's one thing that is a good predictor of the future, it's the expense ratio. If a fund has been spending a lot of money in the past, there's a very high likelihood that it's going to spend a lot of money in the future.

Index funds, of course, are the fund industry's low-cost leaders. But just because a fund has "index" in its name doesn't mean it's necessarily the best investment. Many frugal-minded actively managed funds have been able to outperform a benchmark index consistently, if only because their managers are not struggling to overcome the head wind from high expenses. Say you own a large-stock fund that attempts to surmount the S&P 500 average and carries an expense ratio of 1.25 percent. Each year, the fund manager has to beat the index's total return by the amount of the fund's expenses just to break even. But most managers aren't skilled or lucky enough to deliver above-average returns without taking above-average risk. A search of Morningstar's Principia Pro database of more than 5,300 domestic U.S. mutual funds found 626 portfolios—or about one of every nine funds—with a beta of less than 1.0 that beat the 27.5 percent average annual S&P 500 return for the three years through December 1999. The results send a clear message: As an investor, be your own engine.

Know When to Fold 'Em

It's said that mutual funds are sold, not bought. To the fund companies, funds are products; to many individuals, funds are status symbols to proudly show family and friends.

With blissful investors convinced that their portfolios are stuffed with dazzling jewels, why should anyone burst their bubble? The fund industry certainly isn't pointing out that some of these baubles are just expensive glass. The mutual-fund companies are full of kind advice on when to buy 'em and when to hold 'em—and boy, do they want you to hold 'em—but not on when to fold 'em. And that's something the old song says you've got to know. Investors need to understand the difference between a fund that's having bad luck and one that's dealing a bad hand.

The Internet is a terrific source of independent advice and assistance about when to buy a fund. Many sites champion the view that funds should be bought by wise shareholders and not sold on performance and catchy advertising slogans. Financial Engines is a good choice for online financial planning and counseling, as is Clear Future from Morningstar (www.clearfuture.com).

And when it comes to selling a mutual fund, the Internet also provides an honest perspective. One of the clearest voices is FundAlarm (www.fundalarm.com), which even features a step-by-step primer on when it's appropriate—even imperative—to dump that fund darling. Roy Weitz, FundAlarm's creator, updates the site on the first of each month with an outpouring of often hilarious barbs at the foibles and fumbles of well-known funds and their managers.

For the mecca of fund Web sites, make a pilgrimage to Morningstar's Web site (www.morningstar.com), which features frank opinions and plenty of hard numbers from the highly respected fund- and stock-rating service. Morningstar began analyzing the fund industry when the biggest investment concern for some of today's portfolio managers was what to wear to the senior prom. These Morningstar analysts know their stuff, and they're not afraid to make tough calls.

To be sure, deciding to part with a fund is a tough call in itself. By that point, you're angry, hurt and frustrated about being left high and dry, and you're hoping against hope that your true love will come back. But don't dial the fund family's toll-free number in a panic—it's a sales office, not a crisis line. Take it easy. And even if your fund is doing well, you'll want to check up on it at least every six months.

Here are some important reasons that you might want to sell a fund, along with some recommended Web sites that can confirm your suspicions without having to hire a financial planner to investigate.

This Dog Won't Hunt The fund that once happily pointed the way to profits lately has been lagging not just its benchmark index—hey, anybody can do that—but its peers. A fund can have positive returns and still fall short of its bogey, but when it starts to slip behind the pack, you know something's wrong.

The official fund-company line might be that the manager's style of investing is "out of favor." Of course, investment styles do fall out of fashion. That's why it's important to look at the fund's risk-adjusted returns relative to its peer group over the past three years and longer, if possible.

How long should you wait? Maybe the sector or style is, in fact, out of favor, but the fund manager is on top of the fallen heap. Then it actually might be time to buy more. Give the manager 12 months to regain his footing, and maybe 18 months if he's been compared to Warren Buffett. But if the fund hasn't significantly turned around after 18 months, stick a fork in it—it's done.

Don't expect the fund family to clue you in. Morningstar.com provides investigative tools for free, though you'll need to register first. Morningstar also offers a premium service for a monthly charge. Brush up on basic investment knowledge by clicking on the "University" tab at Morningstar's home page. Track fund performance with the "Quicktake" function. Type in the fund's ticker symbol or name to bring up a snapshot of the portfolio that includes annualized returns against its benchmark index and its peers, top five holdings, asset allocation and recent news. Hit the "Total Returns" bar to see how $10,000 invested in the fund would have fared since 1993; the "Ratings and Risk" section uses Sharpe's work to help provide a careful analysis of the portfolio's volatility.

The Fund Manager Changes It's nice to get mail from your fund, a kind of personal "How's it going?" from the folks in charge of your money. Then one day, you read that a new batter is on deck—someone you've never heard of. Oh, they've got the pedigree, all right. But it's not the manager you "hired" when you bought the fund. Now it's just "Hi, I'm William [or Patty, or Xavier], and I'll be your fund manager today."

If the manager was an important reason for buying the fund, her departure is clearly an issue. The new portfolio manager will likely stamp his own imprint on the portfolio, and that could involve lots of trading. These sales increase portfolio turnover, and unless that eager manager matches capital gains against capital losses, you could be hit with a big tax bill.

Still, don't make a knee-jerk decision to sell. The old manager's portfolio is going to drive performance for a while. Wait three to six months. Then review what you've got. Perhaps the new manager apprenticed with the old one, as often happens. If so, the fund's style and portfolio may remain surprisingly constant. It's the torpedoed, poor-performing funds, where the manager leaves "to pursue other opportunities," that demand more careful scrutiny. The new manager probably has a mandate to clean house.

You Change Life happens. School. Marriage. Kids. Retirement. Needs change. You change. Some money is earmarked for your kids' college, while another pot is percolating for retirement years. Perhaps the best reason to sell a fund is that you've reached a financial goal, or those goals change. The aggressive growth-stock fund you bought as a 30-year-old may not fit your personality at 50. If the kids are going to start college in a few years, or you plan to buy a house, it may be time to ratchet down the equity portion of a portfolio.

Many Web sites are especially good at helping guide investors through these milestones and determining whether a fund is best left out to pasture. Sage (www.sageguide.com) is full of, well, sage advice on investment strategies to fit all lifestyles and life cycles. Sage models itself as an online community, and its open, friendly manner invites you to pull up a stool for plain talk about funds. The site also sends e-mail alerts of daily investing events and discussions.

For a more formal education in the facts of investment life, the American Association of Individual Investors (www.aaii.org) offers step-by-step instructions. Registration is required, but the service is provided free of charge. You'll then have access to some of the most thoughtfully researched and well-written articles about investing in stocks and mutual funds.

Size Matters Top-performing funds gather crowds, but a flood of new money can overwhelm a manager and make it hard for a fund to continue at the torrid pace that attracted investors in the first place. A small-stock fund with $50 million in assets under management can buy undiscovered gems without much difficulty. A manager can pour tremendous effort into researching an idea and then buy a meaningful position. If the stock moves higher, the fund scores. After a few of these big winners, the press and investors start to notice.

Suppose that this small-stock fund's assets swell to $2 billion. This is your fund on steroids. Now the manager is forced to take increasingly larger positions in a security in order to have a meaningful impact on the fund's performance. This leaves a huge footprint on every trade. The Street notices what he's buying, and that can impact the prices of the stocks on his shopping list.

The manager becomes hamstrung. He's stretched thin, hiring support staff and analysts to meet demand. And when he does tend to stock-picking, the game has changed. He can either add positions to the portfolio, diluting the powerful concentration that had helped boost returns, or shift investment style and move into larger stocks where he might not feel as confident.

Rapid asset growth can put a great manager in a slow-moving vehicle that doesn't showcase his talents. It's Mario Andretti forced behind the wheel of a Yugo.

Performance Envy The cocktail party chatter had turned to investing and mutual funds, as it always did. Everyone was talking about Quentin's timely sale of a searing Internet fund just before those stocks fell out of favor. Then Zoe piped up about how her international fund had loaded up on European shares and was now reaping the gains. Not to be outdone, Kara casually mentioned her fund's deft ability to sell stocks short and post superior performance in both up and down markets. When someone asked about your investments, you gamely touted a diversified portfolio that had been producing marketlike returns with below-market risk. An uncomfortable silence followed.

Driving home, you thought about selling your plain Jane funds. That's not necessarily a bad idea—if it really means trading up. Just be sure that the grass is indeed greener. Before you buy an alternative fund, weigh the pros and cons of any sale. Compare your fund's performance with others of its type to determine if an upgrade is indeed the right decision. Once again, Morningstar stands out as an invaluable resource. Now you'll definitely have something to talk about at parties.

Realize a Tax Loss Taxes can be a pretty dry subject—until you have to pay them. Selling a fund incurs a tax on unrealized capital gains—profits the fund has not yet distributed to shareholders. But maybe you've taken a hit already. Perhaps it's time to drop these bombs and buy leaders with better management.

A loss in one fund can be used to offset a gain in another. Selling gives you an opportunity to trade up and realize a tax loss, and this might be wise. For solid help, try the Mutual Fund Investor's Center (www.mfea.com). Under "Learn" at the top of the home page, click on "Select a Topic" and scroll down to "Tax Considerations." You'll find a comprehensive review of the most tax-advantageous ways to sell a fund, including a useful explanation about the impact on a portfolio from unrealized capital gains. If you're not versed in tax-planning terms like "cost basis" and "first-in, first-out," this site will clue you in.

You Blew It Face it. You made a mistake. You went looking for funds in all the wrong places. That attractive Internet play you heard about at the cocktail party has gotten soused. That's what comes from focusing on performance and not on risk. If you own a fund that you should never have bought to begin with, don't regret it, sell it.

Funds aren't static, and neither are you. Perhaps your initial analysis was wrong or the fund no longer has the same appeal. Periodic reevaluation and fine-tuning is essential. As you gain more knowledge, you'll buy smarter. You'll look for low-cost, low-turnover, tax-efficient funds where the portfolio manager has put most or all of his own investment dollars.

Taking Stock

For more than four decades, Sharpe has been encouraging individual investors to think for themselves—to draft a personal declaration of financial independence. You can choose your own investments with a mature view of probability, unpredictability and chance, or you can delegate the task to a professional who shares your philosophy. But choose. In either case, you will be on the path toward becoming an active investor—aware of inherent risks, yet secure with your plan and responsive to an ever-changing investment landscape.

Epilogue:
Variations on a Theme

Wall Street welcomes every investor warmly. It just doesn't accommodate them all. If you can keep that in mind, then investing will be less surprising and more comfortable.

Volatility is hardest to accept in the blue-chip stocks and solid equity mutual funds that many people depend on to build long-term security for themselves and their families once they stop working. Many investors understandably are anxious about risk and uncertainty. Their bottom-line concern—the crucial kitchen-table issue—has everything to do with finding accommodation and assistance. People really want to know just two things: "Will I have enough income to live comfortably in retirement?" and "How can I reach this goal through my investments?"

The nine luminaries you've just met have addressed these two key questions in their own unique way, yet several key ideas about investing tie their experiences together.

First, all of these investment veterans agree on the importance of diversifying a portfolio according to your tolerance for risk. Too often, the promise of spectacular stock-market gains causes us to accept risk that we ordinarily wouldn't. Leave it to Harry Markowitz to explain the powerful benefits of blending different investments into a cooperative team. For nearly half a century, his Portfolio Theory has been the basic instruction manual for investors to diversify and balance their holdings. "You've got to look at the portfolio as a whole, not just position by position," Markowitz asserts. Through his groundbreaking work, investors have found a better understanding of the trade-off between risk and reward.

A second essential element for many of these market experts is to buy smart. Costs matter. According to Jack Bogle, they matter a great deal. Bogle is critical of any investment strategy that isn't low-cost and tax-efficient. And no mutual fund is cheaper and more tax-friendly than an index fund, which Bogle has zealously championed. Over the years, low-priced stock-index funds have outperformed most higher-priced actively managed equity funds. While there are signs that bottom-up stock-selection may be returning to vogue among investors, Bogle, true to form, remains resolute. "An index fund always wins," he tells us. "It wins every single, solitary day, and there's no way around it."

Josef Lakonishok doesn't like to spend much money on investments either. As a value player, he looks for individual stocks that he believes other investors have priced too low. Unlike some of the experts in this book who proclaim that markets operate with near-efficiency, Lakonishok ferrets out the mispricings and anomalies he claims arise from investors' emotional overreactions to unwelcome news and information. Value stocks are attractive, he says, because many investors have abandoned them. Yet these stocks might not be the dogs the market thinks they are. So live rich, invest cheaply.

A third crucial lesson from the teachers of this master class is to start investing now—and stay invested. Jeremy Siegel contends that stocks are more attractive than any other asset. He asserts that despite their risk, stocks actually are safer than bonds. Stocks are uniquely able to withstand inflationary pressures that eat away at the purchasing power of bonds and cash, Siegel maintains. Over many years, in fact, stocks have provided investors with a strong inflationary hedge and a predictable annualized gain. "There's very little place for bonds, primarily because of inflation risk," Siegel explains. "Stocks, being claims on real assets, respond much better to inflation in the long run."

These seasoned authorities also stress the importance of keeping emotions in check. Investors and markets often react defensively to the uncertainty, surprise and chance that exists in any gathering of buyers and sellers. Facing danger, people will sell first and ask questions later. Fleeing from a perceived threat makes perfect sense on some primal level, but when it comes to investing, this can be a shortsighted response.

Richard Thaler describes many of the mental traps that all investors are susceptible to, and tells us how to recognize them. "People exaggerate their own skills," he says. "They are optimistic about their prospects and overconfident about their guesses." Optimism, overconfidence and confusing chance with skill are three of the biggest errors of judgment that investors make. Regretting decisions, getting locked into a single unyielding mind-set, and not seeing the big picture can also be detrimental to our wallets. Perceptive investors can profit from understanding other investors' limitations—as well as their own.

Peter Bernstein, too, puts a realistic perspective on the investment concepts and ideas that his peers have discussed in these chapters. He reminds us that what we don't know about investing is enough to, well, fill a book. In being so direct, Bernstein is not using scare tactics—it's an aware tactic. "A good investor," he emphasizes, "is realistic about the nature of the market, which is a bunch of other people making decisions that may or may not be right. The future is unpredictable, and you have to make decisions and choices from that assumption." Solidify a portfolio around your core beliefs; this will help you enormously when times get tough.

Above all, these critical thinkers want you to take an involved, active role with your investments, even if you hand your money to a financial adviser or create a portfolio of indexed mutual funds. Take your rightful place in the driver's seat. William Sharpe believes that all investment professionals ought to provide their customers with sound, qualified counsel in a cost-effective, colloquial way. "The advice that people are getting seems to ignore risk," Sharpe contends. "Making a decision as to how much to save in stocks, bonds or cash without acknowledging uncertainty, let alone trying to estimate it, seems to me the height of folly."

The well-regarded innovators featured in this book have shown that honest intuition and strong conviction can make you a better and more satisfied investor—whether you buy stocks and mutual funds yourself or rely on an investment adviser. What works in investing for these experts? Basic self-discipline, that's what.

Think about it. If we spent as much time researching and deliberating on our investments as we give to buying a new car or home computer, we probably would make better choices about which stocks and bonds to own and which to forego. Many in the investment business—and what a business it has become— would prefer that you simply get on the bus and leave the driving to them. And in fact, mutual-fund shareholders in particular can sit back with a relatively high degree of trust—the fund industry has been remarkably scandal-free.

Don't get complacent. The best investors aren't swept away by the latest trends and fads. Knowledgeable investors go online or to a public library and research a company and its competitors. Digest the financial information found in 10-Q and 10-K filings, paying careful attention to management's projections about the company's future. Listen to quarterly earnings conference calls for additional clues about a firm's prospects. Ask tough questions of company executives, a fund manager, a stockbroker or adviser— and, most important, of yourself. Then, when you buy or sell, you're acting decisively and with conviction. You take charge.

But will you beat the market? You might, although most of the experts in this book would advise you not to bother. Few investors are able to generate return above a market average, and fewer still can scale a benchmark index with below-average risk. But if you have realistic expectations about what the market can give and what you can accomplish, then your odds of becoming a more contented investor will improve greatly. As Bernstein explains, "You'd like to be going up more than the market, but not if it involves risks that you don't want to take."

Understand that you can only control things within your reach. For investors, the extent of their control includes deciding what to own, when to buy or sell it, how much market- and company-specific risk to take, minimizing mutual-fund costs and limiting tax liabilities. Stellar investment performance, sad to say, is not among the options. So focus on what you can keep, not on what you might get.

The investing pioneers you've just met are telling you as much, and through their perspective and insights are helping you to learn more about your investment portfolio so that you can do more with it. Success in the financial markets comes and goes. But investors these days have tremendous opportunities to gain expert advice and to make educated choices. The Internet single-handedly has created a more egalitarian playing field. Never before has it been so easy and so inexpensive to get into and out of a stock trade. And never before has it been so easy to get into trouble. The Net is a magnet. Its immediacy and ease can be seductive. Overconfident or naïve investors can abuse this power—and it in turn can abuse them. Be careful not to confuse information with knowledge.

Alert, independent investors are better able to navigate these twists and turns of logic and reason. So go ahead—take the wheel. Successful investing may follow a winding road, but the view from the driver's seat is far more spectacular.

Notes

Chapter 1.
The Efficient Frontier:
Harry Markowitz

1. John Maynard Keynes, *The General Theory of Employment Interest and Money,* 1936.
2. Gerald M. Loeb, *The Battle for Investment Survival.*
3. "Planet Stock Market," *Grants Interest Rate Observer,* March 26, 1999.
4. "Some Studies of Variability of Returns on Investments in Common Stocks," *Journal of Business,* April 1970.
5. Charles D. Ellis, "Small Slam!" *Financial Analysts Journal,* January/February 1997.

Chapter 2.
Time and Money:
Paul Samuelson

1. Morgan Stanley Dean Witter Investment Research Dept.
2. Adam Smith, *The Wealth of Nations,* Book One, Chapter X.
3. Peter L. Bernstein, *Capital Ideas: The Improbable Origins of Modern Wall Street* (New York: The Free Press), p. 121.
4. "Equity Ownership in America," Investment Company Institute; Securities Industry Assn., Fall 1999.
5. Montgomery Asset Management, "Wise Investor" Survey; 3Q, 1997.
6. James K. Glassman and Kevin A. Hassett, *The Wall Street Journal,* March 17, 1999.
7. At September 30, 1999, Amazon.com had a market capitalization of $27 billion; Avon Products: $6.5 billion. The market cap

of Yahoo! was $46.5 billion; Merrill Lynch: $24.9 billion.
8. Charles Mackay, *Extraordinary Popular Delusions and the Madness of Crowds.*

Chapter 3.
The Equity Premium:
Jeremy Siegel

1. Jeremy Siegel, *Stocks for the Long Run* (New York: McGraw-Hill, 1998), pp. 249–250.
2. Ibid.
3. *The No-Load Fund Investor* newsletter, September 1998, p. 17.
4. "TIPS Now Offer Attractive Returns," Standard & Poor's *The Outlook*, February 2, 2000, pp. 10–11.
5. "The American Age of Affluence," PaineWebber research report, November 1999, p. 36.
6. Jeremy Siegel, *Stocks for the Long Run* (New York: McGraw-Hill, 1998), p. 108.
7. "Big-Cap Tech Stocks Are a Sucker Bet," *The Wall Street Journal*, March 14, 2000.
8. Ibid.

Chapter 4.
The Average Outperforms:
John C. Bogle

1. John C. Bogle, "Gentlemen . . . To Save Our Business from Ruin, We Must Reduce Expenses," address to the National Association of Personal Financial Advisors, Washington, D.C., June 4, 1999.
2. Morningstar Principia Pro.
3. John C. Bogle, "Marketing Madness," *Bloomberg Personal Finance*, May 1999, pp. 33–36.

4. John C. Bogle, *Common Sense on Mutual Funds* (New York: John Wiley & Sons, 1999), pp. 400–401.

5. Morningstar Principia Pro.

6. Ibid.

7. Ibid.

8. Jonathan Burton, "Lean, Mean Money Machines," *Bloomberg Personal Finance,* July/Aug. 1999, pp. 74–93.

9. Morningstar, Inc.

10. Charles Ellis, "The Loser's Game," *Financial Analysts Journal,* July/Aug. 1975.

11. Paul A. Samuelson, "Challenge to Judgment," *The Journal of Portfolio Management,* Fall 1974.

12. Morningstar Principia Pro.

13. Standard & Poor's.

14. Ibid.

15. Morningstar Principia Pro.

16. John C. Bogle, "Changing the Mutual Fund Industry: The Hedgehog and the Fox." Princeton University, February 20, 1999.

17. Morningstar Principia Pro.

18. "The Mutual Funds: Selling Savvy in the Stock Market," *Time,* June 1, 1959. Vol. LXXIII, No. 22.

19. Investment Company Institute.

Chapter 5.
Uncommon Value, Hidden Growth:
Josef Lakonishok

1. Benjamin Graham, *The Intelligent Investor.*

2. Ibid.

3. Josef Lakonishok, Andrei Shleifer and Robert Vishny, "Contrarian Investment, Extrapolation, and Risk," *The Journal of Finance,* December 1994.

4. Ibid.

5. Rafael LaPorta, Josef Lakonishok, Andrei Shleifer and Robert

Vishny, "Good News for Value Stocks: Further Evidence on Market Efficiency," *The Journal of Finance*, June 1997.

6. Adam Smith, *The Wealth of Nations*, Book One, Chapter IV.

7. Josef Lakonishok, Andrei Shleifer and Robert Vishny, "Contrarian Investment, Extrapolation, and Risk," *The Journal of Finance*, December 1994.

8. Benjamin Graham, *The Intelligent Investor*.

9. Company reports.

10. Company reports.

11. Josef Lakonishok and Immoo Lee, "Are Insiders' Trades Informative?" National Bureau of Economic Research, July 1998.

Chapter 6.
It's All in the Mind:
Richard Thaler

1. In the first example, 84 percent of a group selected a. In the second example, 69 percent of the group chose b. Daniel Kahneman and Amos Tversky, "Prospect Theory: An Analysis of Decision Making Under Risk," *Econometrica*, 1979.

2. Pink Floyd, "Money," *Dark Side of the Moon*.

3. Brad Barber and Terrance Odean, "Trading Is Hazardous to Your Wealth: The Common Stock Investment Performance of Individual Investors," *The Journal of Finance*, April 2000, pp. 773–806.

4. Brad Barber and Terrance Odean; "The Courage of Misguided Convictions: The Trading Behavior of Individual Investors," *Financial Analyst Journal*, November/December 1999, pp. 41–55.

5. Terrance Odean, "Online Investors: Do the Slow Die First?" Unpublished paper, December 1999.

6. Daniel Kahneman and Mark Riepe, "Aspects of Investor Psychology," *The Journal of Portfolio Management*, Summer 1998, pp. 52–64.

7. Werner F. M. DeBondt and Richard H. Thaler, "Does the Stock Market Overreact?", *The Journal of Finance*, July 1985.

8. Shlomo Benartzi, Daniel Kahneman and Richard Thaler, "Optimism and Overconfidence in Asset Allocation Decisions," posted on Morningstar.net, April 1999.

9. Shlomo Benartzi and Richard Thaler, "Risk Aversion or Myopia? The Fallacy of Small Numbers and its Implications for Retirement Savings," April 1996.

10. Paul Samuelson, "Risk and Uncertainty: A Fallacy of Large Numbers," *Scientia,* 1963.

11. Shlomo Benartzi and Richard Thaler, "Myopic Loss Aversion and the Equity Premium Puzzle," *The Quarterly Journal of Economics,* February 1995.

12. Terrance Odean, "Are Investors Reluctant to Realize Their Losses?", *The Journal of Finance,* October 1998, pp. 1775–1798.

13. Daniel Kahneman and Mark Riepe, "Aspects of Investor Psychology," *The Journal of Portfolio Management,* Summer 1998, pp. 52–64.

14. Ibid.

Chapter 7.
Passport to Wealth:
Gary Brinson

1. Gary Brinson, "Investment Management in the 21st Century," *The Future of Investment Management,* Association for Investment Management and Research, 1998.

2. Adam M. Brandenburger and Barry J. Nalebuff, *Co-opetition* (New York: Doubleday, 1996).

3. Strategis Group, October 1999.

4. International Data Corp., October 1999.

5. Company reports.

6. Company reports.

7. Company reports.

8. Company reports.

9. *Nation's Restaurant News,* January 26, 1998.

10. Company reports.

11. Gary Brinson, L. Randolph Hood and Gilbert Beebower, "Determinants of Portfolio Performance," *Financial Analysts Journal*, July–August 1986.

12. Gary Brinson, Brian Singer and L. Randolph Hood, "Determinants of Portfolio Performance II: An Update," *Financial Analysts Journal*, May–June 1991.

13. In U.S.dollars; Morgan Stanley Capital International data.

14. Rex Sinquefield, "Where Are the Gains from International Diversification?" *Financial Analysts Journal*, January–February 1996.

15. Chase Investment Performance Digest, 1997.

16. MSCI.

Chapter 8.
Widows, Orphans and Other Risk-Takers:
Peter Bernstein

1. William Goldman, *Adventures in the Screen Trade* (New York: Warner Books, 1983).

2. WSJ Market Data Group, *The Wall Street Journal*, March 8, 2000, page C1.

3. Peter Bernstein, "Where, Oh Where, Are the .400 Hitters of Yesteryear?" *Economics and Portfolio Strategy*, April 15, 1998.

4. Ibid.

5. Burton Malkiel, *A Random Walk Down Wall Street* (New York: Norton, 1973), p. 193.

Chapter 9.
We're All Investors Now:
William Sharpe

1. Ibbotson Associates.

2. Personal interview.

3. Peter L. Bernstein, *Capital Ideas: The Improbable Origins of Modern Wall Street* (New York: The Free Press, 1992), pp. 75–76.
4. "The Decoupling of Technology," *U.S. and the Americas Investment Perspective,* Morgan Stanley Dean Witter, March 1, 2000, pp. 15–17.

Index

About the Author

Jonathan Burton is a prolific and respected financial journalist. *Investment Titans* grew from his "Leaders in Finance" series, written for *Asset Management*. A coauthor of the best-selling *Electronic Day Traders' Secrets* and a frequent contributor to *The New York Times, Bloomberg Personal Finance, Mutual Funds, Individual Investor, Online Investor* and *Asset Management*, Burton has also written for top publications including *The Economist, The Christian Science Monitor* and *The Far Eastern Economic Review.*